Chicken Soup for the Soul®

Home Sweet Home

Chicken Soup for the Soul: Home Sweet Home
101 Stories about Hearth, Happiness, and Hard Work
Jack Canfield, Mark Victor Hansen, Amy Newmark
Published by Chicken Soup for the Soul Publishing, LLC www.chickensoup.com

The publisher gratefully acknowledges the many publishers and individuals who granted Chicken Soup for the Soul permission to reprint the cited material.

Front cover photo courtesy of iStockPhoto.com/akurtz (© akurtz).
Back cover & interior photo courtesy of iStockPhoto.com/nojustice (© nojustice).

Cover and Interior Design & Layout by Brian Taylor, Pneuma Books, LLC

Distributed to the booktrade by Simon & Schuster. SAN: 200-2442

Publisher's Cataloging-in-Publication Data
(Prepared by The Donohue Group)

Chicken soup for the soul : home sweet home : 101 stories about hearth,
  happiness, and hard work / [compiled by] Jack Canfield, Mark Victor
  Hansen, [and] Amy Newmark.

   pages ; cm

   ISBN: 978-1-61159-935-0

   1. Dwellings--Literary collections. 2. Home ownership--Literary collections. 3.
Dwellings--Anecdotes. 4. Home ownership--Anecdotes. 5. Anecdotes. I. Canfield,
Jack, 1944- II. Hansen, Mark Victor. III. Newmark, Amy. IV. Title: Home sweet home
: 101 stories about hearth, happiness, and hard work

PN6071.H72 C45 2014
810.8/02/0356/4   2014934626

PRINTED IN THE UNITED STATES OF AMERICA
on acid∞free paper

24 23 22 21 20 19 18 17 16 15 14   01 02 03 04 05 06 07 08 09 10 11

Chicken Soup for the Soul

Home Sweet Home

101 Stories about Hearth, Happiness, and Hard Work

Jack Canfield
Mark Victor Hansen
Amy Newmark

Chicken Soup for the Soul Publishing, LLC
Cos Cob, CT

Chicken Soup
for the Soul

www.chickensoup.com

Contents

❶
~On the Move~

❷
~Buying and Selling~

❸
~Dreams Can Come True~

❹
~Remodeling, Redecorating, Repairing~

❺
~Through the Generations~

❻

~You CAN Go Home Again~

❼

~Unwanted Guests~

8

~Do-It-Yourself Disasters~

9

~Downsizing and Retiring~

~What Makes a Home~

Chapter 1

Home Sweet Home

On the Move

Starting Over

A successful marriage requires falling in love many times,
always with the same person.
~Mignon McLaughlin

"This is it," said my husband as we pulled up in front of a funky, little house with a couch on the front porch. My heart sank, but I didn't voice my disappointment. We'd just sold a beautiful two-story home in a city an hour away. Now we were going to live in the college town where my husband had a new job teaching military history at the university. This funky, little house was a rental with four college boys moving out so we could move in.

"It's nice of them to leave that couch for us," I said, thinking how our three small children would look jumping on that broken down thing for all the neighbors to see. With my husband in the Army, we'd lived in a lot of different places in the past twelve years, but never had living room furniture decorated the front porch of any of our homes.

"The couch will be gone by the time our stuff gets here." My husband pointed to a nearby park. "We can walk the kids down there every night to play. I'll be home for dinner now. Won't that be great?"

I swallowed hard. I wasn't sure I wanted my husband home every night. I wasn't sure I wanted him home at all. For years, he'd been a helicopter pilot away on missions. This new ROTC job was my husband's attempt to restore our marriage. I'd been trying to leave him for a year. I just couldn't take being married to a military pilot.

And when he was home, we fought because I didn't trust him. Our children were the only thing holding us together. That, and the hope perhaps we could start over again in this rental within walking distance of my husband's new job.

When we moved in, I didn't care much about the rental, although I did clean it like a mad woman, realizing we'd now be living with bugs, mice, and perhaps a raccoon once we settled into this rattrap place (literally, I placed traps everywhere). My husband put a foosball table in the living room. Each night he and the kids banged up a storm on that table, laughing and loving being together while I plugged my ears and prayed that God would restore our marriage and help me like this dirty old house and that foosball table in our living room.

When my mother-in-law came to visit she was horrified by our move. "How could you sell your beautiful house for this place?" She looked around at the battered rental, the jungle in the back yard, and threw up her hands. "You must really love my son to move here for him."

I kept my mouth shut since I wasn't feeling love. This was something new I was learning. To give thanks for a roof over my head, and three little kids safe in their beds, children so happy to have their dad home every night to play with them before bedtime.

"This house isn't so bad," my husband said a few weeks into our new life. "If we cleaned up the back yard we could sit out there around a fire pit. The kids could make s'mores and we could talk and share a glass of wine." My husband's blue eyes sparkled with longing.

"We could have kept that couch and put it out there too. The kids and the critters would have liked that in this crazy yard."

My husband laughed and I thought how handsome he looked at that moment. After several weeks, my heart was softening towards him and this place. "How about we put the foosball table out in the back yard? You guys make a ton of noise playing that game at night in the house."

"I like it in the living room," my husband said. "It's a lot better than zoning out in front of the TV. Besides, we can't play in the dark. It would be dark out there at night."

"Tarzan might join you out there," I said, looking at all the lush green vines covering the backyard trees and the forest of weeds that had once been a lawn.

"We'll work on the yard this weekend," said my husband.

Within a month, we were sitting in the yard circled around a fire pit as a family. We nearly had a lawn now and I'd picked out a spot to plant a small garden. I'd left my job working for a newspaper in our old town. Now, with only our three-year-old son at home with me and our two older girls in school, I was ready to put my hand to the plow. Any plow. But I decided not to work outside our home because my heart was coming home, and that's where I wanted to be even though this home didn't belong to us. Thank goodness this house didn't belong to us! I couldn't imagine the money it would take to fix it up and get all the bugs and rodents out, but our family was healing here.

Cleaning up that yard, and then growing a garden in a corner of it, my first garden ever, made me love that funky, little rental all the more. I also loved watching my husband become the dad I never realized he could be. The husband I never realized he could be. I also made going to church a priority, and God seemed to be answering all those prayers, because I was falling in love with my husband all over again.

And then September 11th happened and I thought I'd lose him to war. Yet, the Army allowed him to stay at the university teaching cadets instead of sticking him back in the cockpit of a Black Hawk helicopter. I cried when my husband's cadets graduated from the university and were sent into battle, and I cried when my husband arrived home safely every night. I cried because I was crazy in love with him again, and I really liked our rental house now. I was so grateful my husband wasn't in a Black Hawk on the battlefield. I loved walking to the park with my family, and I loved sitting around our fire pit in the back yard. I loved listening to my husband and our children laughing in the living room as they beat the foosball table to death.

That rental wasn't much to look at, and I never succeeded in trapping all the critters scurrying through it night and day (once a mouse ran over my slipper as I ate breakfast at the kitchen table), but that funky, little house became our home. The place where our family started over and the war in Afghanistan passed us by. A baby was born to us there, too, before we moved on to buy another beautiful home. That baby was the first of four more sons we would have!

~Paula Bicknell

Celebrating the Tears

Today I close the door to the past, open the door to future, take a deep breath,
step on through and start a new chapter in my life.
~Author Unknown

I stared with dread at the square on the calendar. The words "Moving Day" seemed to gleam on the page as if printed in neon lights, not black ink. A lump rose in my throat every time I thought of leaving our apartment in Virginia. I'd known when I'd married my husband John, an officer in the Navy, that we'd have to move often. I just hadn't known how hard it would be. I hadn't grown up in a military family. In fact, I'd lived in the same house for twenty-two years before I'd become a wife. The closer the time approached for us to leave the life we'd made together in Virginia, the more depressed I grew.

When the packers came I watched in despair as they quickly wrapped up bits and pieces of our home in sheets of paper and stuffed them into boxes. Then they pulled out rolls of tape and sealed up the cardboard. A few words scrawled on the side of the box, "baby's room-toys," "kitchen-silverware," and the comfortable life we'd had was stuffed out of sight.

That night I sat at the kitchen table and called my mother-in-law. She'd been a self-described "corporate nomad" for most of her married life, never living anywhere for longer than three years. I figured if anyone could understand my anxiety, she could.

"How are you holding up?" she asked.

My gaze drifted over the stacks of boxes now filling the living room. "I don't know how you did it."

"Did what?"

"Moved so many times. This is killing me."

"Physically?"

"No." I sighed. "Mentally. I don't want to leave. I love it here."

"Good."

Her enthusiastic reply surprised me. "You're happy that I'm sad?"

Her warm chuckle brought a smile to my face, even though I was confused. "Let me tell you something, I've lived in more houses, in more states than I can count, and I listened to a lot of the corporate wives moan and groan with each new transfer. I decided early on not to be one of them."

"How'd you do that?"

"Think of each move as a new adventure. I vowed to explore each place as much as I could with the kids. They knew more about every new state than people who had lived there their whole lives because we didn't take anything for granted. Every vacation we'd take a road trip to some new corner or historic sight."

My heart lightened as my mother-in-law continued, "I always said, 'If I don't cry when I move away, I wasted my time.' I don't know about you, but life's too short to waste any of it, don't you think?"

Her motto stuck with me through my twenty years as a military wife. We made the most of every new duty station. We've walked through Revolutionary War forts in New England, panned for gold in California and slept with the sharks in a Florida aquarium. I tried to instill in my kids the same view of life. Every move is an opportunity. A chance to see new things and make new friends. And even though I cried as I left each home, I celebrated the fact that I hadn't wasted my time.

~Kim Stokely

Finally Home

Our dreams must be stronger than our memories.
We must be pulled by our dreams, rather than pushed by our memories.
~Jesse Jackson

I reached for my favorite coffee mug with the message that I had taped on it the day before: "If it was easy, everyone would be doing it!" It was to remind me that what we were about to do was not only difficult, but gut wrenching. How do you pack thirty-five years of marriage into four suitcases? I realized that all the other twenty-nine moves were just practice for our final move — to live and retire overseas.

I laid the coffee mug down on the cardboard box — one of several — that contained precious memorabilia that were being sent to my mom in California. She was going to be the keeper of our memories, which included photo albums, pictures, and mementos from our boys' lives.

As I passed by the living room filled with boxes of various sizes — an accumulation of a lifetime of memories — I had to wonder if this final move was worth all the pain of sifting, sorting, selling, and giving away. I sat with my elbows resting on a box that contained our boys' baby albums and felt a tear slip down my cheek, then another, and another until the mailing label smeared into an unrecognizable blob of black. My thoughts were interrupted by the cellphone ringing in my pocket.

"We have a buyer for our home!" my husband announced.

I gulped back tears, trying to muster some excitement in my voice. But I simply couldn't. After thirty-five years of marriage, there's not too much I could hide from my college sweetheart—Mark.

"What's wrong?" he asked.

"Oh, nothing… I mean… everything!" I lamented.

"Stop what you're doing right now and take a coffee break," Mark demanded. "That's an order!"

The message came through loud and clear. I grabbed my coffee mug, jumped into the car, and drove to the park around the corner to let the cool spring breeze dry the tears from my face. I thought about our new life in Cuenca, Ecuador—the land of eternal spring—and realized that all of these little sacrifices were nothing compared to the paradise that awaited us.

But keeping to our limit of four suitcases presented a challenge. Night after night I practiced packing—using every inch of space allowed. After careful consideration, I realized that my favorite coffee mug would have to be left behind. As I placed it with the things to be dropped off at the thrift store, I stared at the toothless grins of our boys on the front of the cup. It was a Father's Day gift to their dad when they were five and ten years old, but I had claimed it as my own. After sitting on the suitcases to keep them from popping open, I realized that I had made the right decision.

The next few weeks were a blur until we boarded our flight for Ecuador, which was a relief after all our moving and packing. We arrived at our condo complex as scheduled, and I saw that the glossy-print magazines hadn't betrayed us. It was all that I had hoped for and more.

The elevator to the sixth floor gave me just enough time to quiet the butterflies in my stomach! As Mark opened up the door to 6-J, I held my breath.

"You're going to love this view," Mark announced. "Close your eyes and don't open them until I tell you."

Holding both hands over my eyes, Mark ushered me toward the balcony. "Open your eyes!" he shouted. I marveled at the view from our living room, which was a cityscape of Cuenca—complete with the familiar blue domes of the Catedral Nueva (New Cathedral).

As I oohed and ahhed over the landscape and the white clouds in the crystal blue sky, I felt a calm overtake me. Mark grabbed my hand and led me into the kitchen and announced, "Now, open the cabinet!"

My heart swelled as I ran my hand over the rich walnut-stained cabinets with the modern stainless steel handles and thought, "This is the nicest home we've ever had!"

Mark grinned and said, "There's something in the cabinet for you."

I gasped when I saw my favorite coffee mug staring back at me. "I can't believe you managed this! But how? And when?" I choked.

Mark looked at me and smiled brightly. "We couldn't leave the boys behind—could we?"

At the last moment, Mark had managed to fit the mug in his carry-on luggage, leaving his favorite book behind.

As we held each other in a tight embrace, Mark kissed me lightly on the lips and whispered, "Now we're finally home!"

~Connie K. Pombo

Eulogy for a Compost Pile

Compost: Because a rind is a terrible thing to waste.
~Author Unknown

When I was twelve years old I helped my dad build the Cadillac of all compost bins in our back yard. This majestic edifice was made from twenty-four full-sized alfalfa hay bales. It may not have been the world's most beautiful building material, but when we finished stacking the bales together like overgrown toy blocks, we had a large, sturdy enclosure that held in moisture and held off frost. I will always remember the first time my dad successfully got the pile to "heat." He came running into the house with a soil temperature thermometer in his hand, inviting the entire household to come "take his pile's temperature." For the rest of that summer, any visitors to the house were required to visit the compost pile as one of our home's main attractions.

(Yes, my adolescence was an eccentric one. But very satisfying, all the same.)

For the rest of my teenage years, that composter did its duty. I do remember occasionally resenting its existence, particularly when Dad assigned me the chore of emptying food scraps into it after every meal. But as I lived with it season after season, I eventually began to understand my dad's enthusiasm. Everything we grew in our family garden either became a part of our bodies or went right back into that composter, to miraculously dissemble itself and eventually become a part of the produce I ate the next year. To quote the teenage me, "How much cooler can you get?"

In due course, I grew up and began a life of my own... but the composter stayed right where it was. It was a fixture of life at my parents' house, and I visited it at least once during every vacation home. However, eventually the day came when caring for a large house and garden got to be too much for my parents, and they decided to move to a smaller home in the city. Many things about the old place needed sprucing up to ready it for sale, but the real estate agent was the firmest about one of them. The composter needed to be disassembled, ASAP. "Rotting vegetables don't sell houses," she said.

Accordingly, the next sunny weekend Dad and I assembled with pitchforks in hand, ready to take our old friend apart. It felt oddly like a funeral, and we were both very quiet as we tore apart the bales, setting them aside for a neighbor who wanted them for mulch. Then we started on the remaining compost itself, pitching it into a wheelbarrow so we could give the garden one last top dressing.

As we got closer to the bottom of the pile, my dad's pitchfork made a loud clink. Frowning, he reached into the soil... and pulled out a china plate, unbroken and perfect. I recognized it as belonging to a dining set we'd had when I was still a teen. "How on earth did that get there?" I asked.

"Your guess is as good as mine. But if I had to say, I'd say that once upon a time some butterfingers were scraping something into the pile from the plate, lost hold of it, and then decided the plate wasn't worth rescuing."

"I never did that!"

"Now, who ever said that those butterfingers belonged to you?" Dad answered with a grin. "They could just as easily have been mine. Butterfingers tend to run in the family. Come on. Let's see what else we can find."

As we worked to the very bottom of the pile, we discovered many other "butterfingers" finds: a paring knife, a fork, several cornon-the-cob holders, and a truly staggering number of vegetable peelers. ("I thought we'd lost a few more of those over the years than was normal," my dad said mildly.) Other less explainable items included a cat collar (we'd always been dog people) and a Frisbee I couldn't even remember owning, let alone playing with. When we'd finished destroying the pile and had rinsed the final item under the hose — a green plastic yo-yo that I did remember and was very glad to have back (it had disappeared when I was thirteen, after the string had broken during a particularly exuberant 'round the world) — my dad cradled the old toy in his hands. "Lots of history in this compost pile," he said reflectively.

It was a very sad moment. I didn't know what to say, so I just nodded. Dad was quiet for a little while longer, and then he went to the house and returned with a large one-gallon canning jar. I watched while he solemnly scooped some of the compost into it, then, less solemnly, retrieved the long-buried fork and tucked it into the jar as well. "To start the next one," he said with a grin.

My mom and dad now live in town with a much smaller compost pile tucked into one corner of the yard. Contained by chicken wire, it's hardly the Cadillac Composter of days gone by, but it's still perfectly suited to the small, made-for-two veggie garden they now maintain. I sometimes wonder what will happen when the property eventually moves on to other owners and they discover a fork along with who-knows-what other "butterfingers" artifacts in that part of the garden — but it doesn't really matter. The whole point of keeping a compost pile is to be in touch with the cycles of nature, to understand how the leftovers of the past become the crops of the future. And in that way, our old composter will always live on.

~Kerrie R. Barney

The Story People Who Live with Me

*Whenever I go on a trip, I think about all the homes I've had and I remember
how little has changed about what comforts me.*
~Brian Andreas, StoryPeople

We walked into the empty house carrying garbage bags filled with clothes and shoes, big plastic tubs of kitchen paraphernalia and armfuls of bedding. We had no couches, no beds, no television. We arranged our blankets and pillows on the floor of one of the bedrooms and put our clothes in the closet. I carefully unwrapped the flat wooden pieces from the towels I had transported them in, lining them all up on the linoleum kitchen floor, looking at their familiar faces. I felt the warmth of happy memories spread across my skin and couldn't help smiling. My son and I walked from room to room, carefully deciding where each of them should be hung on the bare walls. When we were finished we sat on the kitchen floor, ate our Chinese takeout and took some deep breaths… a familiar ritual we had repeated over and over and over again… sixteen times to be exact.

Sixteen homes in fourteen years, twelve of them in five states since the death of my husband when Jackson was a toddler. This is certainly not the vision I had for his childhood, moving from place to place as work and finances dictated. Over the years, we went from being financially secure and stable, living in a sprawling Mediterranean style home in San Diego, to renting two rooms in a friend's house in Vegas to now being in a sweet little rental cottage built in 1865 on the border of New York and Connecticut. Thankfully, our life is now on an even keel and Jackson and I are both starting to feel settled in our new hometown.

Our nomadic existence is a far cry from the way I grew up—going from kindergarten to high school with the same group of friends. Living in a handful of places—mostly in the home that had been my grandparents and then ours—I had a strong sense of where I was from, home and family.

Through all of these moves, I have looked for ways to create a sense of stability. Little things that we could have with us no matter where we are that would mean "home" to us. For me, the answer was found in a series of brightly painted characters made from old Iowa barn wood by an artist named Brian Andreas. Each piece has a whimsical, amusing and often wise saying stamped on a multi-colored background. My first "Story Person" was a wedding gift. It read, "He loved her for almost everything she was, and that was enough for her to let him stay for a very long time." That began my love affair with these StoryPeople. Over the years, the collection grew into a community of happy and heartwarming friends that my friends and family have been kind enough to add to for milestone occasions—the birth of my son, our first home, my thirtieth birthday. They have accompanied us from one place to the next—the sometimes only familiar part of the décor. They have become our calling card—our announcement to the new address that we have arrived and are going to stay—even if only for a little while.

After the first major downsizing experience, I had to put almost everything we owned in storage. All of my furniture, my mother's china, my husband's surfboards and every piece of memorabilia you can imagine, are still in a storage unit the size of a small airplane hanger in Vegas, waiting for the day when we can all be reunited. As much as I would love to be surrounded by all of the wonderful possessions I have accumulated, I can honestly say, there has been a beautiful simplicity in living without them.

As we went from California to Vegas to Vermont — we picked up a couple more family members: our two dogs Gandhi and Roscoe's Chicken and Waffles (yes, that is the name on his nametag). The four of us have become our own little portable community — happily and hairily pitching our tent wherever fate has landed us. We have also added a few more items — some photos, a Bob Marley wall hanging, some hand-painted mugs from the local ceramics studio in each place we have lived. Each of them creating a sense of familiarity and connection that has helped us on our journey. As soon as we got the keys to wherever we were going to be living, the StoryPeople were the first personal items to go in. From the big beautiful homes we were fortunate to live in, to the one bedroom apartment in San Diego, to the rooms above an old bed and breakfast in Vermont. Our traveling companions hung proudly on otherwise bare walls. They became our anchor, our familiar surroundings (thankfully very portable) and confirmation that this place was ours.

I still look forward to the day when we have a more permanent address and can rescue all our possessions from their dark existence in storage. Although I will be excited to have them back — it will undoubtedly feel like Christmas — I have learned that I don't need them to create a home. Our family of StoryPeople has stood by us through good and bad times, adding the worn-in comfort of a favorite pair of jeans to what would otherwise have been cold, strange surroundings. It amazes me how such simple things can create so much warmth and a sense of security. Of course, the most important ingredient in creating any home is love — and that we have always had in abundance — no matter how large or small our place of residence has been.

~Joelle Jarvis

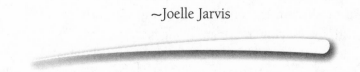

Father Meets Cat Door

It's really the cat's house — we just pay the mortgage.
~Author Unknown

My father loved gadgets and tools almost as much as he swore he hated cats. So when he was visiting my sister and found a catalog for upscale devices, he was in handyman heaven. One of the contraptions he saw was an electronic cat door, keyed to a transmitter that slipped on the cat's collar. Torn between love (gadgets) and hate (cats), love won out and he ordered the door.

On his next visit to me, he pulled out his special gift. "What do you think?" he asked.

"It's a cat door," I said, not overly impressed. All of the cat doors I had previously seen were simply flaps that pretty much let any cat — or other animal — in.

He smiled. "Not just any door. It's electronic. Only your own cats can get in and out. And it has four settings. Closed. In only. Out only. In and out. You can control how much freedom you want to give them."

Up until then, the only cat door my cats used was the back door, with me playing doorman. Being cats, they were never on the right side of the door. If they were in, they wanted out. If they were out, they wanted in. An electronic cat door was just what I needed to retire from doorman duties. "That's a brilliant idea. Where can we put it?"

We looked around the house. The front door had a separate storm door, so that wouldn't work. The back door was an oversized sliding glass door. While my father was semi-handy with tools, there was no way I was letting him put a hole in a glass door. None of the windows on the first floor opened, so we couldn't fit the door into their opening.

"Guess it's the basement," I said.

My father, my two cats, Tiger and Sammy, and I trooped down to the basement. There was a sliding window at the back that opened under my deck.

"This is perfect," my father said. "There's a plug nearby. I'll just remove the pane, get a piece of plywood to take its place, and cut out a hole for the door. Shouldn't take more than an hour or so."

I mentally doubled his estimate, then doubled it again, and wondered how many things he'd manage to break while installing the door. Still, it was nice of him to think of my cats, so I smiled weakly and prepared to do my usual job of assisting, which meant handing him tools and applying bandages when he accidentally cut himself.

Luckily, my father followed one firm rule in DIY: Never start a project when the local hardware store is closed. That way he always had somewhere to go for a needed tool, missing part, or help. More often than not, he needed all three.

That rule proved handy. The cat door project required a trip to the hardware store to get a piece of plywood to cover the window-pane, plus a second trip for a special jigsaw to cut out the shape of the door.

Five sweaty hours, a pile of sawdust, and two bandages later, my father stood back and admired his handiwork. We moved an old chest under the window so the cats could use it as a launching pad to the windowsill. I grabbed the nearest cat, Tiger, shoved her through the door and then coaxed her back in with her favorite treat. The third time I did it, she refused to come back in. When I turned to grab Sammy for her lesson in Cat Doors 101, she hightailed it up the stairs and out of the basement.

An hour later Tiger was sitting outside the sliding doors in the kitchen, yelling to come in.

Realizing that I had forgotten to put the transmitter on her collar, I opened the door for her. "This is the last time," I said. "From now on, this is a self-serve house. Use your own door or stay inside." That evening I put the electronic transmitter on both cats' collars.

The next day, I came down to breakfast to find Sammy outside on the deck. I turned to my mother who was sipping coffee at the kitchen table. "Did you let her out?" She shook her head. Either Tiger had been instructing her sister on the finer points of electronic cat doors or Sammy was smarter than I thought. Either way, both cats were happily using their own private cat door.

When I moved several years later, one of the first things my father said was, "Don't forget to take the cat door."

Taking it was easy. Finding a place to install it proved a problem. My new house had no basement windows, and the only windows on the first floor that opened looked onto the mutual driveway—not the best place for a cat door. The street was heavily trafficked, so I didn't want to use the front door, even if I had been willing to let my father cut a chunk out of it. That left my enclosed back porch. While two sides were floor-to-ceiling windows, a third wall was mostly drywall, and more importantly, it had a power source nearby.

Having done this once before, my father figured he'd have the door installed in no time. As my cats and I watched, my father made a template of the door, carefully traced the outline on the wall, and began cutting. Drywall, insulation, and cladding fell to his blade. Once done, he smoothed the sides of the hole. "Perfect," he said, as he stood up to survey his handiwork, wiping drywall dust off his pants.

"Good job," I said, "and you didn't even need a bandage." Then I quickly grabbed a broom and dustpan and cleaned up the mess on the floor.

Once the floor was swept, he unwrapped the door and carefully mounted it into the hole. It fit perfectly. "How's that for a good job?" he asked just as my mother walked into the room.

She stared at the door for minute, looked away, and then turned back with a puzzled look on her face. "Sam," she said, "why is the writing on the door upside down?"

"Huh," he said, as he peered at the door. A deep sigh escaped his lips. He turned to me. "I don't suppose you'd consider giving the cats a key to the front door?"

I shook my head. "They'd just lose the key or invite all the neighborhood cats over for a party while I was at work."

He sighed. An hour later my dad the semi-handyman and avowed cat hater had the cat door reinstalled right side up. "It's done. But if you move again, leave the damn door behind." He paused. "Leave the cats, too."

~Harriet Cooper

A Patch of Peace

*The human spirit needs places where nature
has not been rearranged by the hand of man.*
~Author Unknown

The shopping mall owns my flowers now. I used to live kitty-corner from the parcel of land on which the center was developed. One morning I opened to a knock at my front door and found a pretty young woman—dressed in khaki work pants, straw hat swinging down her back, hair in wisps, sweaty, dirt-streaked—standing on my porch.

"I'm working across the street on the shopping center development, and I was just wondering if I might dig up some of the wild irises and cattails from your pond so that we can transplant them over there. We're building a drainage pond and need some natural landscaping."

My heart raged at her question. Knowing the land we occupied was also destined for development, I wanted to grab my natural landscaping and run!

We had moved in a few years before precisely because the area was still a patch of country, a spot of peace and beauty. Dairy cows dotted the fields. Great blue herons speared fish in the pond at the base of our yard. Every day I looked forward to coming home to roost on my rented parcel of peace.

Now, I not only watched the development, I heard and even felt its invasion—the beep of the big machines as they backed up, the rumble of earth moving, and the whine of traffic. I mourned for my scarred scenery and the vanished tranquility. I viewed the infestation as the enemy camp. Each night I holed up at home behind the great trees, shutting out the noise, burying myself in the barns with the rabbits and the goats, pretending I had years to enjoy my haven.

But here was reality knocking on my front door in khakis. I looked into her eyes. She was eager to preserve the natural feel. All this wasn't her fault; progress is relentless. Perhaps here was a friend among the enemy. I gave in to the inevitable, granted her permission, shut the door and did not watch her dig.

Once the developers were ready to work on our side of the street, we moved far away and had many adventures. As workers in overalls and hard hats positioned great pipes to direct the course of the stream that fed the pond in my front yard, I tucked the memory of my natural landscaping in my heart. Concrete then covered the pipes.

When we moved back years later, we noticed a sign by the mall: Perry Creek. Who knew our stream had a name? The painted likeness of a great blue heron, peering out among blue cattails, accompanies a polite message requesting passersby to "Please take care of our wetlands." The rivulet, too small to accommodate an actual great, tall stalking heron, is at least deemed a wetland.

In the spring, delicate spots of iris yellow sprinkle the edges of the pond where ducks raise their wobbly young ones. In the summer, water lilies dot the surface. Swaying cattails spike the rim, dotted in turn with red-winged blackbirds. Later in the season, the ducks sail lazily past the lily pads.

My wild irises and cattails greet me each time I round the corner by the local shopping mall. They continue to create a patch of peace for the neighborhood.

~Barbara Crick

The Red Brick House

You can never go home again, but the truth is
you can never leave home, so it's all right.
~Maya Angelou

I was cleaning out my bureau drawer when I found a photograph underneath my sweaters. It was a picture of the house in which I grew up—a big fourteen-room red brick house in Maryland.

Whether our upbringing was good or bad, we usually have vivid memories of our original homes. They are the back drop of our lives. Like most adults, I remember the yard as at least twice the size that it was in the picture. Maybe that's an emotional metaphor. Where we grew up was truly, in our minds, larger than life.

I remember we had two dining rooms. One for everyday with bright red bunches of cherries on the wallpaper. And one for company that had dark walnut panels and a crystal chandelier. The porch, with green and white canvas awnings, was in the back of the house and private, so I could hold onto the awning pole and gleefully spin around it, singing as loud as I wanted. I adored our magical house.

One summer, when I was eleven, I went to a camp about an hour away. But I couldn't wait to be home again. I so much missed the security of my red brick house, where I knew all the nooks and crannies.

I loved the familiarity of the imperfect details. There was a tiny circle of torn wallpaper by my bed, inside of which were little specks of plaster that resembled the man in the moon.

At the end of that summer, when my parents picked me up at camp, I distinctly remember my mother turning around in the passenger seat and reaching to touch my arm as I sat in the back. "There's something we need to tell you," she said.

I put my hands on either side of me on the seat, literally bracing myself. I could tell from her tone this was going to be bad.

"Honey, the house was just too much for your dad and me and I'm afraid… we had to sell it," she said.

"You mean we're not going home?"

I can still see the pained expression on her face. "We have a new home right nearby. A modern condominium."

In shock I said, "When did you sell it?"

"About a month ago."

"Why didn't you tell me?"

"Because we didn't want to ruin your summer." This was all so terribly hard for her to say to me.

"Who's living there now?"

She took a deep sigh and said, "There's more to tell you." How could there be more? "We sold it to a man who's going to build an apartment complex on the land and the house has been—"

I interrupted her. "It's been torn down?"

She nodded yes. I was furious. We didn't drive past the wreckage, thank goodness. We went straight to our little condo.

Responding dramatically like most kids would, I felt that my life had been torn apart along with the house. I went to my bedroom, which my mother had furnished with lovely light blue wicker, and slammed the door. I cried the rest of the afternoon, only pausing to scream at her, "How could you do this to me?"

And so, as I looked at the photograph I had found in my bureau, I had the same little girl's reaction that I did on that day long ago. And it startled me that I could be so self-centered, even at age eleven. "But now I'm no longer a little girl," I said to myself. "I'm certainly old enough to see things from my mother's point of view." And that's when I experienced a profound healing change.

I took the photograph to my bed and sat down with it in my hands. I envisioned my mother in my mind as if she were alive today and I pretended I was in that very back seat on the day that she told me the news.

I spoke from my heart to my mother's heart. "Mom," I said aloud with my eyes closed, "I can only imagine how hard it was for you to tell me about the house. And now I can see that at that stage of your lives, it was a struggle to keep it up. The gardens were so much work and the housecleaning was endless. You must have been so relieved to move to a condo."

I felt tears in my eyes but they were tears of comfort in bonding with my mom this way. "I wish that I hadn't reacted so horribly."

At that very moment, I realized that she'd probably say, "You never meant to hurt me. You were just eleven. I understood you'd feel betrayed and your life would seem shattered. You didn't react horribly at all. You reacted the way any little girl would."

I continued to speak, feeling soothed by the connection. "I remember you surprised me that night over dinner when we heard the sound of a telephone ringing from my new bedroom," I said quietly. "You had your friend call the number of the Princess phone you bought me as a present. I can still see us running into my room and finding the pink telephone under my bed. I know you did your best to make it better for me. I'm so sorry."

"It's time to stop doing this to yourself," I could almost hear her say. "You have nothing to be sorry for."

"Mom, I want you to know that I have the very same crystals from the chandelier. They're hanging in my windows as sun catchers. In the mornings, the prisms of glass cast dancing rainbows all around my living room. The wallpaper in my kitchen even has bunches of bright red cherries on it."

"I love you," I heard her whisper, "and I know that you love me too." In my mind, my mother forgave me, just as she probably did so many years ago on that day in the car.

I got up and safely tucked the photograph back under my sweaters. Then I closed the drawer and said, "The house where I grew up is still a part of me today, the way my mother and my father are still a part of me... and always will be."

I knew that the next time I cleaned out my drawer and came across the photo, I'd feel happy instead of sad. With this newly found compassion for my mother and her compassion for me, I had turned a corner I didn't think was possible, opening doors for a lifetime of healing.

~Saralee Perel

House-Whispering in Tucson

A house is not a home.
~Polly Adler

Sun flows through the living room like the tide, washing slowly over my bare toes. It warms the back of Einstein, a wirehaired Dachshund, who is hovering around me. He looks like an escapee from a fairy tale. A scientist some temperamental sprite cast a spell on. Instead of concocting chemicals in a lab — poof! — he is a dog with bushy eyebrows and a big banana nose playing with squeaky toys.

For the next three months, I will be living in his home, acting as an emissary of goodwill for his moms, who are adapting to a prolonged stay in Hong Kong. Their home is my equivalent of their Hong Kong adventure. As a professional housesitter, it's my job to decipher and adjust to new cultures.

On day one, I typically wander from room to room, like the dogs I also care for, circling around and around until I find it. The sweet spot. The space that makes me feel at home within someone else's home. It could be a patio swing, a study ripe with books, the company of a rose garden, or a surprise shaft of sunlight flowing onto my bare toes.

Because housesitting is a delicate art. You don't squat inside a house like a fat hen filling up all the spaces with your feathers. You don't startle it by jumping in belly-flop style, your presence, and all your belongings erupting in giant waves, displacing all else.

You sense the life already lived there, emanating through photographs of loved ones on the walls, couches that face enormous TVs rather than panoramic sunset views, windows naked, or lost in gauzy curtains, mirrors where you'd least expect them. You listen to the house's voice. Is it soothing? Agitating? Birdsong, traffic, floors creaking like old bones, a refrigerator's quiet hum, fans clicking on and off, fountains sweetening the air, clock alarms calling for their absent owners.

Some houses feel marshmallowy, with bed pillows that seem to multiply and overstuffed couches like great-aunts who won't let you go without one more hug. Some houses have bad breath. The scent of incense or garlicky meals clinging to the walls, not a drop of fresh air anywhere. One house was *Architectural Digest* immaculate, but its glow was checkbook-induced rather than from the heart.

It doesn't matter. You meet each house on its own terms. This is the space where people let their guards down. Take off their masks. How do you best protect such a place? Honor it? Harmonize with it while still being yourself?

You can't always. My most challenging house was coated with animal hair from the eleven rescued cats and three dogs that lived there. At the last minute the owners decided to board up all the kitty doors so the cats would not be tempted to flee.

I spent all week sneezing and praying I'd keep the countless cats inside while ushering the dogs out safely. Especially since one pup had a phobia about crossing thresholds. Once he was inside or outside, he was calm, but that in-between space terrified him into viciousness. The cats would swarm by the door while he hesitated, leering from the tops of filing cabinets, their tales swaying and curling, as if they could hypnotize me into doing their bidding.

In such moments I long for a traditional home all to myself. The truth is I haven't turned the key in a home I've owned since my first marriage, twenty-five years ago. In subsequent years, I've shared homes with another husband and a couple of boyfriends, rented a guest house on five acres of a wildlife sanctuary, rented a room from a midwife, finally falling into housesitting as a favor to a friend.

It made sense. As a writer, my laptop and I could travel anywhere. Did I need one building to house my emotions, my memories, my relationships? "Portable" became my mantra, inspired by the strong, creative women I befriended.

Like Leslee, who valued home as a launching-off point for her adventures. She'd worked with rescued wolves in the suburbs of Detroit, lived alone in the Upper Peninsula of Michigan, snowshoeing in and out of her cabin for groceries while seven months pregnant, swam with the whales in Baja, survived shamanic journeying in Peru. She was one of the most centered, intuitive people I knew.

And Sandy, a native New Yorker who followed an irresistible yearning to explore the Gila National Forest in New Mexico—by foot. She ended up living off that land for four years with nothing but pack burros to carry all her belongings. She walked the paths the Apaches once walked, soaked in the same hot springs that once allegedly soothed Geronimo's spirit. Every cell in her body told her this was home.

What joy, inhabiting the earth in such playful, earnest ways. I couldn't believe that anyone could dream such a large dream and literally walk right into it. I admired that sense of curiosity. The ability to expand the boundaries of home.

I expand my definition of home with every new house I inhabit. Sometimes I feel house-full. Sometimes it feels like I'm on a twenty-city bus tour, and I just want to stop packing.

"I could live here," I think about the adobe ranch house where Einstein and his buddy, Gracie, a rescued Greyhound, live. "I could move right in."

"You'll be out soon," I imagine telling my belongings, which are in storage. "We'll all be together soon."

I walk around, throwing Einstein a rubber chicken. I splash in the whimsical artwork and doors signed by the woman who painted them. I listen to the house humming with the good morning and good night lullabies sung to Einstein by his moms. I hear echoes of the coaxing cheers they give Gracie when she is slow of appetite. "Eat Gracie, eat!"

I can feel it all. The pathways of love created through this family's daily intimacies are as solid as their rooms and as easy to step into. Who needs pet and house care instructions?

For the next ninety days, this house will tell me all I need to know. We'll co-create a sanctuary that honors all inhabitants, present and absent, two-legged and four-legged. I'll thank the desert-tan walls, the hummingbirds in the gazebo, the kiva fireplace, the furry family. And I'll let the inevitable questions rise up under each footstep. Where will you live next? What do you want? Why aren't you settled? Surely my life has opened pathways of love, too. What are they creating? Something solid? A dream large enough for me to walk right into? Will my boyfriend and I be able to live together? Or will I, at last, step through the door into my own home?

"What do you think?" I ask Einstein. He runs toward me, rubber chicken in his mouth, short legs traversing the carpet like the cavalry coming to save the day.

~Jan Henrikson

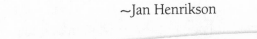

10

The Bubble Bath

There must be quite a few things a hot bath won't cure,
but I don't know many of them.
~Sylvia Plath

The tub in our new house beckoned to me. It wasn't just any tub, though. It was the likes of which I'd never owned before. Never even dreamed of owning. It was a marvelously decadent Jacuzzi tub big enough for two, with jets and all. And it existed in our new house for me to use whenever I wanted!

I couldn't believe our good fortune. We'd been able to purchase our dream home for less than market value, which included this grand tub.

Granted, there was a reason for the bargain price. The previous owners hadn't taken very good care of the home. It needed a lot of repairs.

But they were mostly cosmetic and superficial. A little new carpet, some paint, and we'd be able to enjoy our beautiful dream home.

What was a little elbow grease? When we'd made the offer on the home, I'd been in the process of prepping and painting our Jacksonville house for our move to Nashville. I was an experienced DIYer. I could handle shaping up the Nashville house too.

Or so I thought.

Our new house was only six years old, but the previous owners had been very hard on it. It turned out there was a lot more wrong with it than stained carpet and scuffed walls.

Sometimes we had water pressure in our shower, sometimes not. The air conditioning worked sporadically. The dishwasher backed up on its first use and flooded our kitchen. One of the banisters had a disturbing jiggle, as if it was going to give way each time we grasped it. The roof leaked—a slow, gradual leak in our master bedroom that resulted first in a faint, almost imperceptible stain. We weren't even really sure we had a leak until a heavy rainstorm sent a deluge onto our carpet. The lawn sprinkler system exploded the first time we tried to use it and shot a geyser ten feet in the air until we could find the shut-off valve—an hour later.

Basically, everything we touched seemed to break, crumble, or collapse on us. We felt like Tom Hanks and Shelley Long's characters in the movie *The Money Pit*.

I'd wanted to take a bath from the very first day we moved in, but I had waited. It was going to be my treat after I completed all of my painting projects. (Which I thought would only take a week or two. I hadn't counted on the other repairs the house needed interfering with my painting schedule.)

Plus, with everything else that had gone wrong with the house, I feared my precious Jacuzzi tub wouldn't work either. I didn't dare touch it.

For weeks I only looked at it admiringly. Then one day the temptation proved too great. My arms and back ached from a hard day's work in the yard. I was sunburnt. I smelled. I was in desperate need of some solace.

Even if the jets didn't work, I could still soak in the tub—provided the floor held and I didn't go crashing into the living room.

Apprehensively, I turned on the water. I half expected the stopper not to work. But when the tub filled without leaking, I dared to press the on button. There was a pause, then came a rumbling grumble, a sputter, and those jets started spewing!

I let out a triumphant cry. After nothing but calamities, something was finally working right! And what a something it was. My big, beautiful, beloved tub! Calgon take me away!

I lit a candle, grabbed the bubble bath, and slid into the tub. I squeezed the bottle generously, not sure how much to use in such a large tub. Certainly more than a regular tub. I figured a third of a bottle ought to do it. Then I sat back, closed my eyes, and relished the massaging water jets.

For two minutes I knew heaven.

Then Mr. Meow, our ever-demanding feline, leaped onto the tub's ledge and meowed for attention. I promised him I would pet him as soon as I was done. But that wasn't good enough for him. He came closer, mewing louder. Something tickled my chin. I knew he was flicking me with his tail.

"Stop it," I admonished him, keeping my eyes closed. This was my time. He wasn't going to wreck it.

He tickled me again. With eyes still closed, I swiped at my face to try and catch him in the act. I knew his tricks. I might be able to resist his pathetic cries, but there was no defense against the powers of his tail. He'd use it to taunt me relentlessly until I paid him the attention he sought.

I simultaneously got whacked on the head and tickled on the chin. Either he was becoming incredibly talented or…

I opened my eyes and saw Mr. Meow's butt towards me, his tail swishing, but not to torment me. He was staring intently at the bubbles, engrossed in swatting them.

"Oh no!" I shouted, not at the cat, but because the bubbles had multiplied at an alarming rate. They were now threatening to spill over the tub and onto the floor!

Frantically, I searched through the field of foam for the off button to the jets. But before I found it, I saw that in his quest for a better bubble-batting spot, Mr. Meow had repositioned himself near the candle. His tail now swished mere millimeters from its flame. No sooner had I comprehended the possibility of his fur catching fire than it did.

I jumped up, grabbed him, and doused the flames with my hand.

My rescue was rewarded with a hiss and a nice gash across my belly before Mr. Meow squirmed free and jumped to the floor. Which was now a sudsy swamp, thanks to the bubble waterfall cascading over the tub's edge. He left a nice trail into the bedroom as he ran away.

I leaned over the tub to hunt again for the off button. I managed not to tumble head first into the tub as I shut off the jets. Then I rinsed myself off in the shower, bandaged my wounds, and headed downstairs for the mop and bucket.

So much for a nice relaxing soak.

Well, at least my dream tub had worked, but I learned relaxation was not necessarily synonymous with bubble bath. Just like renovations, it also required effort.

That first attempt at a bath was a disaster. I have since mastered the art of relaxing in my beloved tub. It requires flameless candles, locking Mr. Meow out, and using bath salts instead of bubbles.

~Courtney Lynn Mroch

Home Sweet Home

Buying and Selling

11

Shared Dreams

Kind people are the best kind of people.
~Author Unknown

My husband, Glenn, and I needed more than just a house. We needed a home for the fifteen of us... our Malamute and wire-haired Terrier, five cats, two Hereford cows, their calves, my horse and a shaggy donkey named Augie. When we moved to Napa Valley in 1970, we had no idea how hard it would be to find a place to live with our animal family.

After Glenn graduated from University of California at Davis in veterinary medicine, he took a job that started immediately. We searched for rentals but their owners were leery when they heard about all our animals. Desperate, we were forced to rent a two-room house allowing no pets.

Dear friends offered to temporarily watch our cats and we kenneled our dogs as we continued to search. Our cows and horse roamed a family ranch and Augie stayed back in Davis.

We missed our pets. No dogs shadowed us as we walked through the house or yard; no cats snuggled up to us on the couch. And outside, only unbearable silence. We yearned for neighing, braying and mooing.

Then we encountered a new complication. Soon there would be sixteen of us. I was pregnant with our first child.

"What'll we do?" I asked Glenn.

Ever the optimist, Glenn suggested that we buy a place. We, two new grads with school loans and a depleted bank account, had no business looking at houses for sale, but, we searched anyway. We wanted a cozy older home located on a rural lane surrounded by a couple of acres. Unfortunately, many prospective buyers wanted the same: the country life in a valley abundant with the beauty of vineyards, orchards, hay lands and horse ranches. But there remained a big difference between them and us: they had money and we only had dreams.

One day, our real estate agent drove us past a place on South Whitehall Lane. "This place will be on the market soon at double your price range, but it can't hurt to look."

The minute we saw the two-story house, huge barn, and six acres, our hearts beat faster. The owners waved us in to take a closer look at their home: a living room, fireplace, wood-paneled family room, three bedrooms, one wallpapered with tiny pink and white roses, perfect for a baby girl. I nudged Glenn in front of an upstairs window. "That view. Look at that view." The dark pine-covered Mayacamas Mountains rose up closely to the west, and across the valley to the east lay the oak-studded grassland hills, and in between, all the red and orange leaf change of early autumn.

Glenn's eyes widened when we stepped into an old dairy barn large enough to shelter both livestock and store hay. Mangers lined one side for feeding cattle and individual pens lined the other for isolating sick stock. Water from the "best well around" surged into sinks and troughs.

As we walked through the fenced fields, Glenn gave my hand a squeeze. "This is perfect."

The owners, Bill and Neva, told us the place had been a dairy for decades. They bought it and later their daughter raised a small dairy herd for her Future Farmers of America project. After she had graduated from high school, she moved away. Soon Bill and Neva had difficulty with the upkeep, especially after Bill's father took ill.

Bill told us, "Dad's getting too frail to work his orchard. It's an hour and a half commute there and back. We need to move in with him, help him."

He pointed at the barn needing shingles, the milking shed with missing boards, the nursery trees at least seven feet high outgrowing their one-gallon pots. "We can't manage both places."

Neva lowered her eyes. "We'd planned on living out our years here."

Glenn spent the rest of the afternoon at his desk, figuring and re-figuring, determining if we could manage it. "With my salary, we can make the monthly payments," he told me, "but make a down payment... no way."

I slid an arm around his slumped shoulders. "Something will turn up. Besides, our baby can sleep with us for a while."

It didn't look good. But worse yet, the real estate agent had been wrong; it did hurt to look at a place we couldn't afford. I dreamt about it. I imagined rocking our baby in a chair next to a window watching my dark-haired husband filling the barn with hay, or watching our cats playing on the porch or our stock grazing in the lush pasture, or chickens pecking at bugs in the barnyard. I imagined riding Tinka bareback down the dirt road with our dogs running alongside me. I imagined everything that was not to be.

The next few days we couldn't help ourselves. We drove by several times, just looking and dreaming.

A couple of weeks later the real estate agent called. "Bill and Neva like you two. They were wondering if you're interested in buying their place."

"Sorry," we said. "We wish we could but we can't make the down payment."

Another week passed. Neva asked us to drop by. "This place needs to come alive again. It needs an energetic couple. Animals. Children. A young family to love it as much as we have," she said, her eyes misting. "But maybe something as basic as 'genuine love' could count as part of the down payment. We need the money. That's for sure, but if you really want to live here, love it as we have.... Tell you what we'll do. We'll lend you the money you're short for the down plus take a second mortgage. You can pay us back monthly in addition to your bank note. Would that help?"

We knew they could see the excitement on our faces.

"But," Neva said, "there is one condition." Glancing at Bill, she hesitated before continuing. "Our furniture… there's too much for Bill's father's house. Until we can add on a room, and since you have little furniture, we were wondering if you might store some for us. Our antique dining room set, it's precious… a family heirloom. If we could leave it in the dining room for a while…" She touched me on the wrist. "And in the meantime, of course, you could use it as your own."

"And," said Bill, "if I could return later to clean out the outbuildings. That would help."

So little to ask for offering so much—how could we answer with anything but "thank you."

We submitted our meager offer, which was immediately taken.

On moving day, two crystal goblets and a bottle of champagne sat on the hand-carved oak table alongside a note wishing us the best.

That evening as we sat in two overstuffed rockers they'd also left for us, we toasted the kindness of Bill and Neva, grateful they gave us a chance to step into the heart of Napa Valley, the perfect place for us, our animals, and our children.

~Karen Baker

12

The Home that Found Us

It is said that when Sedona finds you it paves the way.
~Arizona Folklore

I was notified in late August that the movie theater adjacent to my boutique in Houston was to be torn down and my store would have to close for a month. After a day of indignation I re-centered myself and realized this might be a gift of time... an intervention that I needed since I seemed to be burned out. I had even had a dream earlier that year about a major life change coming, so I talked with my husband Bob, who was already retired, about taking off on an adventure.

Three days later, Bob and I left the big city of Houston for the open road. Camping gear, road maps and high sprits in tow, we made our way westward. Fifteen hundred miles and three weeks later, reaching Flagstaff, our map showed a canyon road circumventing the interstate, passing through a town called Sedona and then reconnecting with the interstate. We could make Phoenix before nightfall.

Five miles into the canyon we were awestruck. We viewed overlooks descending thousands of feet into a sea of towering pines. Bob maneuvered hairpin turns, and as if at a tennis match, our eyes darted from one breathtaking vision to another. We had the windows and sunroof open, and the crisp September air was invigorating. We heard a rushing creek alongside the road. After another twenty miles and a 2,500-foot descent, cacti started to dot the landscape, and red boulders, hundreds of feet high, jutted out of the earth in a landscape reminiscent of a prehistoric playground.

My voice breaking, I said, "Bob... are you thinking?"

"Yes," he finished my thought. We had been taken over by a mystical sense of belonging.

The late afternoon sun, shining on the stone towers, turned them into glowing, iridescent works of art. Bob pulled into the first business we saw and ask a person where we might find a real estate agent.

I am a spontaneous person but Bob doesn't like change or surprises. Which is why when I had the dream, a few months before, about the coming of a major change in our lives, I gave him forewarning. He had learned over our time together that when I had a precognition, we could count on it.

At the time, it did not strike either of us as strange that we were spending the afternoon seriously looking at homes.

We returned to Houston and put the wheels in motion to close my business. We researched Sedona homes online and kept re-visiting one in particular.

The following month we returned to Sedona. We arrived the evening before our appointment and decided to find the house we were so charmed by on the Internet. Sitting right at the base of an 850-foot butte, we spotted it. A tear ran down my cheek. Joy, humility, gratitude and a childlike wonder filled me. Turning, I saw tears had formed in Bob's eyes too. Life had been hard for us, and we knew we were finally home.

We knew we would need three months, at least, to make the transition work. We sure couldn't pay for two houses.

The next morning I entered the home carrying a video camera, stating at each new room, "This is our entrance hall and... bathroom, etc." As we continued through the house, everything on our wish list was there—longed for amenities not shown in the pictures online.

We made an offer on the spot, and in two hours it was accepted. The couple had one stipulation, that they be able to lease it back from us for three months. We hugged and laughed.

Back in Houston I had one employee I was concerned about leaving without a job. Coincidentally, she said she had just been given a wonderful opportunity and was thrilled she could take it without leaving me in a bind.

My number one supplier was a major concern. How might my business closing affect her business? Over the years we had become somewhat dependent on one another. I was her biggest wholesale client and she was my main supplier. I called her the day I returned and asked her to lunch. She said she was just going to call me. Over a tasty lunch we laughed hysterically as she related that she and her husband had decided to retire and close the business. It also just happened that my six-year commercial lease would be up in three months.

Everything continued to fall into place in an uncanny way, and three months later we pulled into the driveway of our new home in Sedona. Within five minutes the neighbors were greeting us with well wishes and offers of help. In the second week we were given a "welcome to the neighborhood party." Within two months we were an integral part of the community.

If you're not yet convinced, let me tell you of my birthday, four months later. No one in Sedona knew that I had gone through years of therapy for flashbacks, regressions and the debilitating effects of childhood abuse. Childhood birthdays had not been happy occasions for me.

Upon hearing it was my birthday, a neighbor invited the block over for cake. When I arrived a cardboard glittered tiara was placed on my head. Among the balloons and paper streamers, we played pin the tail on the donkey, blew bubbles and drenched each other in water gun fights. Long past my prime, immersed in the childhood antics I missed so long ago, with a lump in my throat and joy in my heart, I blew out my candles. My neighbor doesn't know how she was so on target—she says the idea of a big child's party "just came to her."

And Sedona just came to us. Wrapped and ready.

~Miki Butterworth

The Auction

Take risks: if you win, you will be happy; if you lose, you will be wise.
~Author Unknown

"We must be crazy to even consider buying a house we can't see inside," I told my husband Don. That morning we drank two pots of coffee as we sat at the computer, waiting to find out if we had the chance to do just that.

"Desperate is more like it," he replied.

"Well, don't worry." I shrugged. "It's about as likely as us winning the lottery." In this case the prize would be our dream home and the end of a frustrating two-and-half-year search during a drought in the Seattle real estate market.

For thirty-three years we'd lived in suburbia, raised our children and remodeled our home to suit our growing family. Now we were empty nesters. We longed for the late day sunlight, blocked by the hundred-foot Douglas fir forest that had grown up around us. There were too many steep stairs inside and too much traffic outside. Our dream was to move to a neighborhood in the city with easy access to downtown, the Pike Place Market and the waterfront. Most of all, we wanted open skies and westerly sunset views over Puget Sound.

Two days earlier, driving away from another disappointing open house, we noticed a vacant home on one of our favorite streets. We still disagree about who actually spotted it. Perched on a hillside in the middle of the city block, the 1950s brick and wood bungalow with large picture windows looked perfect. It was the kind of house that never seemed to come up for sale.

As we pulled to the curb, I noticed an official-looking notice posted on the front door. "Maybe it's for sale by owner?" I tried to contain my excitement. By the time we were up the front steps I'd fallen madly in love. "Look at the view—the mountains, the water—it's exactly what we want."

Don pointed to the note. "Yeah, but read this. It's a foreclosure, going to an online auction. With this location and view, there's no way we could afford to bid high enough."

I wasn't about to give up. "We have to try. Come on, we're here. Let's at least look."

We skulked around the overgrown yard, peeking in the windows, trying not to draw attention to ourselves. "The hardwood floors are beautiful." From the kitchen window I spied an old stove and worn countertops and linoleum. "It's all original."

Don checked out the exterior. "Brick and siding looks okay… gutters and downspouts are in good shape."

I felt hopeful as we headed home. "It needs a lot of work inside, but we've done that before. With a foreclosure, there may not be much competition."

He shook his head. "Contractors watch for them all the time. Some builder will nab it, do a quick renovation and sell it for a million."

"We have to try." When we returned home, I pulled up the online auction website to read the rules. We would have to submit proof of finances and a large deposit. But most daunting, the winning bidders were not allowed inside the house until they officially owned it!

Then I noticed the auction date. "Oh no! It's the day after tomorrow. If we're going to have any chance at all, we'll have to act fast."

I couldn't sleep that night thinking about the risk we'd be taking if we actually got the winning bid. But my mind kept returning to our dream of living in that neighborhood, enjoying sunsets and unobstructed views away from the dark, gloomy woods. Back on the Internet the next morning, I found county records and a few old real estate photos that gave us an idea of the house history and floor plan. We already knew the kitchen and bathrooms needed remodeling but the rest was still a mystery.

I convinced Don to return to the house that afternoon. In spite of some concrete cracks and dingy paint, it appeared livable. We stood on the front porch and took in the view one more time. I turned to him. "I know we'd be starting over but look where we'd be living!"

He grinned. "Okay—we might as well try. I think I have one more remodel left in me!"

I couldn't sit still the next morning watching the online auction site as the timer counted down to the noon closing. Bids rose slowly on the screen. One minute to go. My heart raced. The last bid we'd submitted still stood on the screen in front of us.

"The high bidders are all waiting to jump in right at the end, like us," Don said, confirming what I'd been thinking. Our strategy was to hold back with our last and final offer right before the bell.

I counted the seconds off. No other bids came up. The bell rang and the screen went blank. Then the following words came across our computer:

CONGRATULATIONS—YOU ARE THE WINNING BIDDER!

I was stunned. When I finally caught my breath, I screamed out loud and did a happy dance across the kitchen floor. "I can't believe it! We did it! We actually got the house!"

"Not so fast," my ever-cautious husband responded. "It's not over yet. Remember, our bid has to be accepted."

A few minutes later a man from the auction company called. Our bid was below target. We had no idea what that amount was, but we would be notified in a week or so if the mortgage company currently holding the title was willing to accept it.

That week turned into three grueling weeks. I was sure we'd get the house. Don was sure we wouldn't. The wait was killing us. Finally, Don received a call on his cell phone in the middle of a dental appointment. The caller told him our bid had been rejected. "But you're very close," he added. "You have one last chance to bid higher if you do it right now!"

Our dentist waited while my husband made the big decision that changed our lives. He offered the maximum amount we'd originally planned to bid during the online auction.

"That ought to do it!" the man said. "I'll get back to you soon."

Two days later, we got the good news—the house was ours! Then reality hit—we still had another month of waiting before closing, when we could actually step inside our new home.

When that day finally arrived, our Realtor received the key and walked us through our house. "No bad surprises," Don said with a sigh of relief as we made our way through the main floor.

"Some good surprises too," I added as we took the stairs to the basement. The garage was deep enough for two cars and a workshop, and there was plenty of space for guests and an exercise area.

We've been in our new home for six weeks now and there are many remodeling projects ahead. Don still teases me. "Aren't you glad I spotted this place?"

"Yes dear." It's easy to agree with him now as I stare out the window at blue sky, snow-capped mountains and ferries gliding across Puget Sound. "Aren't you glad that I pushed you to take the risk?"

~Maureen Rogers

The Hunt

I work on the assumption that a house is successful if it's pleasant to live in.
~Alexandra de Garidel-Thoron

"Hey, Karen—I love what you've done with your house!" Pleased with my friend's compliment, I smiled and looked around my living room, enjoying my new color scheme. After all, Max knew his business as a successful real estate agent.

"You really have an eye for color and a knack for transforming an ordinary home into something warm and inviting. What do you say we go into business together?" Max continued. "I know I can easily sell this house and find you another one to fix up—something that just needs a facelift. Then when you're done with that one, we can do it all over again. It will be a great money-making proposition for both of us!"

I looked over at my husband, David, curious to see his reaction. After all, he was the handyman. It sounded like fun to me but how much fun would it be for him?

With a shrug of his shoulders, David replied, "Whatever makes you happy, honey, makes me happy."

Before we knew what hit us, the three-bedroom ranch-style home was sold to the first prospective buyer, giving us just thirty days to find another. How hard could that be? I loved to house hunt.

But, alas, at the end of thirty days, we found ourselves storing all our household possessions in a friend's barn, borrowing a camping trailer from another friend, and heading for a nearby lake to set up home for the summer with our four kids, ranging in ages from six months to six years. The kids loved swimming in the lake and digging in the sandy beach. They didn't seem to mind sharing the double bed at the end of the tiny trailer as the four of them lay crossways together. Our bed at the other end of the camper was the converted kitchenette table.

As the hunt continued, the summer days rolled by and lake living, with a community bathhouse and campfire cooking, lost its appeal. David also didn't appreciate his hour-long commute to work in the city. I decided we would never do this again. The next house we bought would be for keeps.

Three weeks before school began, we found a quaint two-story, dormer-windowed, Cape Cod-style home — only two blocks from the home we had sold! With just the right paint and wallpaper, I knew I could enhance its charm. Once more I delighted in digging through piles of wallpaper books, scouring through myriad color swatches and designing window treatments to create the precise effect I had visualized. And, once again Max "oohed" and "aahed" as he admired the transformation.

I was excited about discovering my talent for "decorating on a shoestring" with pleasing results. "Now, don't get any wild ideas about selling this house," I exclaimed. "The dust has hardly settled."

"I'm here when you're ready for the hunt to begin again," Max said with a grin. "We really do make a great team, don't you think?"

I was convinced that wouldn't happen anytime soon. After all, I was just beginning to enjoy the finished product and the fruits of our labors.

Then, with just a stroll around the block, it happened. There it was — my dream home — being erected on a neighbor's vacant lot. As I meandered through the rooms of the tri-level home, I could envision my family gathered around the kitchen table in the spacious kitchen, watching TV and playing games together in front of the brick fireplace of the family room, entertaining friends and family beside the massive living room fieldstone fireplace and enjoying dinner around the table in the formal dining room under the sparkling crystal chandelier. And, for heaven sakes, with four bedrooms, we wouldn't have to think of moving ever again. It would be our home sweet home!

As the contractor explained he was building the home on spec, I thought, how perfect is that! All I had to do was decide what I wanted for final colors and finishes and someone else would do the work. Even David should love that idea! Better yet, the kids wouldn't have to change schools, only their bedrooms. And, the nest egg we had put together from the profits of our real estate endeavors with Max would handle the down payment.

With David's familiar words, "whatever makes you happy, makes me happy, honey" ringing in my ears, Max put a "For Sale" sign in our front yard one more time.

"My family will think I'm crazy selling and buying another house so soon after moving into this home," I told David as we looked out the window at the real estate agent's sign. "Let's not say anything yet."

"Well, Karen, it won't be long before they'll be coming to our house for Thanksgiving," he replied. "We'll have to tell them sooner or later."

"Let's make it later," I retorted, wanting to postpone it as long as I could.

The week before Thanksgiving found us settled into our brand new home, complete with all my decorating touches. Still struggling with how to share the news with my family, I suddenly came up with an idea. After all, they really didn't need to know until the very last minute.

As David basted the turkey one last time, the doorbell rang. "Surprise!" I sang as I opened the door and greeted my astonished family clutching the directions we had taped to the front door of the former Cape Cod home.

After the initial shock wore off, Mother hugged me. "This is the perfect home for you, Karen. Does this mean the hunt is over?"

I smiled and thought, of course! But then again, who knows! For a bona fide house hunter, is the hunt ever over?

~Karen R. Kilby

15

Thumbs Up!

Jack and I spent eight years gut renovating our little suburban farmhouse. We built red oak floor-to-ceiling cabinets in the entrance, added wide plank floors, constructed new kitchen cabinets and counters, and even put in a dunking claw foot tub in the small guest bath. It was perfect! Well, it would have been perfect except that we had outgrown it now that Emma was six, Tucker was four, and Sam, our puppy, was now a sixty-five-pound Lab.

To test the waters we decided to put our house on the market ourselves. We figured it would take two to three months to sell. To our surprise (and fear) it sold in two days. We knew we had to act fast.

We called a real estate agent to show us houses. Jack and I were very specific about the property we wanted. We wanted a dead-end street (or a "cul-de-sac" as they say in Connecticut). Something private, with just enough land where the kids could play with Sam and I could plant the perennial garden I had dreamed of all my adult life. We loved the idea of finding the perfect location and then transforming the house that accompanied it into what suited us. We also wanted to stay in Stamford.

Jack and I sat down with the kids and explained that we had

outgrown our house and that we thought it would be fun to start looking for a new place. We asked each of the kids to tell us what things they would want in their dream house.

And when I say dream house, their desires were just that. Dreams. Emma wanted enough land for a horse and paddock, a lake to fish in and a forest to keep a real-life Simba lion. Tucker also wanted a lake where he could keep a fishing boat like his Grandpa's, plus a cave to explore with his many Batman action figures and Sam.

After culling through dozens of listings, Jack and I found fifteen properties we were interested in. They were scattered all over town and I knew it would be hard coordinating the hunt. Jack was in town that next weekend, but scheduled to be out of the country for the following three weeks, so our window for family exploration was short, as would be the attention span of our two little angels.

How could we make this fun and keep them engaged and us focused?

Then came the idea.

The next day the kids and I took a trip to the local arts and crafts store. We bought a piece of poster foam board, some construction paper and tape. When we got home we stapled a map of Stamford to the board. That night, Jack and I sat with the kids and looked at the specs for each of the houses we were considering. If we all agreed that a house was interesting, one of the kids would cut out the picture and attach it to the map. By the end we had selected eight houses to visit.

The next day the kids took out their construction paper and traced out eight thumbs. Emma used green construction paper, her favorite color, and Tucker chose Batman blue. Next, they cut them out and put them in two separate Baggies.

That Saturday we awoke early, had breakfast and packed a special snack bag along with our map board, thumbs and tape. Then we were off to start our adventure.

We went through the first house quickly, as it was so close to the main street and had such a tiny yard. The kids couldn't wait to run out, meet at the back of the car and post their thumbs down.

The next house was somewhat controversial as Jack and I shook when we saw Tuck run towards the looming cliff in the back yard. Thumbs up for him and after some discussion between siblings, Emma agreed with her brother and posted a thumbs up as well. Jack and I just gave each other the look.

This went on for the balance of the properties. After walking through and around each house the kids would get a twinkle in their eyes, run back to the car, open their Baggie, reach in and grab their blue or green thumb. Then they would carefully pull off a piece of tape and attach their thumb next to the corresponding property on the map. Great giggling would ensue as they would count the ups and downs on the map.

We made it through five listings that first day: six thumbs up and four thumbs down. Tucker really wanted the house with the huge rock ledge in the back so he could climb. With his young history of cuts, bruises and stitches, we didn't feel this would be wise. Emma liked the house with the pond in the back so she could go fishing and swimming whenever she wanted. Given the two huge snapping turtles we saw in the back, that didn't sit well with us either.

Although the kids were optimistic, nothing inspired Jack and me. The next morning we set out again on our hunt. The first house seemed like a contender. Perfect size, quiet street. The only drawback was that it was a bit too far from the schools and town. I was feeling a little better.

The second and third houses that day were nothing special. The last house was a nice-size split-level on a beautiful, tree-lined cul-de-sac right down from the elementary school, but from the curb it was less than appealing. The inside wasn't much better: it was dated, with shag carpet and shiny silver-felted wallpaper on the bathroom walls and ceiling. The kids loved going up and down the three levels. Despite its overwhelming décor there was something homey about it. It wasn't until we went into the back yard and walked through the overgrown yard with what was left of an aboveground pool that Jack and I fell in love. The property was adjacent to a 100-acre nature center and preserve. Suddenly the kids' dream lists didn't seem so crazy.

When we got home the kids were exhausted, as were we. They went off to bed while Jack and I added our own thumbs to the board.

One property got all four thumbs up. The ugly tri-level on the jungle-like property. We went back the next day and made an offer.

~Jeanne Blandford

16

Puzzling Out Our Problems

To us, family means putting your arms around each other and being there.
~Barbara Bush

t is amazing just how long it can take to lose one's home. When my family first became unable to pay our mortgage in late 2010, I thought we would have to move right away. I really believed that the sheriff would come to evict us right after we missed our first payment. And believe it or not, that's what I actually wanted to have happen. For years, my parents and I had tried everything possible to stay afloat in this tough economy and keep the family home. Now that the last of our savings had been exhausted and there was no option but to move, I was oddly relieved. I knew it would be hard, losing the house to foreclosure and moving into a small apartment instead, but it seemed like the best way to make a fresh start. I was ready to go.

Little did I know that missing a mortgage payment was just the first step in a process that could last for months or even years. There were all kinds of bureaucratic hoops that had to be jumped through before the foreclosure process could really begin. And in a way, jumping through these hoops paid off. After almost a year of suspense and a mountain of paperwork, our mortgage company finally agreed to let us put the house up for a short sale instead, a much better option for my parents' long-term financial health.

Still, this introduced its own set of stresses. The huge jumps in utility costs meant that even without a mortgage payment we couldn't afford to keep living where we were. But if we moved before we had a firm offer, the bank would consider our home to be abandoned, and all the arrangements for the short sale would be null and void. So we embarked on a long-term waiting game, doing our best to keep the house in show condition while we continued to live in it.

Now, my family has been through a lot together. The very fact that as an adult I was living with my parents at all—in my thirties, I was diagnosed with a chronic pain disorder that made it impossible for me to live on my own—was proof that we generally faced even the most extreme challenges as a team. This time was different, though. The stress of losing our home was so extreme that we started turning on each other, sniping at each other and arguing over the dumbest things. I knew there had to be something I could do to raise everyone's morale—but figuring out what that was proved to be a challenge. All the fun things we'd once done to bring us together as a family were now way beyond our financial reach. What could we do instead?

The answer turned out to be hiding in our attic.

I'd originally found the old thousand-piece jigsaw puzzle when I was cleaning. Despite the fact that I loved its picture—the puzzle depicted a beautiful stone cabin in Scotland, surrounded by a peaceful Highland loch—I'd put the puzzle into a box of things to be given away. But one evening, when we were all gathered around the TV watching yet another news report about the mortgage crisis, I knew I had to do something to distract myself or go crazy. I brought down the puzzle and emptied its pieces onto the table.

The effect of this was rather startling. Suddenly, the television was forgotten. My parents made their way to the table as if magnetically attracted. My dad instantly sat down beside me and started helping me turn all the pieces right side up. My mom picked up the box and surveyed it with surprise. "We haven't put together a puzzle as a family since you were in grade school," she said. "I'd forgotten we even had this."

"I know. So had I."

She looked at the box's picture sadly. "I always wanted to live in a place like this, you know," she said. "This picture always felt like home."

"Yes, I know. It always did for me, too." I gave her a hug. "Maybe we really will live someplace like it someday. After we've had some time to get back on our feet."

My mom looked startled. I think it was the first time she'd thought that there might be a future worth dreaming about at all, and it obviously took her aback a little. "Maybe," was all she said. But she sat down at the table too.

As we started putting the pieces together, we quickly discovered that each of us had different "puzzling" gifts. My mom had an uncanny ability to find parts of straight lines, easily piecing together horizons and the edges of buildings. My dad was able to see subtle changes in color on pieces that just looked like plain old patches of blue to Mom and me, which let him piece together huge expanses of lake and sky. And when all else failed, I had a knack for seeing the actual shapes of the pieces themselves, for knowing exactly which "outie" matched up with each "innie." It ended up taking all three of these talents to put our puzzle together. And as we started figuring out which one of us could best work with which section of pieces, an amazing thing started to happen.

We started thinking like a team again.

No more sniping, no more stupid arguments. Now, when the stress of our situation got to be too much, we had something to do. Piecing together our Highland cabin required so much concentration that we could forget our other problems, at least for a little while. And it turned out that doing the puzzle had other benefits, too. Our real estate agent told us that having a jigsaw out on the table gave our house "a real feeling of home"—sort of the visual equivalent of the scent of baking bread. Several times now, we've come home to find that a prospective buyer has actually stopped to put a few pieces together, which our real estate agent says is fantastic. It means our visitors are much more likely to remember our house as a fun place to spend time. And thus, much more likely to make an offer.

Maybe someday soon, somebody will. In the meantime, my family has long since finished that first puzzle and moved on to complete three more. We've started a "Puzzle Exchange" with a few of our neighbors and friends, so everyone can have new puzzles to solve without having to spend money at the store. But I haven't traded away that first one. I painted it with puzzle glue so I could keep it forever. Wherever my family ends up, I'm planning to hang it on the wall, to serve as a reminder of the wonderful future we still can build.

And someday, when we're once again living in the house of our dreams, it will remind us of what we accomplished together.

~Kerrie R. Barney

17

How to Speak Realtor

Next to the writer of real estate advertisements,
the autobiographer is the most suspect of prose artists.
~Donal Henahan

Last week we moved into a new house. Well, some of our stuff moved. The rest is somewhere else. I don't know exactly where that somewhere else is, but the movers assure me that someday they'll figure it out. Honestly, I'm trying to look on the bright side about this. If the boxes are lost, I don't have to unpack them. Still, it would be nice to have plates to eat on.

Anyway, I learned a few things on the road to a new house. The first thing I learned is that you have to see a lot of yuck before you find the house of your dreams. I also learned that there are still people on this earth who think white carpet is a good idea. Clearly, they don't have a twelve-year-old boy and his dad living with them, as I do.

But thanks to my real estate agents—who, by the way, were awesome, fantastic and wonderful—I actually learned a foreign language. Not Spanish or Mandarin Chinese. Nope, I learned to speak Realtor. I'm not fluent by any means. All the technical terms frankly just sailed in one ear and out the other. But I did learn a few useful phrases that I plan to use the next time I look for a house. Which, according to Harry, should be when I'm ninety-seven.

Cozy Eat-in Kitchen
This kitchen has two cabinets, a stove and a mini fridge. The only reason you eat in here is because there is no place else to eat. SEE: Intimate Family Room, below.

Intimate Family Room
Your entire family will be squished together on the floor watching *American Idol*, because the room is too small for your couch.

Dripping with Charm
The roof leaks.

Priced Below Market
Yes, if this was 2005. Otherwise, it's way too much money.

The Bank's Loss Is Your Gain
Really? When have you ever seen a bank give away something for free? Once I got a toaster, but a house is a different thing entirely. And the toaster never worked anyway.

Ready to Move in
It's empty except for the family of spiders that have taken up residence in the bathtub.

Views! Views! Views!
On a clear day, if you stand in the living room next to the window, turn slightly to the right and squint you can see a mountain. ALTERNATE DEFINITION: A supermodel is your neighbor and she forgets to close the blinds. Harry searched for this house, but we never found it.

Handyman Special
The sellers broke everything and you can now pay them for the privilege of fixing it all yourself.

Ready for You to Make Your Own
The sellers took everything, including the built-in appliances, lighting, and carpet.

Professionally Staged
The house looked awful, so we paid someone to come in and make it look better. Once we take all their stuff away, the house will look awful again.

Entertainer's Dream
A group of rowdy teenagers broke into this vacant house and had a party. They left the empty keg, beer-stained carpet and cigarette butts in the overflowing toilets for the lucky buyer.

Motivated Seller
They are desperate, but not so desperate that they won't laugh at your prudently low offer.

So you see, I am fairly fluent. And just in case you were wondering, yes, the house I bought had one of those terms in its ad. We ended up with the Entertainer's Dream, equipped with the features listed above!

~Laurie Sontag

18

Barely Listening

Courage is what it takes to stand up and speak;
courage is also what it takes to sit down and listen.
~Winston Churchill

We were selling our old house and moving to the beach. The first showing of the house was uneventful. I waited at my neighbor's house until the tour was over. The potential buyers were underwhelmed.

The next showing went a bit differently. After the tour, I watched the real estate agent and her clients drive away and returned home from my neighbor's to change clothes.

I was upstairs, undressed, when my front door opened and the agent and her clients re-entered, talking loud enough for me to hear. As they started up the steps to the bedrooms, in sheer terror I jumped into my husband's small closet and hid beneath the closely packed suits, shirts, and shoes.

The buyers were measuring the upstairs bathroom. Then they proceeded to our master bedroom where I cowered with fear in the closet. I held my breath, determined not to cough or sneeze and scare them to death or worse.

They sat down on the side of the bed only three feet from me and began to discuss what price they would offer us. A couple of eternities went by.

With my long history of claustrophobia, I knew this wouldn't end well. I started hyperventilating, wondering what piece of clothing I could substitute for the usual brown paper bag to breathe in.

I contemplated sliding to the closet floor to breathe under the door but the floor was covered with John's shoes and rolls of Christmas wrapping paper that I still hadn't put back in the attic. "Organization" was not my strong suit.

Still, the agent and her clients talked. And talked. And talked. They wondered how quickly we could vacate the house if they purchased it. I could have told them: "Just as soon as the coroner and hearse arrive to pick me up."

I knew I had to get out of that closet soon. I thought about jumping out, throwing my arms in the air and yelling, "Tada!"

I thought of stumbling out and pretending I had amnesia and didn't know who or where I was.

As my whole life passed before me, the front door suddenly opened and I heard my husband yell, "Hello, anybody here? I'm John."

The three quickly got to their feet and hurried downstairs to say hello to John and continue their discussion in the car.

There is a God.

~Mariane Dailey Holbrook

Home Pee Home

A little girl is sugar and spice and everything nice—
especially when she's taking a nap.
~Author Unknown

"**B**uckle up," I said.

"Where are we going?" asked Zoe from her car seat in back.

"On an adventure to look at houses."

"What kind of houses?" she asked, as she rifled through her snack bag loaded for a three-hour expedition.

"We're thinking about getting a new house."

"Why? Our house isn't broken."

"You're right, but since you're going to kindergarten soon, we want a house near a good school."

"But I like my house. You always drive me to school, so I don't need a new house."

"Well, don't worry, we aren't getting one today. We're just looking." So much for my psychology training. We'd barely pulled out of the driveway and already the troops were dissenting.

"Hey, let's listen to some music," I said cranking up the volume on the *Annie* soundtrack. I had to pace myself; Zoe had become quite the debate expert when she had an opinion. I knew I was pushing my luck, because she'd come home from preschool at 11:30 and we'd be gone for a long time. When Zoe reached that horrible level of tired where most kids conk out, she opted for nuclear meltdowns where she'd spin out her final energy and then crash, leaving a distraught and depleted mother in her wake.

We were meeting a real estate agent to show us around, and agreed to meet at a designated location. The agent suggested I transfer Zoe's car seat to her vehicle so the agent could get to know us and explain some things about the neighborhood. I eyed the pristine Mercedes with the ivory interior and every nerve fiber and muscle twitched with anxiety.

"Oh, it's okay, it'll be easier if I take my car and follow you, then Zoe can listen to her music and eat the snacks that I brought."

"Don't worry," she said, "I just want you to sit back and relax."

How bad could grapes and Cheez-Its be on ivory interior? At least Zoe had already finished the peanut butter sandwich.

"So what kind of house do you like, Zoe?" the agent inquired.

"My house. I don't want a new house."

"Maybe we could put her music on," I suggested.

Luckily the houses were all pretty close, so actual car time was kept to a minimum. Zoe liked getting in and out of the car and racing up the stairs or driveways of new houses, now seemingly disconnected from the thought that any of these houses could replace hers. There were houses that were still occupied, though the owners weren't present, and houses that were totally vacant.

Zoe began an independent scoring system, developing criteria for what made a house "good." The first thing was it had to be cartwheel-worthy. Empty houses fared better in this category. At the homes where furniture was present, before I could set the rules about not cartwheeling, she'd either clunked on a table or come close to a delicate object. Houses with rugs, versus stone or wood floors, were also winners because of their softer thud factor. In fact, Zoe developed a signature scoring system saying, "I'd give it three cartwheels," if it was pretty good. The next most important feature was how good the echo in the bathroom was when she'd belt out "Tomorrow."

We had seen six houses and I knew we were living on borrowed time. We still had two more houses to see. We drove up a steep and oddly pitched driveway, with a sharp left turn, to see a rather nice house with large double doors. "Geesh, who can drive up that thing," I said as the agent made a second attempt, complete with the sound of screeching rubber.

Immediately upon entering the home, we were in a six by six space facing a doublewide staircase that rose straight up to a narrow landing, which led to the rest of the house. I felt dwarfed in the hole of this space and strangely vulnerable with the guillotine glass panel chandelier that hung above me.

"Oh my gosh," I said. "I feel like Alice in Wonderland. Everything is so odd." Zoe raced ahead of us and found a large carpeted area worthy of multiple cartwheels and whirling dervish spinning. I could tell she was getting punch-drunk dizzy. It wasn't long before she fell, got a rug burn, and began a mini-meltdown. "Okay, honey we're leaving in a minute," I said, as I quickly dashed through the rest of the house trying to get a feel for it. The hallways were long and narrow and there seemed to be a series of extra high walls that divided the front from the back of the house, as well as a thirteen-foot retaining wall in the back yard. But the view was nice and the lot above the retaining wall was on open parkland.

"Time to roll," I said to the agent. "We've seen enough for today." I scooped up a whining Zoe and carried her down the long stairway. Too tired to go nuclear, she actually slept on the forty-five minute ride home. That evening at dinner, we talked about the house, with Zoe giving her full account. Even though she gave it "four cartwheels," she said she still liked her house with the "fuzzy staircase" better. I liked parts of the house, but between the scary driveway, imposing staircase, and weird high walls, it just didn't feel right. Still my husband was intrigued, and we made arrangements to see it again. We visited that house six more times trying to make a decision.

On our last visit, Zoe was once again with me. The novelty of doing cartwheels had worn off and she was just plain pooped, so I lay her down on the carpet in the master bedroom while I looked at everything in scrupulous detail. When I was ready to leave I went to wake Zoe. I realized she had peed in her sleep, soaking both the carpet and her clothes. She awoke crying and grumpy and immediately began stripping off her clothes. There were no towels to blot the rug and no spare dry clothes. I mumbled a lame and embarrassed apology, adding, "Well, nothing like home pee home." I carried my naked, crying Zoe to our car parked at the bottom of the driveway—I still hadn't dared to drive up.

The next day we asked our agent to put in our offer to buy. When it came time for inspection, I walked around with the inspector getting his opinion of the condition of the house.

"Well, on the basis of the smell of urine in the carpet, it's pretty obvious they have animals," he said.

"Hmm, it's a funny thing how animals pee to mark their territory and claim their homes," I said. "If only it were that easy for us."

~Tsgoyna Tanzman

A Gift from the Past

Men work together… whether they work together or apart.
~Robert Frost

e married each other after bitter divorces. Our families thought we were crazy to jump back in so soon. "Give the wounds time to heal," people said, but we were anxious to begin our life together. Love would repair the damage.

On the practical side, lawyers, ex-spouses, and broken-down cars had drained our savings, and we needed a house big enough for four children—immediately. That made us real estate bottom feeders. Most houses we inspected had been abused by previous owners. One didn't even have a kitchen sink, just a hole in the floor where the pipes had once been. These houses were scarred with broken woodwork, rotten porch steps, and holes in the walls from things thrown in anger. Staircase railings wobbled at the touch. The houses smelled like bad relationships.

"I'm sorry we can't buy anything better," I told Carol.

"We have each other," she said, snuggling close. "Home is where we are."

Among the wrecks was an estate sale far from the city. It would be a long commute. The grayed siding had never been painted, and the kitchen counter must have dated from the 1940s, with its black rubberized surface and curtains covering the shelves under it instead of doors. The bathroom—a single bathroom for the six of us—also had only a curtain, no door. Some wallpaper was peeling, and the furnace wheezed.

But no one had smashed into the walls or railings or taken a crowbar to the sills to pry open a stuck window. There were even beautiful features. The living room had a shiny new hardwood floor and a massive fieldstone fireplace. And above the ugly kitchen counter was a set of fairly new cherry cabinets. It was better than anything else we saw, so we snapped it up that same day.

The most immediate problem was the weatherbeaten barn that sagged like the back of an old horse. The entire structure swayed when you walked on the second floor. We wouldn't have to worry about that for long as it turned out, for it would collapse completely under our first winter's snow. The house was a blend of the old and new, just like us. It had been worn down by time and use, but the owners had not mistreated it. The elderly Ingrahams who had lived there for fifty years had made improvements when they could as they raised their big family. They must have envisioned the totally renovated home they would create someday. But when their children finally were independent, the couple was too old to finish the job. Carol and I were sure we could bring the house to its full potential.

One Ingraham spouse had a sudden stroke and died, and the other passed within days. Stunned, their children held an auction. The house had only been on the market a few days when we bought it, so many of the Ingrahams' possessions remained: old salves and pills in the bathroom, crumbly sponges and half empty bottles of cleaning solutions under the kitchen sink, a well-worn armchair, and in the back of a closet, ancient board games from half a century earlier and a few Christmas decorations in a crushed box.

I was uncomfortable; it felt as if we had elbowed out the elderly couple. We had bought a family's home, not an empty building. The couple's ghosts seemed to hover, wary of our invasion. Did they disapprove of us? The nerve of strangers wearing rubber gloves and making faces when we threw out their medicines and salves. I just felt unworthy spying on their secret ailments. After all, they were a wholesome, traditional family who never divorced.

Yet we had young children like they did and our own salves and pills. Our own worn chair sat in the corner where theirs had been. When our four children thundered upstairs or rolled screeching down the little grassy hill outside the kitchen, it must have sounded like it had fifty years ago when the Ingrahams first moved in. The house was getting another chance. Why not us?

Our kids found a rubber replica of "throw up" in a closet and began giving dramatic, gagging performances as they flung it onto the floor at our feet. One night they discovered a *Parcheesi* game with split corners and a worn board. "Look Dad!" they yelled as if it were buried pirate treasure. "The Game of India!" We sat around our chipped kitchen table and rolled dice from the tumbler. The kids ganged up on Dad, of course, and laughed triumphantly as they sent my pieces back to start. Exaggerating my groans made them enjoy it more. In the kitchen I imagined the couple's ghosts watching us. Did they remember how their kids and grandkids had thrown up that fake vomit and played *Parcheesi* with them? Did it reassure them that we were not so different after all? A long line of owners had kept this house alive over the last 100 years. Now it was our turn to rebuild the house—and our family.

When I slapped the first coat of red paint on the bare siding, I knew the old man would be relieved. When I built new kitchen cabinets to match the cherry cabinets and dragged out the black rubberized counters, I could almost hear Mrs. Ingraham sigh, "Oh! At last!" That lovely ghost offered us a housewarming gift in spring when her bulbs and flowers blossomed—tulips, crocus, snowdrops, rose of Sharon, lilacs, Jack-in-the-pulpit, and so many others. Forget-me-nots covered the backyard in a bed of blue mist—a gift of life from the dead. I mowed around the flowers to let them sing until they withered. We would not forget. When my wife revived the herb garden and I salvaged some red oak cabinets broken by the collapsed barn roof and built a chest from the intact boards, I knew the Ingrahams would approve. They knew how to make the best of what they had.

We became friends with the dead couple, for tending things

together creates bonds. So what if they were dead and we were alive? The house needed all of us. Maybe I'd dig out one of their unbroken Christmas ornaments from the closet of treasures and hang it on the Christmas tree for them. There would always be room for those ghosts. My wife and I wanted to build our marriage better than the first ones, and I was glad to have that house be the place it happened.

~Garrett Bauman

What You Take With You

Memory is a way of holding onto the things you love, the things you are, the things you never want to lose.

~From the television show The Wonder Years

It felt surreal to watch my dad push the "For Sale by Owner" sign into the cold winter ground. We had moved into the little white house when I was only four years old. Now I was almost a teen. It had seemed like we would stay in this house forever. Now I knew that we wouldn't.

I didn't want to move. I didn't want to leave this house and its memories behind. I loved our life here. How could we just pick up our lives and leave behind everything that happened here?

That night, we gathered around the table for dinner.

"It will be so nice to have a bigger house. Our family just barely fits in this tiny dining room," my mom said. She glanced across the table at my two younger brothers and me. "I can't believe how much our family has grown since we bought this house. Back then we were only a family of three."

"I'll just be glad to be closer to work. It takes me almost an hour to get there," my dad said as he passed a salad bowl. "Why don't we spend next weekend driving around and looking at some of the houses we saw online?" My mom nodded her head.

I pushed my meal around on my plate, uneasy. "I don't think I want to move," I said tentatively.

My mom cocked her head and frowned. "Why not?"

"I like this house," I said. "We've lived here forever. This is where I learned to ride a bike. I helped dad put the windows in the family room. I wrote my name in pen on the basement wall. I don't want to forget all of those things."

"We're going to move into a new house, where you'll have lots of fun and make new memories," my dad said. "I promise."

I hung my head. "Okay."

We spent the next several months looking at houses. I didn't want us to find one. I knew that it would just bring us one step closer to leaving our home. One day, we looked at an old Victorian home on the Mississippi River. It had a nice yard with a big tree for a swing. The staircase was curved, and there was a secret door underneath it. There were enough bedrooms for my brothers and me to each have our own. And it was only ten minutes from my dad's job.

My parents loved the house. I wasn't so sure. The house was nice; that wasn't the problem. I just didn't know how I was going to leave behind a home filled with such great memories.

It took a while to iron out the details, but a few months later my parents told us that we were buying the house. Not long after that, a buyer started showing interest in our old home. Soon papers were signed, and we began to prepare our old house for a new family.

One day, my mom and I sat on the living room floor, packing our belonging into big brown boxes. I still wasn't at peace about the move, and my mom could tell.

"I know it's hard to leave good things behind, Logan," Mom said as she tore off a piece of packaging tape. "It's hard for me too. But God will bring new blessings. When one door closes, he always opens another." She tousled my hair. "Could you pass me another box?"

I didn't feel completely at ease, but I knew she was right. "Thanks Mom," I said. We unfolded the next box together.

All too quickly, the big day came. We crammed our final possessions into the back of our van. Then we went back into our house for one last look. I walked up the driveway where I had learned to ride a bike. I walked through the living room where my mom had read us picture books. I looked out the windows that my dad and I had put in. Then I went to the basement where I knew my name was scribbled on the drywall in ballpoint pen.

It was gone, covered by a few strokes of new paint.

I guess that's just the first memory to go, I thought as I slid my finger over the spot where I had written my name years ago. Then I noticed something that I had missed before. There was a crisp cut square around the place where my name had been. The saw lines told me everything that I needed to know. Somebody had very carefully cut out the square of wall with my name on it and replaced it with a new piece. So that the memory wouldn't be left behind.

And suddenly, everything felt better. I understood what I had been missing all along. We might be leaving our old home behind, but we were taking our memories with us. Just like that square of wall. It wasn't really the house that mattered, it was the memories that we had filled it with. We could take those with us no matter where we lived, and we would add to them in our new home.

I walked slowly up the stairs and found the rest of my family. "I think I'm ready to go," I said.

My mom smiled at me, knowing that I had found my peace.

As we walked out of the house and piled into the van together, we said goodbye to our old home. It was still sad to leave that place we had loved so much behind. But we had our memories tucked inside our hearts. That's what mattered.

~Logan Eliasen

Renewed

Home is home, though it be never so homely.
~John Clarke

ot one kitchen cupboard door hangs straight. The furniture is secondhand with ugly, dated upholstery and the odd stain. None of the floors are level — when you walk from one room to another, you get the distinct feeling of walking the deck of a ship at sea. There are unusual odours whose source we have been unable to find and little black bugs we can't get rid of.

It is paradise.

My husband, two sons and I live most of the year in a comfortable home in a small Ontario city that is perched on two lakes. We have all the necessary comforts and room enough for us and the dog. The house started out as a two-bedroom bungalow but has grown with our family's needs. It has a nice yard and garden, though certainly nothing worthy of a magazine spread. We like to think we live simply, but every corner betrays the need to declutter our overabundance of "stuff." It was never in our long-range plans to own a second property, let alone in another province, but a summer holiday in 2005 changed our course forever.

The tourism people of Newfoundland and Labrador launch a wonderful ad campaign each year. The stunning images and toe-tapping music intrigued us and we made plans for a family trip. With two boys aged seven and five at the time, we boarded a plane and headed east, about as far east as you can go in Canada. From the moment we caught sight of the rocky coastline on our descent to St. John's, we were enthralled. For two weeks, we toured the area in our cherry red rental van, continually surprised by the beautiful vistas around each curve. A highlight for the boys was the whale-watching excursion, which brought our boat perilously close to mammoth humpbacks. For Mark and I, the stunning landscape, kindness of the people we met and relaxed pace made for a most satisfying holiday. There seemed little doubt we'd be back.

In the fall of that same year, I had an idea: What about buying property in Newfoundland? My husband and friends will attest that once an idea takes root within me, it becomes something of an obsession. And so I began looking at real estate pages online. Casually, you understand. Just for fun. No, I would tell myself, this was a crazy idea. It's too far away. But then, didn't we know many families who owned properties in Florida to which they went each winter? And that's in another country! It is land after all, I would reason, a fine legacy to leave our sons. With no hope of us ever being able to afford a vacation cottage in Ontario, maybe it wasn't such a crazy idea. The wheels continued to turn.

A few affordable properties caught my eye. By now, my husband Mark was on board and eager to get more details from the real estate agent. I had a moment's pause. Could we really do this? Well, not without actually setting foot in the cottages we were considering.

A weekend trip is not unusual for many couples. An easy three-hour flight meant it was manageable. But for us, this was an incredibly big deal. I remember landing in St. John's under grey skies and wondering what we were getting ourselves into.

A white-knuckle ride down the coast in pursuit of our real estate agent finally landed us in Renews. At the time, the population of this outport community was about 400. It boasted a post office, a general store, a church, a parish hall and a scattering of houses. We looked at two that were for sale.

The first was a roomy two-story house close to the rocky shore. While it certainly had potential, it needed too much work.

The second place was considerably smaller. But what it lacked in floor space it made up for in land—high up on a hill with almost two acres of rolling meadows. The afternoon sun poured through the windows, which offered a glorious panoramic view of the town and the harbour. It had a warm, cosy feel to it, and we immediately felt at home.

When we met the owner, who offered us tea and cookies, I voiced the question that had been preying on my mind: How would the residents feel about people from Ontario buying property in their community? His response was priceless.

"My dear," he began in his charming Newfoundland accent, "once they get to know you it will be like they've been waiting for you to come." That clinched it. Papers were drawn up and the deed was signed.

In the eight years since we bought our little yellow cabin on the hill, it has become our sanctuary. Each summer, we look forward to breathing in the sea air from our deck as the clothes blow on the line. Neighbours became friends, and over time, like extended family. We keep in touch throughout the year and have forged an enduring bond with them.

Renews, Newfoundland has a very special place in my heart. It will always be our family's beloved second home, waiting for us to return, open the windows and wake it up after a long winter's sleep.

~Joanne Webster

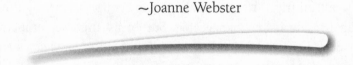

Home Sweet Home

Dreams Can Come True

Meant to Be

He is the happiest, be he king or peasant, who finds peace in his home.
~Johann Wolfgang von Goethe

"I'm sorry," said my landlord, as he pounded a stake with a For Sale sign on it into my front yard. "I haven't gotten a lot of construction jobs this winter, and I have to sell this property to make ends meet."

He looked genuinely apologetic. "When it sells, I'll help you move."

It was a small consolation, but I accepted his offer.

Looking back, awaking that Sunday morning to the sound of my small rental home being put on the market was probably the best thing that could have happened to me.

For years I'd been saving up, putting a little money away in a special account each month from my teaching salary, anticipating the day I'd find the perfect home.

I dug out my list of thirty-five things I wanted in my dream house. Years before, I'd doodled what I thought was a pretty good floor plan for a perfect home during a rather dull school board meeting. I found that drawing also among my saved papers.

"Sharon," I said, calling up a local real estate agent I knew personally, "it's time I looked for a house of my own."

"Oh boy!" she exclaimed. "Can't wait! Do you know what you're looking for?"

She was silent while I read her my entire thirty-five-point list.

"And where are you going to find this home?"

"I thought that was your job."

She laughed. "I mean, in what area of the peninsula shall we start looking?"

Times, as my landlord had noted, were certainly tough, and it seemed like every other house on the entire southwest Washington coast was up for sale. But I hadn't given much thought to which end of the peninsula I wanted to live on.

"I'll have to get back to you on that."

I spent the next couple of days driving around, checking out different towns, making notes, figuring what I'd spend on commuting to work, how far it was to a grocery store, etc. Finally, I had my target area narrowed down to a radius of seven miles from my school.

The following Sunday I went out looking for any interesting home with a For Sale sign within my arbitrary boundaries. There was only one home, tucked down a driveway a little way off the road, which seemed to call to me. I'd driven by the sign many times, but previously had not gone down the gravel drive to check it out.

"Sharon, can you get me into a house with someone else's realty sign in the yard?"

"Of course. Just tell me the address and we'll go see it today."

It had been raining all week, and I huddled underneath the short porch roof as Sharon unlocked the door.

"It's been empty all winter," she explained, "but the heat's been turned on low to keep things from mildewing."

"Funniest thing," I told her as we stepped inside, "I sketched the front of a house on my wish list that looked just like this one. It had a high peaked window in the front, and the attached double garage, and everything."

She smiled. "Did you bring your list?"

"Right here." I waved my paper at her.

I walked briefly down the hallway to the bedrooms, back through the utility room and kitchen, popped my head into the rec room and then sat down on the two carpeted steps leading to the sunken living room without saying a word.

"So…" Sharon said softly, "what do you think?"

"I think the Christmas tree goes right there." I motioned to the tall peaked windows facing us. "This house has the exact floor plan I sketched, and thirty-two of the thirty-five things on my wish list. Walking through this house was like coming home."

Sharon smiled. She got out her pencil, opened her file folder and started crunching the numbers. "You'll be able to assume the loan on this house at the current rate if you have enough saved for the down payment."

I tentatively returned her smile. "How much do I need?"

She handed me her notepad. The circled number was about a hundred dollars less than I had in my special "Someday I'm Going to Buy a House" savings account. My grin took over my entire face.

Together we figured out what the payments would be, and my dream house became a reality. That was twenty-seven years ago, the house is now paid for, and I've never even missed those last three things on my wish list.

And yes, every year, the Christmas tree goes right there, exactly where I planned it on that rainy Sunday afternoon in February, way back then.

Some things are just meant to be.

~Jan Bono

Dream Home

Home interprets heaven. Home is heaven for beginners.
~Charles Henry Parkhurst

My boyfriend and I had been planning to get our own place. We were in our early twenties and we wanted to stop living with roommates and trying to collect the rent from them.

One night we were at a party close to where we lived. It was a beautiful night so we escaped the crowd, walked down the beach to lie on the sand, and looked up at the stars. While gazing into the starry universe I said, "If we're going to do this, be together and live on this island, then we should live on the beach. The North Shore of Oahu is the ultimate place to be. There's nowhere else like it on earth."

A few days later I had a dream, one of those vivid dreams that you don't want to wake up from. In the dream my boyfriend and I were in a small beach house, sitting on a bed looking out sliding glass doors to the lanai (deck) that lay on the edge the beach. The vast sea shined as far as I could see. In the dream I was super happy and walked onto the wooden lanai that was painted a brick-red color. I had the dream several times and was always happy to go to that place.

A year later, a friend stopped by to ask for our help. We sat at the kitchen table listening to his sad story about his break up with his girlfriend. Because he wasn't a full-time Hawaii resident he needed someone to live in his house now that they had broken up and she had moved out. He came to his place only twice a year to surf and spent the rest of the time on the mainland, so he asked if we would consider it. We knew the house was across the highway and also on the beach. He told us he'd rent it for less than what we were paying at the time.

Before he left he simply said, "Think about it."

We watched him walk down the hill and out of sight before we broke the silence. "Think about it? Of course we want to live in that house!"

Moving in was a cinch because we had only the basics. It didn't take long to set up our own place — at last!

Being beach people, surfers, and sailors, we settled right in to the constant sound of the ocean; morning, noon, and night. Every day was a new moving picture.

The house needed lots of work, so we began fixing and maintaining it. One morning I was cleaning the lanai by hosing off the salt. Just outside the sliding glass doors, a piece of dark green deck paint flaked off. Underneath the color was brick red! My heart fluttered as I blasted more of the green paint off to reveal the red, the exact same color that I had seen so many times in my dream. I called my boyfriend at work and told him — we couldn't believe it. I knew right then this was where we were supposed to be.

Twenty-six years later my boyfriend is now my husband of twenty three-years. And we are still renting our dream home on the beach. We've patched, painted, rescreened and fixed the fuzzy wooden windowsills that salt air got the best of more times then we can count. We've re-roofed, termite tented, and trimmed the surrounding hedges and coconut trees many times too. We've watched the surf outside change with the seasons, and even experienced hurricanes and fast moving water wash under the house and through the yard.

Some of our best memories are of playing in the waves on boards and boats, enjoying the tranquil summer water, fishing, diving, floating around, and watching the sunset after a long day of work. We've thrown dozens of parties and danced the night away on the lanai with all our crazy friends.

We were married on the sand in front of the house. We raised our son here and celebrated birthdays and holidays throughout the years by decorating the house in every imaginable theme.

Our son just left for college. The room that went from nursery to grammar school clutter to teenage mess has been cleared out.

From where I sit on the lanai I can still see through the layers of paint to the brick red color. I know we'll soon be prepping and painting again. But it's all been worth it because this place is most definitely home sweet home. Aloha!

~Kerry Germain

Building a Dream

Motivation is when your dreams put on work clothes.
~Author Unknown

For as long as I can remember, one of my dreams has been to build my own home. In my mind, I saw myself on this beautiful piece of land with sweat on my brow, dirt on my nose and a hammer in my hand as I pounded nails, laid block, sawed, painted and performed other acts of manual labor to physically create, foot by foot and wall by wall, my very own home. At one time, back in my really idealistic days, I not only wanted to create my own house, but I wanted to create everything in it—all the furniture, the rugs, the curtains, a stained glass window here and there. I figured if I was going to dream, I might as well dream big.

Since I'm the kind of woman who has had my own workbench and power tools since I was eighteen, I didn't really think this was an out-of-reach plan for me. I've been known to go into my garage on a weekend and create a new piece of furniture just because I'm bored.

I couldn't find any local schools that gave courses in home building or even carpentry, so I did what I could to get free home-building "lessons." I participated as often as I could when our local zoo had community builds. During those builds I worked side by side with many local contractors and carpenters, and picked up a lot of hints and tips from them. I also volunteered several times with Habitat for Humanity. Both of these experiences were great ways to get free, firsthand training in construction practices and to also feel the joy of building something meaningful and lasting.

I always kept the dream-home idea in the back of my mind, but I never did much to pursue the dream for the first forty years of my life. I needed the right soul mate to pursue the dream with me, a man like my early crush — Mark Harmon — who said in a magazine article that he wanted to meet a woman who could live happily in the woods. A woman who was comfortable with sawdust in her hair and sweat dripping off her nose. All my life I had wanted to meet a man who thought like that. Instead, I met men who wanted me to wear high heels and make-up, and who thought they should be the ones who owned the tools.

Fate finally brought me my dream man at the same time that fate engineered an inheritance for me. At the time, I was writing articles for the Home and Garden section of the local paper and the stories I heard of other people's adventures building their own homes finally pushed me into action.

Little did I know what an overwhelming and complicated process it would be. Little did I know that the process of building a home is not so much sweating and swinging a hammer, but making hundreds of decisions to take all the ideas you have carried around for forty some years and make them fit together and fall into place to become a house.

We did find our perfect piece of land. It was so perfect that I almost hated to clear any of it to make room for the house, but I was itching to actually live there.

And then came another challenging part — drawing up our plans. It's easy, when you are a kid, to draw a house that you would like to live in. But trying to draw up your own plans as an adult is very complicated. Will the rooms be big enough? Or are they too big? Are there enough closets? Are the hallways wide enough? Are the windows in the right places? Where should the electrical outlets go?

My partner and I complimented each other well in this process. I have always been frugal, with simple tastes. My tendency would have been to spend as little as possible and end up with a house that was too small and built from shoddy materials. My better half thinks more logically about these things. He knows that you get what you pay for and it is better to build too big than build too small. He ensured that we got the quality of house that we wanted. And I ensured that we did it as inexpensively as possible.

I spent a lot of my free time looking at building magazines, visiting building websites, shopping for doors and windows and flooring, and even switch plates and doorknobs. I couldn't drive down the street without examining all of the houses I passed. And I found out really quickly that most of the things I had pictured in my dream house were way out of our budget. Unless you have an endless supply of money, building a house is a lot about compromises.

As for the actual construction process, we subcontracted most of it. I did lay a few blocks, just to say that I did. And I stained all of the wood trim and doors myself, and we have a lot of wood trim. My husband and his friends framed the interior walls, and he and I put cedar siding on the front and back porches.

During the whole process, I learned a lot about house construction but I also learned something more exciting. What I learned is that the dream is not the house of wood and block and glass and tile we built. The dream is my better half, my significant other, the person who accepts me with the sawdust in my hair and the sweat dripping off my nose and the dirt on my chin. It is not the house we built together that has made my life so exciting and fulfilling; it is finally finding the right person that I wanted to build that house with. And it is not so much the building of the house as it is the life and the future we are building. I think that was probably the real dream all along. I just never really thought I'd ever find it.

~Betsy S. Franz

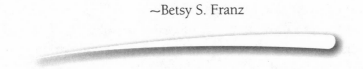

In My Dreams

The road leading to a goal does not separate you from the destination;
it is essentially a part of it.
~Charles DeLint

When we lived in the city, we had one car and two small children. We would pile into the car at daybreak and drive Daddy to work on days when I needed the car for errands. The children were often cranky early in the morning, but the one pleasant part of the drive was looking at the pretty suburban homes we passed. There was one particular block along the main street where giant maple trees towered over ranch-style houses. I fell in love with a gray house with brick veneer and a big picture window. It had a large front yard with two maple trees that made me gasp in awe in the fall. Directly across the street was a working truck farm tended by two gentlemen farmers who were always out in the field. I longed for that house and that neighborhood. I would tell myself, "In your dreams!"

We eventually moved from our city apartment, and bought a second car and an affordable, small house where we reared our children. Whenever I drove past that house in the suburbs, I imagined myself sitting on the front porch, decorating the interior, hanging wreaths on the front door for every holiday. In my dreams!

Life went on, the kids grew up. I divorced, remarried, and relocated to my new husband's condo. Every day, on my way to and from work, I passed that house. One day I noticed a "For Sale" sign in the front yard. I dialed the number. My heart sank when I heard the asking price. It sank even further when the "For Sale" sign was removed.

A year later my husband and I decided to purchase a home. Our real estate agent showed us several houses within our price range. I liked something about every house we toured, and my husband found something wrong with each one. We were getting annoyed with one another; it was late in the evening and we were all worn out. The agent said, "I do have one more house in mind, but the original homeowner is elderly and it might be too late to show it. So, why don't we set up an appointment for tomorrow?"

We explained that we were leaving for vacation in the morning. She called, and the owner agreed to show us her home. At dusk we followed the agent as she drove down that oh so familiar street. The farm was to our right and my dream home was to our left. I held my breath, trying not to get my hopes up. I had seen the "For Sale" sign go up again in the front yard two months before, and unbeknownst to my husband, I'd called and inquired. The price, which had been reduced twenty thousand dollars since the year before, was still twenty thousand dollars above our price range. I thought that the agent would turn into the subdivision just up ahead. Instead, she signaled a left turn into the driveway of my dream home. I gasped and told my husband, "Honey, I have longed for this house for twenty-five years."

But I had to tell her: "I'm sorry but this house is out of our price range. I called about it recently."

She replied, "The owner reduced the price again this week."

I could hardly breathe. The porch light came on and illuminated the front of the house. I wanted to caress the gray siding, kiss the bricks, hug the real estate agent, and jump for joy. When the front door opened, I saw a hand and arm hold the door open for us. My immediate thought was that the arm looked like my beloved grandmother's, who was long deceased. I looked into the eyes of a woman who looked just like my grandma and who was as dear.

The old lady welcomed us into her home, which smelled just like Grandma's; the scent of Cashmere Bouquet powder and home cooking took me back to my childhood. My senses were alive, my heart was thumping, and my eyes scanned the photos of her great-grandchildren displayed on the living room walls. According to the real estate agent we were still ten thousand dollars out of the ballpark. My husband and I conversed quietly and put a bid on the house; it was a low bid, and I knew the chances of it being accepted were slim. The agent told us that the woman was anxious to relocate to a retirement home.

"I'll let you know as soon as you return from vacation," she said. "I'll call you next week."

I'd waited all year for our Florida vacation. We walked my favorite beach; seagulls screeched overhead, the salty ocean breeze blew. But my mind was back home. As my feet sunk in the sand I imagined my feet sinking into the carpeting of my dream home. The sweet powdery smell of that ranch house overpowered the salty sea air and lingered. Instead of the seagulls' calls, I heard the elderly homeowner's voice in my ear: "I like you folks; you'd make nice neighbors for my neighbors." I hung a prayer on every breeze that whipped my hair.

When we returned home, the agent called to say our bid had been accepted. I whooped and hollered. For the past fifteen years, I have flung open my front door and inhaled the earthy scents that drift across the street from the farm. I hear horns honking all day at the gentlemen who have worked the land for decades and provided produce and joy to passing motorists.

My husband has mowed our lawn, grown a garden that rivals the farmers', raked leaves and shoveled snow off the drive. I've decorated my dream home, hung our own family pictures on the walls and decorated the front door with seasonal wreaths. We have chased nine grandchildren across the large front lawn and photographed them in the crook of those magnificent trees. I wake every morning with a prayer on my lips, "Thank You! In my dreams, indeed."

~Linda O'Connell

27

A Leap of Faith

Living at risk is jumping off the cliff and
building your wings on the way down.
~Ray Bradbury

My cousin was getting married for the second time. While she did not want a big formal wedding at forty-eight years old, her children insisted she have a special day with loved ones in attendance and pictures to remember the day. So they helped her plan a small intimate ceremony with thirty of her family and friends in a little chapel in the mountains of Tennessee.

My husband and I drove the 200 miles from our home to attend. When we arrived, the first thing we noticed was almost every car in the parking lot was from our county. My next observation was that the place was packed! We were there for an hour total and saw five different wedding parties. My cousin told me that the location was booked solid until after Christmas—three months away—and she had been on a waiting list to get any date before the end of the year. There would be somewhere in the neighborhood of one wedding every hour all day long from 10:00 to 5:00, or about eight weddings in a day at the tune of $2,200 each. This looked pretty lucrative and I realized there was no place to get married within 200 miles of our home.

I watched as a very small staff handled all the details of a simple ceremony and was amazed at how quickly things were pushed along.

It seemed to be a great idea in theory, but it was all a little too "assembly line" and hurried for my taste. I could hardly keep my mind on the nuptials—I was thinking about how I'd like to do this and offer more full-service weddings and receptions. By the time my cousin was toasting her groom, I had already hatched a plan.

Driving home that next day it was all I could think about. I finally decided to share my latest brainstorm to my husband, sure he would get a good laugh all the way back home. His response almost knocked me off my seat when he said, "You are not going to believe this but I was sitting there thinking the exact same thing!"

So with absolutely no experience in wedding planning, building a business or running a business, and at a very precarious time—less than thirty days after September 11th—I took a leap of faith. Named after my youngest granddaughter and a hundred-year-old oak tree that stood guard over the entrance to our property—Ashley Oaks was born.

We arrived back in Georgia Sunday afternoon and Monday I had the name registered with the county and had started calling contractors. I sat down with pen and paper, and figured out each step and what I would need to learn about that step. What I didn't know would fill an encyclopedia, but one baby step at a time I learned what I needed.

I called SCORE, a division of the Small Business Administration that has seasoned businessmen who volunteer their time counseling and encouraging people starting new businesses. I got my first dose of their encouragement when my counselor barked, "Lady, you must be crazy! You don't exactly live in an area that could be considered a destination-wedding venue. No one is coming to Rockmart, Georgia to get married!"

I thanked him politely and hung up—and moved on to the next thing on my list, not the least bit discouraged.

We already had the property, with a five-acre lake and a 2,500-square-foot building that could be converted to a reception hall. It would be a weekend business, which meant I could keep my full-time job. So I really had nothing to lose. Except of course, my home!

What kind of crazy person moves to the country for peace and quiet and then opens a business that routinely draws crowds of over 100 people to your home almost every single weekend? In all my careful planning I wondered how that part could have escaped me.

Once my website was up and running, my phone began ringing off the hook with excited brides-to-be who wanted to discuss every detail of their upcoming "big day"—at all hours of the day and night. They called at 7:00 on Sunday morning; they called during dinner; they called at 11:00 at night. I had appointments for consultations every weekend—including Sundays, birthdays and holidays, as well as drop-ins that "just wanted to look around" right in the middle of my family get-togethers! All this and we had not even had our first wedding yet. Business, it appeared, was booming. Personal life—not so much.

Then came summer and the actual weddings began. If I thought personal life was just a memory before, I was in for a rude awakening. Ever had 100 people wandering aimlessly around your yard? I had people parking all over my newly laid sod instead of in the desig-nated parking area. I had people in my flowerbeds stomping on my roses. I had children wading in the koi pond. I had people lounging on my front porch and doorstep. I had curious children peeping in my windows. This part-time home business did not stay in the box I had carefully designed for it. It was not "part-time" and it had literally taken over my home!

To say this required some adjustment is an understatement. But adjust I did. And once I got over the initial shock of it all, I found it to be a very exciting and rewarding adventure. It was so much fun getting to see all the beautiful gowns, the elaborate cakes and the individual creative ways the girls chose to decorate that helped make each wedding different. In the nine years that I ran Ashley Oaks I never got tired watching all the beautiful brides as they walked down the aisle to their Prince Charmings.

I always enjoyed helping the brides as they worked with me to plan the day they had dreamed of their whole lives. In the grand scheme of it all, what are a few dead roses when you can end your workday knowing that you have been a part of someone else's beginning?

~Andrea Peebles

28

The White Swan

Ships are the nearest things to dreams that hands have ever made.
~Robert N. Rose

"Wake up," Peter said, gently shaking me. "We're starting to sink."

It was the middle of the night and I rubbed my eyes, trying to understand what Peter was saying. Half asleep, I pulled myself out of bed and grabbed my robe. Was the boat really going under?

Peter and I lived on a boat, and although it was moored in a marina, the water was still pretty deep. As I got off, all I could think about was losing my precious home. It barely crossed my mind that we could have gone down with it if Peter hadn't woken up and realized what was happening.

I stood on the pontoon, trembling. Peter had gone into the bilges to see if he could find the problem. Meanwhile, the boat was slowly and steadily going down. I worried about Peter still being on board, but he had to see if he could do anything to save our home.

When we bought the boat, it needed a complete overhaul both inside and out. We didn't have much money to spend, but there were a few old boats in our price range. I have no idea why, but I was drawn to this boat from the moment I saw it. I didn't care that it was a complete mess inside. It didn't have proper cooking facilities or a decent bathroom, and the furniture was threadbare. I saw the potential in the old wooden Broads cruiser, a forty-five-foot motorboat that had been used as a hire craft on the waterways of Norfolk, a county in the east of England.

We were getting married the following year and this would be our first home. Peter had introduced me to boating and I had fallen in love with the way of life. We decided that we wanted to live permanently on a boat. I knew the boat needed a lot of work to make it livable, but it had the potential to become a snug and comfortable home. Peter had always enjoyed renovating, so we put in an offer.

"Are you sure this is the one you want?" Peter had asked at the last minute.

"Yes, I love it," I had replied. "As long as you're okay with doing the work."

I felt slightly guilty. I knew Peter would be doing the bulk of the renovating and that it would be hard work. However, he assured me he was looking forward to it.

The boat had a center wheelhouse and we decided to turn this into the dining room. In the stern we had a combined sitting room and galley. Peter fitted out the galley with a cooker, fridge, microwave and washer/drier. The bedroom, bathroom and a small office were at the bow, and we even had central heating fitted. The only thing the boat didn't have was a name.

"It's about time we decided what to call our home," Peter said one day.

I had been thinking about a name for weeks, but hadn't come up with anything. Looking around and seeing the ducks, moorhens, and swans float by, I was suddenly inspired.

"I know," I exclaimed. "We'll call it 'The White Swan'. What do you think?"

"Perfect," Peter said. "That's just the right name for our new home." We christened our boat with a glass of champagne.

We spent an almost ideal start to our married life on The White Swan. It was only upset by my health, which gradually became worse due to Crohn's disease. Finally, one year after we got married, I had an operation. After eight weeks recuperation, I was much improved.

The boat was my sanctuary during my recovery and I felt sad leaving it to go back to work and to a normal life.

Now I was watching our beloved boat and home sink and I started to cry. I couldn't believe that this was the end of our boat. I wanted to rush onto it, but I realized that I couldn't help and would probably get in Peter's way.

Suddenly, my husband emerged.

"It's okay," he said, smiling. "The bilge pump had stopped working, but I've got it going again."

I breathed a sigh of relief and rushed to hug Peter. We still had our home and there was no permanent damage.

The following day Peter fitted a second bilge pump as a precautionary measure and the boat was later taken out of the water to be checked. A small hole was discovered and mended.

We lived on The White Sawn three more years before we sold it and replaced it with a steel cruiser, feeling the need for more space. The new boat was sixty-eight feet long, spacious and comfortable, but I still felt sad when we let our old wooden boat go. Peter had transformed it into a perfect haven and it was our first home as a married couple. It journeyed with me through my illness and was my refuge through some very dark and difficult days. However, it didn't leave us without a bang. We sold it to a family at a marina a little further upstream, and Peter sailed it there himself. When he arrived, he went to jump off, but the boat moved and Peter fell in the water! He arrived home soaked to the skin, convinced that The White Swan was paying us back for selling her!

~Irena Nieslony

29

Payoff Party

There is something permanent, and something extremely profound,
in owning a home.
~Kenny Guinn

"Oh my gosh," said my friend Anna Marie, "I've never known anyone who actually paid off the mortgage on their house."

"It took a bit of doing," I said. "But I was determined. By putting a little extra on the principal every single month, I was able to shave off years of payments."

"So what are you going to do to celebrate?" she asked.

"Ever hear of a mortgage burning party?"

"I have to admit," she said, "I didn't know there was such a thing."

"Then I'll teach you all about it," I replied, "because I'm going to need some help."

So Anna Marie helped me design, address, and mail the party invitations. We ordered a large sheet cake with "Home Sweet Home" written on it in frosting. Then we rolled the big steel-drum burning barrel to the center of the front yard.

"You're actually going to burn something at the party?" she asked.

"Oh, absolutely!" I exclaimed. "I printed off numerous copies of the amortization schedule and you and I are going to make a big basket of paper scrolls tied with pretty ribbons. The party guests will get to throw a scroll into the fire while we say blessings for the home."

"Terrific idea! Then everyone has a chance to participate."

On the day of the party, Anna Marie and I inflated one colorful helium balloon for every thousand dollars the house cost. I kept that particular information to myself, privately enjoying the symbolism. Then we tied them to the back of every chair throughout the house.

The guests began arriving just as the sun was going down. Some of my friends arrived wearing T-shirts that looked like tuxedos and others wore sequined dresses with tennis shoes or had feather boas draped from their shoulders. My vote for best outfit went to a guy dressed in full-fledged volunteer firefighter's gear.

"You didn't tell me it was a costume party," said Anna Marie, who wore a simple sweater and slacks outfit.

"It isn't," I told her. "I have very creative friends."

And those friends got right into the spirit of things, happily eating cake and drinking champagne, tossing the amortization scrolls into the burn barrel, dancing on the lawn and cheering loudly until the wee hours of the morning. I was glad my nearest neighbors were also in attendance.

The next day, I discovered a large piece of cake in the refrigerator, wrapped carefully in cellophane. It was the piece with the picture of my house on it, cut from the very center of the sheet cake. A Post-it note proclaimed, "It's all yours!"

I saved that piece for my next birthday, invited Anna Marie to join me, and we celebrated homeownership all over again. Home Sweet Home, indeed.

~Jan Bono

The New Wing

A dream which is not interpreted is like a letter which is not read.
~The Talmud

I wandered down a hallway in my house and discovered a wing I had never noticed before, complete with two empty bedrooms and a bathroom. I was delighted to have found this extra space.

I examined every detail of these newly discovered rooms, which were unusual in their design, with multiple levels, and would be lots of fun to decorate and use. Then I woke up and realized it was a dream, one I had frequently. I was disappointed.

I mentioned this recurring dream to my brother once and he said he had the same dream all the time, too. And when I surveyed my co-workers today, almost everyone reported having the same dream, usually involving the discovery of an extra wing in their houses.

The psychologist Erick Fromm said, "A dream is a microscope through which we look at the hidden occurrences in our soul." More like hidden spaces in this case, right? Why do we have this deep-seated need to find more space in our homes? I always thought it was just me, so I'm fascinated by the fact that almost everyone in our office reports the same thing.

There's a website called The Dream Well (thedreamwell.com) where I found an article by Amy Campion in which she reports that this common dream can be frightening for some people. She says that our reaction to finding one or more new rooms in our dreams can give us some insight into ourselves. Some people view these new rooms as a challenge or an obligation they don't want. Others are excited about the opportunity to expand their lives. And some people find the rooms fully furnished, while others find them empty, filled with possibility but also needing a lot of work! According to Amy Campion, "Dreams of new rooms can be exciting dreams of emerging new potential and the promise of growth and experience."

I'm glad that everyone in my office reports they are excited when they find the new rooms and disappointed when they wake up and realize it's not true. I guess we're an adventurous lot, willing to take on new challenges. It certainly makes sense, since we put out a new Chicken Soup for the Soul book every month, and we are a busy and creative group of people. I sure hope that our common dream really does mean we're up for any challenge.

Or maybe I'm overanalyzing and I just want more space! After all, we have four grown kids, two getting married this year, and we've already cleaned and organized the old toys and created a playroom area for the theoretical grandchildren. It could be as simple as that.

~Amy Newmark

Home

There is nothing more important than a good, safe, secure home.
~Rosalynn Carter

Has it really been fourteen years since I was placed into the invisible hands of the government? Fourteen years since social services first gained control of my life?

After all this time, I remember it so clearly, as if it were only yesterday. I was eight years old and sitting in a group home waiting patiently for my mom. Unfortunately, she did not return. Three months later, I found myself in a foster home. From that day on, my life became a case file; just a large manila folder held snugly under the arm of a complete stranger.

I learned to accept a foster home as I saw it; a place that I stayed. It was not a home to me but merely a house with four walls and a roof, just a building that social services deemed fit for my living requirements. It was a place that I slept and ate in, but it held nothing for me—no love, no family and no values.

I spent the first five years of foster care envying my friends, secretly wishing for everything that they had. I wanted to know what it felt like to be so loved. I yearned to have a real home. I wanted so much to belong, to know what it was like to not feel like an intruder in somebody else's home. I ached deeply to not spend each day believing that I owed those people something for accepting me into their house.

At thirteen, right after I spent three months in the hospital for anorexia nervosa, I learned that I would be leaving the foster home that I had been in for the past five years, and I was going to be placed in a new foster home. I really didn't believe things could get much worse. It felt as though my world was crashing down upon me once more. I cried at the cold realization that my foster family was not going to show me the meaning of "home."

The tears fell for days as I slowly began to understand. A home in my world was like a fairy tale, a far off place of magical beings and magical events where everything would end in love and happiness. I envisioned a world that could make me feel wonder and fascination, but deep in my heart, I felt like such a place could not truly exist. I had never known "home," and I suspected that this would always remain the same for me.

I was sent to what they call a relief home after I got out of the hospital. It felt comfortable, and the family was very loving. I felt at ease the moment I stepped within the warm, cozy walls. But I knew I could not get too comfortable, because shortly, I would be sent to my new foster home. Then, when my two weeks in the relief home were nearly up and my anticipation and terror of being sent to a new home were in full force, the world I had come to know changed.

My relief family sat me down at the kitchen table one evening just before bed, and they all looked at me. The mom spoke in gentle, soothing words.

"We know that you have gone through a lot after finding out that you were not returning to your first foster home." She went on with a quiet breath, "And we don't want to scare you off, or force you into any decision that you don't want to make, but we really want you to stay here with us and be a part of our family."

I stared at her in shock. I couldn't believe what I was hearing. The others smiled.

"We want you to think about it. Take as much time as you need." I nodded and quietly rose from the table and went to the room where I had been staying while I was living there. I put my pajamas on, lay down in bed and silently cried. They weren't just tears of sadness, but also tears of happiness and tears of relief. A part of my life was ending and now a greater part of my life was about to begin. If I would let it.

Later that night, as my tears finally began to dry, the youngest daughter popped her head into my room. "Are you asleep?" she asked. I shook my head in reply. "Have you made a decision yet?" This time I nodded, and she waited for my answer. Without thinking any more about it, I replied with a quiet "yes."

"She's going to stay!" she yelled as she ran out of the room.

I slowly got out of bed and prepared to be welcomed by my new family. I smiled as I walked out the door. For the first time in my life, I felt I belonged. For the first time in my life, I felt comfortable and cared for. For the first time in my life, I was a daughter and a sister. I was finally a normal girl.

For the first time in my life, I truly knew home.

~Cynthia Lynn Blatchford

Home Sweet Home

Remodeling, Redecorating, Repairing

The World's Worst House

Home wasn't built in a day.
~Jane Sherwood Ace

When my husband Mike and I were first married, we lived in a tiny rented house near downtown. It was old. It was ugly. Parking was bad. It was on a noisy street. We talked about the day we would be able to buy our own house. But that would be a long way off. Property in this area is really expensive. Still, we could dream.

Sometimes, we'd hop in the car and go for a drive. We loved the back roads of Santa Barbara. We'd drive all around Santa Barbara and the surrounding towns, talking about our future and dreaming of our someday home. One evening, Mike drove the back roads that lead to Summerland, a charming, quaint beach community just south of Santa Barbara. He drove up behind a little cottage and parked on the street next to it. What a view! You could see the ocean and all the way to the Channel Islands! And what a great yard! It was huge. It was getting dark, so I couldn't clearly see the house, but it looked cute. Rustic, but cute and homey, nestled in amongst the other Summerland cottages, like it had been there a long time and was comfortable in its surroundings.

Mike told me that night that someday we would live in that cottage. After laughing hysterically, I told him there was no way we could afford to live there: In that cottage, with a great yard and a view of the Pacific. He told me we would.

Mike is a contractor and had worked on this cottage one time years earlier. He explained that the cottage was rented to tenants, but the owner was a client and someday, he'd figure out a way for us to buy it from her.

One day, our dream became a reality. The owner decided it was time to sell, and knew Mike wanted to buy it. We made a deal that worked for all of us, and before I knew it, we had agreed to buy the sweet, cozy little cottage… without seeing the inside. Mike had seen the inside once when he worked on it, so he wasn't worried. A little paint, maybe some new carpet. And of course I'd hang some cute beach-themed things on the walls, light candles and put new towels in the bathroom. It would be perfect. Mike assured me we could make it really cute and we'd be able to spruce it up in no time. No worries.

Finally it was ours. Paperwork signed and keys in hand, Mike, my in-laws and I opened the picket fence gate that lead to our dream home. Well we tried to open it. The latch literally fell off the gate and then the gate fell down. No worries. We all laughed and continued walking. The outside of our cottage was pretty run down. "Paint," my father-in-law said. "Not to worry."

We walked up the creaky, crumbling steps and onto the creaky, crumbling deck that led to the crooked front door. We pushed the door open—no key needed because the lock was missing—and stepped inside. The first thing that got to us was the smell! All four of us instinctively covered our noses with our hands. And we had to duck down when we walked! There were cobwebs everywhere. We couldn't believe that people had actually lived here.

This was the worst excuse for a house that any of us had ever seen. We just stood there looking around. The living room ceiling appeared to be much higher on one side than the other. The reason for that was that some of the ceiling was missing. The house was single-wall construction, which meant the sun was actually streaming into the living room through holes in the boards that were supposed to be our walls. Insulation? Ha! No insulation whatsoever. I was completely in shock.

We all quietly wandered around the rest of the so-called house. It looked like the windows would also need a little help. They were louvered windows, and several of the louvers appeared to be missing. "No worries. We'll buy new energy efficient windows," said Mike, as he looked at me reassuringly. I figured he knew what he was talking about since he was in the business.

I guessed at where the kitchen should be. There were only a couple of doors on the cabinets and when I opened one of them, it led straight to the outside! Paint was peeling, there were no door-knobs, the doors were off their hinges. The laundry room, if you could call it that, had a dirt floor. Mike, following behind me, admit-ted he didn't remember the cottage being in such bad shape when he had worked on it.

The bathroom had to be better, since the woman we bought it from said it came with the original, beautiful claw-foot tub. Well, that was something. We headed for the bathroom, looked around and commented on how big the bathroom was for such a small cot-tage. My mother-in-law agreed as she tried to smile. It did seem quite roomy. It occurred to us all at the same time. It was so roomy because there was no tub in the room. The renters stole it when they left! This was going from bad to worse.

The last room to check out was the master bedroom. Small, but nothing awful. Until I looked into the closet. A closet with no roof. It was wide open. When I stepped into the closet to verify that it was actually the sky I was seeing, my foot fell through the floor! That's when I lost it. I cried harder at that moment than I think I'd ever cried before. All I could think was, "We just paid how much money for this? This has to be the worst house in the world."

I ran (carefully) out of the house, down the rickety stairs, past the dumb gate and got into the car and cried. Hard. For a long time. Mike and my in-laws came down to the car and explained that although the cottage was awful (and they agreed it was), there really wasn't anything that couldn't be changed to make it better. And it had the most awesome view. No worries. They promised.

Two months later, we moved into our cottage, complete with functioning gate, sturdy stairs, energy-efficient windows, a new kitchen with cupboards, a claw-foot bathtub and master bedroom closet (with roof). Mike and my father-in-law worked day and night to get our place ready. They literally put their blood, sweat and tears into it. It was now a brand new house. And when we sit on our deck and watch the boats sail by, I think about how lucky we are to live in the world's worst house.

~Crescent LoMonaco

More Power

Nature abhors a vacuum. And so do I.
~Anne Gibbons

My husband decided that he needed to remove our old carpeting and replace it with wood flooring. For some reason many of his home improvement projects occur when I am out of town on business trips. This is probably due to the fact that it would be quieter around the house with me out of screaming range. My youngest son's room would probably not have been painted bright blue if I'd been home when that improvement was made. Oh well.

The carpet replacement job was well underway when I left town for a gourmet foodie convention in San Francisco. The old gray carpet was stripped away and safely delivered to the local dump. The work of cleanup and preparation for the new flooring seemed a fairly benign activity to undertake while "Mom was gone" so I wasn't even worried.

Upon my return I saw that the floor debris was completely gone and the subflooring not yet in place. I actually admired the cleanup work and thought that for once my husband had completed a job without leaving a monumental mess for me.

Back in the kitchen, inspired by the foodie offerings at the convention, I looked for my favorite sauté pan, prepared to whip up a tasty treat to reward my deserving husband. I reached up to retrieve it from the pot rack in the kitchen. As I pulled it down I noticed it was a bit dusty, and I chalked this up to not using it for a few weeks. Later on I needed a strainer, which was also located on the pot rack. This item was equally dusty, and upon closer inspection was covered with dog hair as well.

All of the pots and utensils were coated with dirt and hair. What had happened?

I went to the closet to grab my vacuum and do a bit of clean up. I glanced over at the Shop-Vac and saw the cord was still wound up neatly from the last time I had used it. However the leaf blower was there, cord sprawled all over the floor, the attachment still in place too, indicating that my husband had recently used it.

Even though I knew it was the wrong time of year to be blowing fallen leaves, I could not resist asking what the heck he'd been doing with that leaf blower. Sure enough the answer I received explained the dust and dog hair that covered all of my cooking equipment on the pot rack. In a brilliant ploy to save time and be efficient, my industrious husband had operated the leaf blower inside our house. I had a cartoon-like image of him screaming "woo-hoo!" as he waved the leaf blower around the kitchen. He opened the back sliding door to our deck and proceeded to blow, through the kitchen, all of the accumulated dust, wood scraps and even the hair from our Norwegian Elkhound. Did I happen to mention the dog is a male? They probably did a high five—paw to hand—to each other for a job well done.

Happily the wood flooring went down without further incident, and we enjoyed it for many years while living at that house.

~Kathy Gail Passage

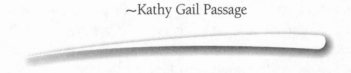

34

Shut Up and Chip

*Perseverance is the hard work you do after you get tired of
doing the hard work you already did.*
~Newt Gingrich

My husband rolled his eyes and I knew he was thinking, "Please, God, not another hare-brained idea." We'd moved into a new country home that summer and our large barren yard begged for landscaping. Alas, our budget begged for other things, like paying the mortgage. I often flipped through house and garden decorating magazines with landscaping lust in my heart, but we couldn't afford it. I coveted an elegant, stone patio where I'd entertain friends and neighbors with cool drinks and tasty barbecues.

I frequently drove past the blackened remains of an old house on my way into town. All that remained after a long ago fire was part of the red brick chimney, feebly standing sentry over the ruins, which were being devoured by kudzu vines.

One day as I drove by the burned house, I had an idea. I hit the brakes, turned the car around, and asked neighbors about the house. When I found the owners, I admit I pleaded, though it probably wasn't necessary. No one else was waiting in line to cart off their old chimney.

So I excitedly shared my brilliant plan with my husband. He inhaled deeply, feigned enthusiasm, and pasted a tight smile on his face.

For the next several weeks, my husband, our ten-year-old daughter and I tackled the bricks. Armed with a sledgehammer and a machete, we repelled both kudzu and snakes. We made trip after trip to the old house, overloading the trunk of our family car, making the suspension groan. While unloading back at our house, I became so adept at pumping up the wheelbarrow's flat tire that I nicknamed it Old Baldy. Soon, we had a mountain of used fire-scorched bricks, mostly still mortared together in clumps of various sizes.

"Now what?" my husband asked, when we finally had a big pile of brick clumps. I produced protective eye goggles, heavy work gloves, hammers, and chisels. Each family member was assigned a goal to clean ten bricks daily. The task seemed impossible, but slowly, with thirty cleaned bricks added to the tally most days, the stack grew.

Initially, we laughed and made jokes, hoping to keep spirits high and hammers chipping. "Santa's going to be surprised when he goes to slide down that chimney this year and finds it in our back yard," I teased my daughter as we incessantly chipped.

I tried to convince the family that great sculptors had started this way. "Okay, Michelangelo," I prodded my husband, "Forget about David. Bricks await your masterful touch."

Finally, the project seemed too long and whining ensued. My daughter swore that someone was sneaking into the yard at night, adding clumps of bricks to the unfinished pile. My positive speeches finally degenerated to a cranky "just shut up and chip." The family threatened to have those words chiseled on my tombstone, as long as they didn't have to personally wield the chisel.

Mortar chipped off some bricks cleanly. Others were stubborn. Some bricks broke and were tossed to the side, smaller pieces to fill in where needed. At last, the already-cleaned heap grew higher than the shrinking still-to-be-cleaned mound.

Laying the charred gems, brick-by-brick, into an intricate pattern was painstaking work. But by the end of the summer, after we'd swept sand between the pavers, we had a large patio and a luxurious fire pit. We spent many summer evenings on the patio.

Fueled by rave reviews, my husband eventually remembered the original idea as his own. This time it was my turn to roll my eyes.

~Hope Sunderland

35

What Real Men Do

*Although every man believes that his decisions and resolutions involve
the most multifarious factors, in reality they are mere oscillation
between flight and longing.*

~Herman Broch

New Year's resolutions never seem to work out for me. For example, a few years ago I resolved to make the workplace better for everyone by offering my boss a few timely suggestions on how to run the organization more efficiently. I've been gainfully unemployed ever since.

Then last year I resolved to lose ten pounds. Instead, I ended up gaining fifteen.

And this year I promised my wife that I would devote more time to home improvement. It was either that or agree to go to more cultural events. How was I to know she'd want to start improving things immediately?

"If it was up to me, I'd go with the Bold Look of Kohler in Cashmere," said a professorial-looking guy in a corduroy blazer, who was seated beside me.

We were sitting on model toilets in the bathroom display section at The Home Depot perusing the store's latest catalog as our significant others scoured the various sections for impossible-to-resist after-Christmas bargains, which were periodically announced over the public address system.

"Attention: Now on aisle twenty-seven—scum-resistant shower curtains, buy two, get one free.

"While you are there look for the fit and trim vanity mirror that takes off ten pounds. We'll take off ten bucks.

"And be sure and visit the lawn and garden section for five-gallon jugs of fish emulsion fertilizer—now available with a handsome sea bass-shaped trowel."

There were a number of other guys settled on the adjacent model toilets, plus a few guys with The Home Depot catalogs tucked under their arms waiting for an opening. After all, there was no sense trying to concentrate on catalog perusal without being in the usual catalog-perusing position.

"I like the Innocent Blush one," another guy said, peering over the top of his reading glasses. "But what about this Thunder Grey one I'm on. That makes a statement."

"My wife would never go for a dark color in a toilet," a beefy guy at the opposite end of the row said sadly. "She'd probably want to go with beige."

I felt his pain. The chances of talking my wife into a colorful toilet were about the same as the chances of getting the special-order padded seat with built-in climate control to go with it.

We all turned the page.

"Here's something," I said. "A he-man-sized tub with sensual fingers massage jets."

"Oh yeah, wouldn't that feel good after a grueling day of football," the beefy guy said.

"You bet," a short guy, who was seated on an American Standard in Daydream Blue, chimed in. "My back is always killing me after five or six hours on the couch. Not to mention that carpal tunnel thing from using the remote."

"Well, you're all in luck," I said. "This weekend it's forty percent off and, it says here, they're easy to install."

There was a moment of silence; then we all laughed.

"I've got a garage full of easy-to-install stuff," the guy with the reading glasses said.

"Me too," said the American Standard guy. "Matter of fact, I've got an easy-to-install garage door opener in my garage."

"How's it work?" I asked.

"Danged if I know. I never got around to installing it."

"Hey. Check it out. Page six," beefy guy said. "They got one of those shoe organizers on sale. You know, for the closet. I'm thinking that would make a great Valentine's Day gift. What do you think?"

"Great idea," several of us said, circling it in our catalogs.

"We're being signaled," said one of the standing husbands.

We turned our attention to a woman holding a complicated-looking faucet and waving from a green granite kitchen two aisles over.

It was my wife. "Oh man," I said. "Look at all those fittings." Reluctantly, I stood and headed her way.

"Tough break, fella," a husband with long white sideburns said as he took my place. Then he asked: "What page are we on?"

"Fourteen. Fashionable shades and vertical blinds," they told him.

I kissed my wife on the cheek as she handed me something called a deluxe dual tap with multi-function sprayer. I thought about my last home plumbing project, and how long it took for the house to dry out, and realized that I probably should have chosen the culture thing for my resolution after all.

~Ernie Witham

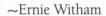

36

Our Own Downton Abbey

The past is never dead, it is not even past.
~William Faulkner

She was like an old lady when we first saw her. She had been grand and attractive at one time but now needed a major facelift. She was built in an era when life was different in a certain social circle, when people had servants and dined in dining rooms, and when the mistress of the house might not even enter the kitchen.

When we bought this California version of a grand European house we started an amazing journey on the road to restoration. We didn't want to remodel her and make her modern; we wanted to restore her to her original grandeur and keep her in the style in which she was built.

She had such amazing potential. She was built in 1907 and had big rooms and lots of bathrooms. She didn't have any showers, only claw-foot bathtubs, which was not very convenient when you have three young sons. She had lots of closet space, which was unusual for a house her age. She had ample windows in every room, so the house was sunny and bright. And she had lots of rooms; enough so that each of my sons had his own room, my husband and I had our room and an office, and there were rooms left over that served as guest rooms when our big family and wonderful friends came to stay.

Every room had a fireplace, including the kitchen, because that was the original source of heat. When she was built, there had been no central heating… actually no gas or electric heat at all. Sometime in the 1930s six gravity furnaces were added, and right now in the entry hall there is a master panel that can control all of them from that central location.

In 1907 when she was built there weren't very many cars on the road. The usual mode of transportation was by horse and carriage, so there is a place in front of our house, right at the street, to tie up your horse should you arrive on one! And we have had people on horseback or people in horse-driven carriages actually tie up to the rail and have their pictures taken.

There is a wonderful dining room with a fireplace. We have had many fun times in that room sharing meals with friends and family. We use to have fires in the fireplace there, but one Thanksgiving, with a house full of people ready to sit down and eat, we lit the fire and… smoke poured back into the room. Soot and ashes were everywhere. What a disaster! That had never happened before. After we discovered the bird's nest we never used that fireplace again.

When we moved in, there was a big room where the kitchen should have been but there was no functioning kitchen left. There was only one cupboard, a small counter space and a sink. For the first few years, until we remodeled the kitchen, I cooked for five people, including three hungry boys, on a twenty-four inch stove. That was pretty tricky and not a lot of fun. There is a big butler's pantry with lots of storage space. Too bad the butler can't be found. I keep looking for him but the old owners must have taken him with them. And then there was the servants' dining room—right next to the kitchen, just like in Downtown Abbey. We opened that up and made it part of our new, big kitchen.

Our house has a bell system for calling the help—sort of like an old-fashioned intercom system. Each room has what looks like a doorbell on the wall. It rings a bell at a central box in the kitchen. No matter how many times I ring those bells the butler still doesn't show up.

Our restoration project took us a long time to complete. We did a lot of research and tried to keep everything as it would have been back when the house was built. We were lucky because all of the light fixtures, light switches, bathroom fixtures, including the claw foot tubs, and many other things were all original and in wonderful condition. The former owners did paint though before they put the house up for sale. The outside. The inside. Everything. There must have been a sale on this paint—a color nobody was buying. It was like the color of tobacco… drab, dark, dull and not at all attractive. The entire house was that color. Every inch of her. All of the woodwork, the inside of every closet, the bathrooms, the kitchen, the bedrooms, the halls—everything was the color of tobacco. Ugly! Needless to say we repainted every inch of her… inside and out.

We love living in our house. We love having people come and stay with us. We love having family celebrations and fun parties for absolutely no reason. Living in our house is like living in a period drama/comedy. The year she turned 100 years old we had a party for her. Everyone came dressed in the style of the early 1900s. Except the butler. He didn't show even though he already had the outfit.

Even though we have owned and lived in this house for many years, we have always felt like her caretakers, keeping her strong for her next owners—whether the owners be our kids and grandkids who might move in after we move out, or another family who buys her if we decide to sell. She is historic. She is an important part of the past and we have had the honor of living in her and enjoying her and maintaining her. We know that she will be around a lot longer than we will and that many more generations will have the privilege of getting to know her. Now… if only someone would answer that bell!

~Barbara LoMonaco

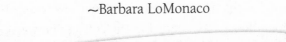

A Carpenter for Life

Nothing is forever, if you have enough power tools.
~S.A. Sachs

"Daddy, will you teach me to use a band saw?"

My father's sisters operated heavy machinery at Grandpa's shop so it didn't surprise Dad when I posed this question to him. The only difference between my aunts and me was age. They were in their twenties, while I was barely nine.

Dad took my request to heart. First, he taught me to weave rocking chair seats, rewarding me with shiny quarters. Eventually, I nailed slats and drilled holes in posts for rockers. My newly learned skills transformed me into a carpenter-in-the-making by the proud age of eleven.

And then our house burned down. The fire was so hot that most of Dad's equipment in the shop next door was damaged. That ended my carpentry lessons.

Twelve years later, my husband and I were married. Soon we had a family. After graduate school, Herb landed a position teaching at McPherson College. His books were everywhere in our house, filling stand-along bookcases, tucked in the crevices between cushions, perilously perched in piles.

One night, while Herb was reading, I ventured, "I think I'll try building some bookshelves here."

"You can't do that!" Herb said.

I blinked in surprise. "Why not?"

"We need to contract a real carpenter for a job like that," he said. "It's too expensive for our budget now."

I recalled my days with Dad; he had taught me the basics. I secretly drew the blueprints, imagining how the finished project might look.

One day while Herb was at work, I could stand it no longer. Mustering courage, I zipped to the lumberyard to purchase power tools—a rotary saw, skill saw, drill press, and sander. I hid the tools in my underwear drawer and behind canning jars in the basement.

That January, Herb traveled again on a three-week trip to Germany with his students. As soon as he left I carefully measured the living room, purchased oak planks from a lumberyard, and meticulously created built-in, ceiling-to-floor bookshelves on the longest wall of our living room. With a manual in one hand and a jigsaw in the other, I finished them with fancy scalloping, even around the picture window. When Herb returned, his jaw dropped. Then, he admitted that he loved it!

The following autumn, I planned early but said nary a word to Herb. As was his weekly ritual, he brought Friday classes to our home to hold discussions. Because our living room was small, the space was very crowded.

Adjacent to the living room, a narrow side room with a long row of windows faced the southern sun. The room had no real purpose.

"Why waste that space?" I thought. "When Herb leaves for Germany again this January, I'll knock out the wall and enlarge the living room!" In the days that followed, I secretly created a blueprint.

The day he left, I called a builder. He carved out the wall between the living room and side room and edged the new archway with maple molding. Sunlight flooded the room! Above the south row of windows, I installed more bookshelves. My confidence grew as I mitered a charming cornice above the long side windows.

The extra book space was great. However, the long, flat floor seemed drab.

"Aha!" I thought. "I'll transform it into a split-level!"

And so I did. I measured, sawed, and nailed floor joists in place. Installing slabs of 8'x12' subflooring. The last piece, however, confounded me. Hard as I tried, it wouldn't wedge over the joists into its allotted space. I trekked outdoors in the snow, climbed a stepladder, and seesawed my torso across the windowsill to heave the heavy subflooring into place. Then, I quickly jumped from the ladder and tore inside to nail it down and call the carpet installer before my neighbors called the cops.

This time when Herb returned home, he shook his head in disbelief. But he took our friends on tours of the house and bragged about my carpentry skills!

The following year, the kids and I purchased Herb's dream gift at Christmas—an antique cast iron stove. We scheduled an expert to install it. After all, my house had burned when I was a child, and I couldn't afford to make a mistake.

But I am an impatient type. I wanted to finish the job while Herb was in Germany so I called the fire chief and insurance company for their wisdom. They graciously came to the house, gave suggestions, and explained regulations in detail.

Quickly, before Herb returned, I laid a base and a semi-circular firewall of bricks for the woodburning stove. A professional carpenter dropped by to saw a hole in the roof and install a quaint little chimney. When he completed the job, I had an extra week to retrofit wainscoting around the lower half of the family room.

This time when Herb came home, he shook his head. In disbelief, he jokingly said, "I'm taking you with me on future trips, to save my sanity!"

Twenty years and forty countries later, I have been cured of "doing it myself." The children are gone, my saw blades are rusty, and my osteoporosis is acting up. Plus I'm too old to wiggle my derriere out the window. With graying hair, Herb and I cozy by the fireplace and luxuriate in our books.

And I am the woman who did it! Dad would be proud of me!

~Jeanne Jacoby Smith

Mending All

There's nothing to match curling up with a good book when there's a repair job to be done around the house.

~Joe Ryan

In his poem "Mending Wall," Robert Frost playfully asks his neighbor why they need a stone wall when there are no cows to stray. The taciturn neighbor replies: "Good fences make good neighbors."

Although I might not always have agreed with that sentiment, recent experience has taught me otherwise. Good fences do, indeed, make good neighbors. And so do good trees, good roofs and good driveways.

When it comes to home maintenance, I am neither handy nor ambitious. My idea of spending a sunny spring day involves a book and a chair rather than a scraper and a paintbrush.

But over the last dozen plus years, I have come to realize that not all people share my philosophy of home repair. When something starts to wear, fray, peel or crumble, most people are inclined to grab a tool and get to work.

I always figured this was a personal choice and that my laissez-faire approach was as valued and respected as the can-do ethic evidenced by my neighbors. After all, I didn't try to convince them of the necessity of pursuing leisure and they didn't try to persuade me to change my hedonistic ways.

On occasion, our philosophies would clash. When one neighbor wanted to extend the sideyard fence, I chafed at the idea of spending several days of what, to me, appeared to be pointless labor. But when he offered to do the work himself and split the bill, I happily went along.

Some time later, the opposite neighbor pointed out that the lower branches of the two large pine trees bordering our shared fence were impinging on his yard. Thus, I was obliged to trim the lower branches of the two trees.

So it was with some surprise that I found myself attacking the large pine tree in our front yard. The lower branches of our "maintenance free" tree had grown so big that they were brushing up against our car. Thus, even though no neighbor had asked, I tackled the job of trimming its as well.

At my wife's urging, I began the dreaded task. Using my handy pruning shears, I lopped off a couple of dozen low hanging branches and hauled them onto the lawn. For the next three hours, I cut, trimmed and bundled the branches into manageable piles for the garbage man and raked and bagged the remaining mess for recycling.

Amidst all of my sweating, grunting and groaning, I was periodically interrupted by various neighbors. One of my immediate neighbors came over to encourage me in my task. He commented on the great improvement and urged me to trim even more of the offending branches. He even lent me his pruning saw to make the task easier.

Some time later, the neighbor from the other side dropped by to survey the job and praise my efforts. According to him, the removal of the lower branches had made a huge difference. He offered me a beer and cheered me on.

As the job progressed, other neighbors dropped by with nothing but kind words for my work. Suggestions were made; encouragement was offered. Apparently there was a huge pent-up demand on my street for the trimming of this particular tree.

When the job was finally completed, I was exhausted. My face was covered with sweat, my clothes were covered with pine needles and my arms were covered with scratches. I had to admit that the tree looked better with its new clean lines and open bottom. But had it been worth it?

According to my wife, yes. And according to half a dozen neighbors, yes. And to the extent that it bought me a couple more years of peace and quiet, even I had to admit that it may have been worth the effort.

The problem is that the removal of the pine branches has highlighted the poor repair of our driveway. With more cracks than a discarded Easter egg, our piece of macadam is long overdue for repaving. Not by my estimation, of course. But if those looks I'm getting from my neighbors are any indication, I've got some more work to do.

~David Martin

Curb Appeal

The best things in life are unexpected — because there were no expectations.
~Eli Khamarov

Our home renovation was almost complete but we still needed a new headboard and footboard for the master bedroom. I browsed among the displays and asked about the antique-style bed. The saleslady told me, "It's cherry wood, but not really cherry wood, because people can't afford real cherry wood because it's too expensive, so it's a cherry finish that resembles cherry wood." The cost of the non-cherry wood bed rivaled the price of a mini-vacation. Buying a new bed would have to wait.

The next morning I awoke while it was still dark. I heard my husband, Jim, in the shower. Before leaving to teach third graders, I put on my jogging clothes and running shoes, and stumbled out the door into our sleeping neighborhood and a drizzle. The street was empty except for garbage cans waiting for the early morning pickup. A block away I discovered several pieces of furniture abandoned on the curb and paused under a streetlight to inspect the trash. I stared in disbelief when I discovered a treasure... a beautiful, antique bedstead.

The tall, curved headboard appeared to be mahogany, bordered by exquisite carvings, and accented with an inlay of lighter wood decorated in a floral motif. Sturdy bedposts stood like sentries. Propped next to the headboard was the matching footboard. I could hardly breathe, not from jogging, but from the excitement of finding this breathtaking four-poster bed that was now… mine.

Raindrops rolled down my cheeks as I pondered my next move. My petite frame was no match for this massive bed. I would need my husband's help. Then, my heart sank when Jim's truck appeared and I watched the red taillights grow smaller as he drove to work. I was on my own and needed to rescue this bed before the drizzle ruined the wood or the garbage truck hauled it away.

I strained to raise the headboard to a standing position and slowly maneuvered it to the middle of the street. I walked it from side to side, like a giant crab, and worried my neighbors would come outside for their morning papers and stare at me.

I was out of breath when I delivered the headboard to our garage floor. Then I sprinted back and returned with the footboard. My rescue complete, I crouched over the wet wood and tenderly dried it with paper towels. I hauled bricks from the construction pile outside and positioned them to discourage warping.

Feeling euphoric, I grabbed a quick shower and rushed to school.

That evening I showed Jim my find.

"This bedstead will look great with our other furniture," he said. "But it's so heavy. How did you get it home?"

"Determination and adrenaline," I replied.

The next day, our contractor attached the headboard and footboard to our bed frame and paused to trace the carvings with reverence. He asked, "Where did you buy this beautiful antique?"

"I found it among someone's trash. It had 'curb appeal.'"

"I don't believe you. It's too valuable to have been thrown away. You must have bought it at an antique shop."

I beamed with happiness.

That night I lay on the soft mattress, snuggled between crisp sheets and thought, "Now I lay me down to sleep. This awesome bed is mine… to keep."

~Miriam Hill

Drawing a Blank

To be able to ask a question clearly is two-thirds of the way to getting it answered.
~John Ruskin

I've developed a condition that, unfortunately, comes with age. It's called Missing Word Syndrome — or MWS. It causes me to forget the correct names of things and substitute placeholder words. Just like a synonym is another word for the one you can't spell, a placeholder is another word for the one you can't remember. And lately, forgetting words is my... what do you call it... specialty. My recall deficit disorder first presented itself when my husband, working on the electrical system in our house, sent me on a parts run to The Home Depot.

Before leaving, he showed me the part and told me its name, but by the time I reached the parking lot, I'd already forgotten it. I should have called him I know, but I didn't want to admit that it took only ten minutes for my brain to misplace the word. And besides, I'd forgotten to bring my phone.

Forging ahead, I walked into The Home Depot on Super Bowl Sunday, which, by the way, is the best time to shop there because the place is empty. Anyway, I needed one of those gadgets that attach a switch box to drywall. I thought I could just search the electrical department until I found it. But after a half hour with no luck, I instead searched for an orange vest — one occupied by someone of my generation. Besides being more knowledgeable, I figured he'd understand my problem.

"Can I help you find something?" the gray-haired clerk asked.

"Yes. I'm looking for one of those flat metal whatchamacallits that has three hangy-down dooley-bobs that hold the whole dooziehoozit to a switch box."

The clerk stood blank-faced.

"You know, it's one of those gray doohickeys that looks like a boat thingy."

He slowly scratched an eyebrow. "I think I know the gizmo you're talking about. Tell me, do the hangy-down dooley-bobs by any chance bend?"

"Yes, they do," I said.

"And if you flipped over the boat thingy, are the hangy-down dooley-bobs actually sticky-up doo-dads that look like smokestacks?"

"Come to think of it, they do."

"And are there sticky-out flippy-doos on the sides?"

"Yes, it has those." Now we're getting somewhere, I thought.

"So, let me get this straight," he said, "the thingamajig you're looking for is one of those whatchamacallits with the hangy-down dooley-bobs and sticky-out flippy-doos."

"Yes, exactly." It was so nice to talk to someone who really knew his stuff.

"Follow me," he said, leading me down the electrical aisle. But, frankly, a man who could understand me like that, I'd follow anywhere.

I flashed him a smile and asked, "So, what are those gadgets really called?"

"Believe it or not," he said, "they're called battleships because that's exactly what they look like."

My heart sank. Of course, how could I have forgotten?

He pointed down the aisle. "You'll find them right there between the frazelhoozies and the madinglehoppers."

~Pam Tallman

The Best Tool in the Toolbox

Don't you stay at home of evenings? Don't you love a cushioned seat in a corner, by the fireside, with your slippers on your feet?
~Oliver Wendell Holmes

With winter approaching, and the possibility of temperatures plunging into the low sixties down here on the Texas Gulf Coast, I found myself longing for a cozy fire in the fireplace. Not wanting to deal with hauling in logs and sweeping up ashes, I stopped by a fireplace center near my home to check out the gas log sets. It was my birthday week, and I couldn't think of a better gift for myself than being able to curl up with a good book next to a crackling blaze.

I was pleasantly surprised by the choices there, and the salesperson assured me that the logs could be installed in less than thirty minutes. I picked out my favorite box of faux wood, and we agreed on a date for the delivery. But things took a turn for the worse when the installer arrived. He informed me that the gas pipe sticking into my firebox was too long, so the fire burner for my fake log set would be off-center.

"No problem," he promised. "Just call a plumber to cut the old pipe to the right length, rethread the end and we're back in business." He even recommended an excellent plumbing company.

A couple of days later, when the plumber arrived, he doled out more bad news. The pipe was located too close to the floor of the firebox. He wouldn't be able to cut it off or rethread the end unless he removed it from the wall. He estimated that it was about two feet long, and if removed, he might not be able to get it back in place without making a hole in the sheetrock to reconnect it to the gas line.

"I can give you the name of a good handyman," the plumber said. "He can either patch the hole we need to make in the wall or cover it up with a fake door just in case he can't match the wall texture and paint."

A cold shiver ran down my spine. I'd only been in my house for less than a year, and had gone through a nerve-racking, twelve-day whirlwind remodeling ordeal before I moved in. The dust hadn't yet settled in my brain, and he was suggesting that I stir it up again. "Thanks, but no thanks," I replied.

To say I was despondent is putting it mildly—my birthday home-improvement wish had just gone up in smoke. But I wasn't ready to throw in the towel just yet.

Instead of giving up, I moseyed on over to the Internet to check out some other options. While bouncing around in cyberspace, I discovered something called a "convert to gel gas log set." These are fake logs that you simply place on the grate in your fireplace (vented or not), then set a can of gel fuel underneath (which is artfully hidden by decorative lava rock), light with a match and enjoy a cozy, crackling fire. It's not quite the real thing, but this option eliminated most of the cost, plus the installer, the plumber, the handyman, and a heck of a lot of stress.

Within a week, my log set arrived on my front porch, and the shipping was free. Things were looking up. By the time the first cold snap arrived and the temperature plummeted to fifty-eight degrees, I put a match to the can under the logs and curled up in front of a cozy fire. For this home improvement project, it seems that the Internet was the best tool in the toolbox—no mess, no fuss. My only dilemma now is which favorite book to read while sipping hot chocolate in front of the fireplace in my toasty warm living room. Ah, home sweet home!

~Gloria Hander Lyons

Chapter 5

Home Sweet Home

Through the Generations

The New Kitchen

Don't save something for a special occasion.
Every day of your life is a special occasion.
~Thomas S. Monson

I started dating my now-husband, Tony, in 1985. We grew up in the same neighborhood. He wasn't quite the boy next door, but more like the boy two blocks over. It was back in the days when people sat on front porches and kids spent summers playing outside. While my family was the typical mom, dad, and two kids, Tony lived in a multi-generational Italian household with his two brothers, his mother, his grandmother, and his mother's bachelor identical twin brothers known collectively as "the uncles." I thought his family was a bit unconventional.

"Show her the new kitchen," Tony's mom said during my first meet-the-family visit. She was obviously proud of their latest home improvement project. We were in a basement TV room, so Tony led the way upstairs to the main level of the house. "Did she say new kitchen?" I asked myself as I surveyed the harvest gold appliances, wood-paneled walls, dark cabinets, and wall-to-wall commercial carpeting. It was in pristine condition but screamed of the early 1970s.

I suppose kitchens are not a common topic among young couples just getting to know each other, but when you are considering the possibility of a long-term relationship with someone, knowing why his family calls a ten-year-old kitchen "new" could influence your decision.

"It was remodeled around 1971, after my dad died, and we never used it after that," Tony told me later, when I finally mustered up the courage to ask about it. He went on to say, matter-of-factly, they didn't cook or eat in the new kitchen. I recalled seeing a small makeshift kitchen area with an enormous green oil furnace as the focal point in the basement next to the TV room. That kitchen, I learned, served the household of seven while the new kitchen upstairs enjoyed a museum-like distinction. Still a boy when the new kitchen got its facelift, Tony never questioned its off-limits status, nor could he offer an explanation for it.

Well, new kitchen or not, something told me to give our relationship a chance. At least there was no red velvet rope strung across the new kitchen's doorway. That could have been a dealbreaker.

Holiday dinners in this large Italian household were major food events with fifteen to twenty people on hand. Like an army of ants following a trail to the nest, family members dutifully carried prepared food up the steps to the dining room, and later, in similar fashion, carried dishes down to the basement sink to be washed by hand. The stove and dishwasher in the new kitchen sat untouched.

Even relatives, friends, and neighbors seemed to be on board with this arrangement. Was I the only one who thought the whole concept of the new kitchen was a bit bizarre? Or, like me, were they simply too polite to say anything?

Tony and I married, and eventually moved 500 miles away from our hometown, returning for visits only a few times a year. As we settled into our new surroundings, the new kitchen story became an anecdote for me, something I could use to amuse friends or co-workers.

As the years passed, we got older, but the kitchen stayed new. Keeping with its museum-like status, the table and counters began to double as display shelves for the many knickknacks and dolls Tony's mom collected.

One Thanksgiving, after Tony's grandmother had passed on and his mom could no longer host holiday meals, we carted an entire precooked meal back home with us. "Thanksgiving in a cooler," I called it. When we arrived, there was so much food to reheat that the basement stove and microwave oven were insufficient. "Let's use the oven in the new kitchen," Tony suggested. "There's an oven up there?" asked one of the uncles. Out of sight, out of mind, I suppose. After thirty years sitting idle, the stove fired up and helped warm our meal.

Later, stuffed and contemplating the cleanup task, Tony smugly proposed, "Let's use the dishwasher." After all, we were the next generation of adults. Couldn't we change the rules? As we positioned buckets in the basement to catch the water pouring through the ceiling, we realized it's probably best not to try to change the rules.

These days, the uncles, now in their late eighties, are the lone members of the household. We made the long trek home for a visit this past winter. One of the uncles greeted us with concern. "You can't use the sink in the new kitchen," he warned us, which seemed odd since we never did use that sink. "I tried to let the faucet drip to make sure the pipes don't freeze, but nothing comes out," he said.

The new kitchen had finally gotten old.

When I sat down to write the story of the "new" kitchen and attempt to decode its significance, I had an epiphany. When I was about ten years old, my dad returned home from a weekend religious retreat with a small gift for me—a black and silver Cross pen. Unlike the plastic BIC pens with chewed caps found in various drawers around our house, this pen came in its own box with little elastic bands holding it in place. At that point in my life, it was the nicest pen I ever had, and I wanted it to stay that way. I kept the pen strapped in its box for more than two decades, confirming once every few years that it still worked by scribbling a few lines. I don't think that pen ever wrote a complete sentence.

So there it was, an insight that had been with me all the time: The new kitchen, like my pen, was the nicest one they ever had, and they simply wanted it to stay that way. Perhaps they weren't so unconventional after all.

~Barbara A. Page

My Father's Desk

What we remember from childhood we remember forever—
permanent ghosts, stamped, inked, imprinted, eternally seen.
~Cynthia Ozick

awn. I tiptoe out of the bedroom so as not to wake my husband or the dogs. I pour a cup of black coffee and enter my small home office. The streetlight outside the long window casts tiny strips of light through the white shutters. No reason to open them yet; it's still dark outside. Still standing, I place my big orange coffee mug on the stone coaster and switch on the desk lamp.

I lower myself into the gray leather office chair and roll up to my old wooden desk. The rounded corners and the desk's blond wood are battered now, but there was a day when the finish was shiny and new, the corners were smooth, and the desk presided steadfastly over my father's office in his pediatric practice.

He sat behind this same desk where I sit now sipping coffee and listening to my house wake up. Dad sat there for almost fifty years, counseling moms, talking on the phone, reviewing bills. I can still see him there, white coat, pen at the ready, listening and advising, black rotary dial telephone at hand. His desk looked the same during his entire practice: at one end, a wine-colored leatherbound accounts journal with entries in his almost illegible "doctor's" handwriting. In another spot, a prescription pad. Recent issues of the *Journal of the American Medical Association* and the *Journal of Pediatrics*. The only concession he'd ever made to modern times was an updated push-button phone. Otherwise, his desk ended its service with the same practical accoutrements he first placed on it in 1949.

Now, though, my huge twenty-seven-inch iMac screen rests atop the desk's scarred surface, a red mug full of pens and pencils sits to the left, and a small Medicine Buddha to the right. At one time, this was where my father conducted the business of healing, and it's now where I craft essays or chapters, the words sometimes healing old wounds of my own.

My father wasn't the kind of man who watched football or went out with the guys. His focus was internal and his only real hobby was immunology. Like me, he was an early riser whose mind kicked into gear just before sunup. Most days he was at the office by 5:30, so he could sit at his desk reading immunology journals, partly to aid his diagnostic skills, but primarily for the fun of it. Decades have passed since these publications rested on the desk's wooden surface. Now, my papers, calendars, sticky notes and writing books clutter the desktop, all tools of my craft, something I, like my father, also do for the challenge and for fun.

There was a time I thought my father and I had nothing in common. Our politics, our approaches to life and even our lifestyles belied our shared genetics. Sitting at his desk, though, I feel connected to him and recognize the ways we have always been alike.

When I run my hands over the desk's worn surface our shared past vibrates in every ding and scar. The spot where a five-year-old kicked the leg in a tantrum. The scratch where my dropped metal toy nicked its smooth surface. And the scrapes made by careless movers as they transported the desk from Rochester, New York to my first home in Florida and then my second, and then to my home in California. The imperfections mark chapters of my father's life and mine, engraved in the grain.

For more than sixty years since it was first delivered to his office, the desk sat impassively, adding nothing but taking nothing, either. Now, this sturdy but average piece of furniture is my only remaining physical connection to my childhood home.

My father loved his work, but he knew it required a sharp mind. As he aged, memory problems appeared, first minor and then more severe. He reluctantly accepted that he could no longer think clearly enough to care for patients, and gave up his medical practice. He was seventy-eight.

I can see him now, furtively clipping the medical journal articles detailing new studies on dementia and Alzheimer's, scraps my mother found later squirreled away in the back of the desk's drawers. He'd told no one. My heart breaks, thinking of his growing recognition of the reality and horror of his disease, of how he must have sat at this desk and made the decision to quit his practice. Of what that cost him.

"What will happen to his desk?" I asked my mother when she called to say he'd be retiring.

"We'll give it away," she said. "Or do you want me to ship it to you?"

Intuitively, she understood that of her three children I was the only one who saw more than a battered old piece of furniture. Instead, I saw the repository of a new doctor's hopes and dreams, the place where a young husband and father earned a living to support his family. My father hadn't been easy—all three of us had endured his strong Sicilian parenting. We wanted a kindly TV dad, but we got a father who eschewed Dr. Spock in favor of "spare the rod and spoil the child."

I saw Dad differently. As a young adult, I'd glimpsed his heart, that of a man who had been insufficiently and cruelly parented himself and who was doing the best he could. I'd been a confrontational and rebellious teenager, and he a strict disciplinarian, a fearsome figure to be avoided. But one day, just before I left college, he took my mother and me out for ice cream. I watched him sitting alone and quiet in the dusk licking his cone and I was overcome with sadness. He was lonely. I was, too: I longed for a stronger connection to him, but neither of us knew how to forge it. But once I'd seen his heart I could no longer hold a grudge.

I wanted his desk.

When Dad retired, I had already been away from our home-town more than twenty-five years. "Home" could have meant any of the apartments or houses or states where I'd since lived. But always, "home" was the place I had grown up and the things that were part of life back then. Taking my father's desk meant I could anchor any place I lived with a piece of home. With a piece of him.

I told my mother to ship me the desk. And then, I couldn't stop thinking about it.

Our first family home was a two-bedroom apartment above my father's medical office in Rochester. When office hours were over, I'd run downstairs to visit my father as he sat at his desk finishing the day's paperwork.

At home, he mostly raised his voice. At the office, he was kinder and laughed more. I was jealous of his young patients — they seemed to get a side of him that we didn't. Who knows, maybe I was claiming my father as my own when I went down those stairs to visit him a few times a week. I'd stand on the other side of the desk that seemed massive (at age four I could barely see over it) and he'd get up from his chair and walk around to greet me with a joke and a hug.

Many years later, my husband and I would drop in on him dur-ing office hours when we'd visit from Florida. My father would set aside his reading and come around the desk for an awkward hug. From childhood to adulthood, I had struggled to connect with him; his desk seemed to be some kind of quiet, stately presence, a mute witness to it all.

Today, though, even at more than four feet wide, the desk seems small, maybe too small. Every so often, I think about getting a larger desk, a new, modern one, sleek and shiny, but then I wonder, what will happen to this old relic? It's not even an attractive antique.

I puzzle at my connection to this shabby old piece of office fur-niture that I hadn't seen in years before a moving van deposited it at my Florida house some fifteen years ago. As time passed, I rarely visited my father's office and had never thought about the desk. And yet some invisible cord bound me to it.

Standing on the right-hand corner of my desk is a photograph of me with my parents, the three of us smiling into the camera. It was taken in 1997, when my parents visited me at my Florida home. Dad was already in the grip of dementia but he'd hidden it well. We're posed at a bayside restaurant near Tampa, an anachronistic place with fishnets hanging from the ceiling and a roaring fire, even in the summer humidity. Our happy smiles remind me what keeps us in any moment is that we don't know what's to come.

My father was deteriorating, but I didn't want to see it. We laughed a lot on that visit and I have photos to prove it. He and I had worked through our issues over the years; or rather, I had worked through them, learning to see him differently. In doing that, I learned that he could be fun—that together, we could have fun.

My mother died eighteen months later. My siblings were busy with their lives, and for the first time, my father was entirely alone. Before we convinced him to sell the family home and move into assisted living, he visited me in California, where I had moved. On our daily walks, we'd talk. No subject was taboo.

"Are you afraid to die?" I asked him.

"No," he told me. "I had the career I wanted, married the woman I wanted, had the life I wanted. I do miss your mother, though." Tears formed in his eyes.

Later, when I told my brother about the conversation he admonished me for "making" my father cry, but to me it was a rare moment of connection, one I'd longed for my entire life.

Framed in silver, four photographs from his visit now sit on my office shelf adjacent to his—my—desk. In one, he stands alone, leaning against a Monterey pine, framed by the overcast sky and a gray Pacific ocean. His eyes are already clouded over in the pictures. That evening, in a restaurant, he went to the restroom with my husband and, fearing he couldn't find his way back to our table, pleaded in a tiny voice, "Don't leave me." He would live another eight cruel years, his once keen mind clogged with disease.

I sit at my father's desk every day, and think of him most days. When I settle in to write, I feel his heartbeat in the grain of the wood.

Life zooms by, our family and our childhood homes left to memory. My parents are gone. I'm thousands of miles from my siblings. But when I feel alone and rootless, I sit at my father's battered old desk — our desk now, and find home.

~Carol A. Cassara

Loft Living

You never know what events are going to transpire to get you home.
~Og Mandino

When my husband, Mark, and I were newly married, we signed up for a chocolate tasting event held in the old International Market Square building in Minneapolis. As we noshed on chocolate confections, we saw a sign announcing loft space for sale in a separate section of the building. Giddy from a thorough sugar buzz, we decided to tour the model and see what downtown loft living was all about. When we got to the fifth-floor showroom, we were greeted by soaring ceilings, huge windows, original brick, and hardwood floors throughout. We were stunned. This was what loft living was all about? No wonder it was all the rage.

Whether it was from all the chocolate we'll never know, but that night we felt like we could conquer anything—even downtown Minneapolis. Right then and there we decided we wanted to be loft owners and a couple of months later we moved into our new home.

Now, the International Market Square is an interesting place. Originally, the brick buildings were the home of Munsingwear: an undergarment and hosiery company that, incidentally, invented the logoed golf shirt. There are five buildings that comprise the International Market Square, all joined by a glass atrium in the center. Four of the five buildings house interior design studios, showrooms, and architectural offices, and the fifth building has been converted into multiple loft spaces with a penthouse on top.

After we moved in, Mark and I thoroughly enjoyed exploring every nook and cranny of our building. On snowy Minnesota days when it was too cold to go outside, we would walk laps around the five floors surrounding the atrium. We would stroll past each of the interior design studios and window shop for our dream lighting, rugs, furniture—everything! We even discovered that we could enter one door on the fifth floor after hours and take a sneak peek at the events going on below. We got to see bridal expos, speed-dating events, ballroom dances, and one night, a trapeze artist hanging from the glass ceiling over a fancy dinner party below. How they got her up there is still a mystery to me.

On one particularly warm summer evening, Mark and I planned to eat dinner on our balcony. We noticed a long line of people winding around the building and up the block. Curious, we put dinner on hold and headed to the fifth floor to overlook whatever event had garnered such a large crowd. We entered the atrium area and were surprised to find people everywhere! On every level they were pressed against the railings, some sitting with their legs hanging over the edge, intently watching someone below. We pushed our way to the railing and saw then-Senator Barrack Obama speaking. It was a noisy affair, and so crowded that we decided to make our way back to our loft and finish the dinner we had started. We took our salads onto the balcony and ate happily. After about fifteen minutes, we heard the large industrial doors beneath our balcony open, and a group of people emerged—the campaign team with Senator Obama in the center. He pumped his fists in the air and did a little victory dance, like you would see any football player do after making a touchdown, while high-fiving his team. To the side was his security detail, and they were giving Mark and me the "eye" as we sat chomping on lettuce and tomatoes directly above the proceedings. Imagine our surprise when later that year Obama was voted into office. We were able to say that the President had been to our house!

Though we were surrounded by enough happenings to give us

stories for the next decade, the discoveries didn't stop there. A couple months after we had moved in, my grandparents came over for dinner. When my Grandma Lois first arrived, she placed her hand on one of the butter-yellow cement pillars in the center of our living space and said, "These pillars used to be green." We were amazed to discover she had worked for Munsingwear as the secretary of the men's hosiery buyer in the very building we lived in!

Grandma told tales of the sewing machines that filled the floors; of the huge washrooms with metal lockers where the workers hung their coats; of the riot that had taken place; and how dreadfully hot the building had been.

"We used to take salt pills," she said, "to replace all the salt we lost from sweating while we worked."

I looked around, glad for all the modern conveniences our loft had, including central air conditioning. It was amazing to think that my grandma had worked in this building with no idea that one day her granddaughter would be living in it—walking on the same floors she walked on, touching the same brick walls she had touched. It boggled my mind. Mark and I had known our home possessed a lot of history, but now it had become personal.

I learned a lot from my grandma about her experiences at Munsingwear, and the history of the International Market Square has become a special connection for us. We love to share our stories and impressions of the building we have in common. Our tales are vastly different—hers set in the backdrop of the post-WWII era, and mine in the fast-paced 21st century—but each memory occurred in the same place... my home.

~Laura Smetak

45

Love Lives Here

The past is not a package one can lay away.
~Emily Dickinson

A blond middle-aged woman with a thick stack of papers entered the conference room where I sat with my wife Margie, who was seven and a half months pregnant with Savannah, our first child. We had just signed the papers transferring ownership of our two-bedroom home in town to a young couple in their late twenties, with one young son and another child on the way. Now we were signing papers that would transfer ownership of our just-purchased sprawling three-bedroom suburban home just in time for the birth of our baby.

The woman with the papers was direct: "I told them that they didn't have to come, that I would bring the papers to them. But they wanted to meet you."

She was referring to the sellers. For the first time, I truly felt nervous. Then they walked in.

Alvin and Marian were in their mid-eighties. They had built the house in 1952, next door to another house owned by a brother. Alvin and Marian lived in the second floor of that house until construction on what would be ours was completed. Over the years, they would add a two-car garage, family room, a second full bathroom and a patio, along with frequent appliance, bathroom and kitchen updates.

Now they were moving to an assisted-living facility about a mile up the road from the home where they had lived for more than half a century.

"We've never sold a house before," said Alvin. "I wanted to see how it works."

While that could have been taken as an interest in the selling process and all the relevant paperwork and fees, I sensed there was more to it than that. We weren't just buying a house. To them, we were buying a home that they had put their hearts and souls into for so many years.

We had wanted an older house, one filled with character and memories. When we had done the walk-through, it was clear that the couple sitting across from us now had spared no expense in maintaining their home over the years.

The roof boasted a defrosting system that melted snow, which was a big plus for these western Pennsylvania winters. There were covers that eliminated the need for cleaning out the gutter downspouts, custom oak cabinetry and paneling, state-of-the-art electronic appliances, a basement kitchen making use of the former main kitchen appliances, three gardens, and landscaping that looked like it had been done by a professional.

After we signed the papers, we began the process of moving in. In a desk that the couple left behind, Margie found a CD. I agreed to her suggestion to find out what was on it.

We placed the disk in her laptop and saw about fifty images of family photos. Holiday celebrations seated in furniture that was not ours, though the rest of the room looked the same. Happy people enjoying one another's company. Presents opened. Grandkids everywhere. This was not something to be thrown away.

Alvin and Marian had left us their contact information in case we had any questions about the house. We immediately mailed them the disk, along with a note explaining the find.

Not long afterwards, I met Alvin and Marian's son Marlin, and his wife Karen. Marlin helped care for his aunt and uncle's house next door that his family now rented out, and we kept in touch on an infrequent basis.

One day, Margie and I were contemplating what to do with the back yard. We had our own ideas, and with our busy careers, gardening and landscaping were things we did not have time for. There were also the rigors of taking care of our young daughter, now on the verge of turning two.

"Did you want to keep those rose bushes?" Margie asked me one day. I shook my head. We decided the rosebushes didn't fit into our plans and would need to come out.

But drawing from my past experience, I remembered that those who tended roses were a different kind of people. They didn't just trim and spray them, they nursed and nurtured them. They were more than just flowers. They were a labor of love. And something inside me said that Alvin and Marian's white and pink roses, like the house, had a story of their own to tell.

Alvin had come to the house not long after we moved in with a spare igniter he had for the furnace, and we returned the favor by giving him the sign bearing his name that had been attached to the coach light in the front yard. Could those roses also hold a sentimental value for him?

I contacted Marlin and Karen and asked if they'd like to have the rose bushes to transplant to their new yard. My instincts proved to be correct.

Marlin came over one evening when I was still at work and dug up the bushes. It turns out those roses had been part of Alvin and Marian's wedding. That treasured piece of family history may have been lost forever had the house gone to someone else or had we not had the foresight to think of them.

It started with the meeting in the real estate agent's office. Then it continued with the visit by Alvin. Then came the disk with the photos. Then Marlin and Karen. Now the rosebushes. It was a carefully crafted puzzle beginning to fit together.

Love lived here. Not just a family. Alvin and Marian weren't just interested in the house-selling process. They were interested in whether we deserved to be in their home.

I felt that we were meant to live in that house. A house on its own is simple brick and mortar. The family and the love that resides within truly make it a home. The generations-old rosebushes symbolize undying love. And I hope someday I'll live up to that high standard that Alvin and Marian created.

~Ken Hoculock

46

Showing Off

My father used to play with my brother and me in the yard. Mother would
come out and say, "You're tearing up the grass." "We're not raising grass,"
Dad would reply. "We're raising boys."
~Harmon Killebrew

The property in rural, southern Ohio where I grew up was straight out of a Norman Rockwell painting. Consisting of nine acres with a gigantic front yard, a wooded ravine, and a small pond, it was the perfect place to raise seven boys.

Situated next to the ravine, our house dominated the landscape. From the sink at the kitchen's corner window, Mom could look over the entire back yard, where nothing escaped her surveillance.

The only reason that we lived in such an awesome house was because of my Dad's Herculean efforts. Dad was a hard-working man, but not averse to the occasional clowning-around-for-a-laugh. And Mom knew that all too well.

One summer, Dad and his older sons decided to build a tree house in an elderly oak just beyond the backyard fence. This led to a beautiful Saturday afternoon in June, with my Dad hammering away on the only portion of the tree house that was done so far—the floor. At the time, my brothers and I were working beneath the oak, doing menial tasks that Dad assigned.

Suddenly, we boys heard a branch snap and looked up—seeing one corner of the floor give way.

My brother screamed "Dad!" while I watched in horror.

Dropping his hammer, Dad grabbed for the nearest branches, but they were too far away. He slid on his hands and knees down the sloping floor, and his body launched headfirst over the side.

In the kitchen at that precise moment, Mom happened to step to the sink, where she witnessed Dad execute a perfect somersault in midair and land safely on his feet.

Immediately, she stormed out onto the back deck and yelled "Jack! Quit showing off in front of the boys!"

After Mom traipsed back into the house, Dad looked at his sons, and we all busted up laughing. If Mom only knew…

~John M. Scanlan

47

That Wall Had to Go

Spontaneity has its time and its place.
~Arthur Frank Burns

That wall had to go. It turned one wide hall into two narrow ones just off the small entry hall of our house. Why have two narrow halls when one wide hall would be so much nicer? And besides, it would expand the entry hall and make everything much brighter. Yes, the wall had to go.

My husband's idea was to demolish it one weekend when we had no other plans. He is extremely handy and did all our home remodeling projects himself with the help of our three sons. I helped too and really became quite good with a hammer and a paint roller. The wall project was scheduled to begin in two weeks but, in the meantime, I had my own plan.

What is it that you tell your children about walls? Don't write on them. Don't draw on them. Keep your hands off them so they don't get dirty. Well, that was all about to change in my house. I went shopping and bought all of the supplies I needed and put them in a big box. I moved the box into the hall. And then I called my three sons—ages nine, seven and five—and asked them to come in so I could talk to them.

Groaning... lots of groaning. "Mom, do we have to come in?" They were playing outside and didn't want to stop playing. They didn't think anything I could possibly tell them could be important enough for them to have to interrupt their play. But, being the good boys they were, they came in. I sat them down on the floor in front of the wall in the hall and started to talk.

I explained that we were going to be remodeling and that the wall was going to be taken out. But before that happened I had an important project for them. I wanted every inch of both sides of the wall covered with their drawings and their words, or whatever they wanted to put there! Just squiggly lines were okay too. My boys just sat with their mouths open and stared at me. They knew I was a little wacky and did strange things that most moms didn't do, but they thought that I had really lost it this time. All these years I had been telling them to not draw on the walls and now I was telling them I wanted them to draw on the walls.

I divided the wall into sections—one for each boy and one for my husband and me. We wanted to play too! We could draw or write whatever we wanted. No restrictions, no rules and no critiquing the other guy's work. Just fun! The boys were a little reluctant and it took some demonstrations on my part to get them going. I showed them my box of supplies. In it were markers. Lots of markers. Hundreds of markers. Markers of every color under the rainbow. I picked one up and started to draw. I drew a flower. Right there on the wall. Now my boys were getting excited. They figured out that I really meant they could draw on the wall. They each picked up a handful of markers and started in. What fun!

One of my sons was being bullied at school. He drew a picture of the bully on the wall and then drew a mustache on him, gave him a huge, ugly nose, pimples, and put him in a pink dress. We all laughed at the way the bully looked. I think that made my son feel good and suddenly that bully wasn't as frightening as he had been. My other sons drew whatever they wanted and I contributed too. When my husband came home, he drew too. We had a wonderful time. We played tic-tac-toe. Each day, for two weeks, we would draw something else on our wall—both sides—things that had happened at school, things that had happened in the neighborhood, things that had happened with friends. Each event was duly noted on the wall.

We had the most interesting wall in the entire neighborhood. Maybe even in the whole city. My kids invited their friends in to see this masterpiece. Some of the moms were not too pleased with me because they thought their kids might get the wrong idea and start drawing on the walls at their homes. Too bad! I assured them that my boys knew that this was the only wall in the house they could draw on and that I wasn't worried.

After two weeks of the artists-in-residence program there was literally no blank space left on our "canvas." Both sides of our wall were covered with the most interesting combination of drawings and words, in a rainbow of colors. Now came the even more fun part—the day the remodeling was to start. It was time for the wall to come tumbling down. All five of us—my husband, three boys and me—had hammers and safety goggles. The boys had done enough work with their father over the years that he didn't have to explain safety procedures to them. They all knew how to handle a hammer and the purpose of the goggles.

On the count of three the demolition began. Each person bashed in the section that he had created. I remember my son standing there looking at his picture of the bully and saying, "Take this! This is for you!!" And then smashing him in the nose and pink dress with the hammer. The bully crumbled into a thousand pieces. Hmmm—this was possibly not the most politically correct behavior but it certainly was a good way for my son to get rid of his anger. And no one got hurt.

That wall was down in a day. Within the next few weeks, my husband put in all of the support beams necessary and then we got rid of the old studs. Suddenly, where two narrow halls had been, there was one wide hall. What a difference. We redid the floors and painted the walls. I made a stained glass window to go next to the front door and my husband installed it. The sunlight flooded in and reflected off of the bevels of the glass. The effect was beautiful.

This remodeling project was finished. We had all participated in making it happen and we were all very proud of the way it turned out. By the way, my sons loved to tell the story of how their mom made them draw on the walls. And contrary to what some of the moms thought would happen, my sons never, ever drew on any other walls in our house again.

~Barbara LoMonaco

A Place of Love

Home makes the man.
~Samuel Smiles

ome. The word kept running through my mind as we drove along the dusty road deeper into the country. All around us oak tress drooped in the sweltering sun. I peered through the dust at the little farmhouse we were nearing. It stood alone at the end of the road, looking more tired than I felt. I swallowed a knot of fear in my throat.

My mom had moved us to California in search of a better job. We lived close to the beach and I woke up each morning to the smell of salt in the air. It had been great, but then my mom's company closed and we had to go back to Texas. I was okay with that, happy to be going home, settling into the city again and returning to my old school.

But my mom told us that the cost of moving had eaten up all our savings, and she still hadn't found a job. That meant we couldn't afford to rent an apartment in the city, so we had to stay with someone until we saved enough money to get our own home. Then she told us the real shocker. We'd be living in the country with our grandmother, whom we'd never met before.

Stepping onto the creaky porch, I put my suitcase down and looked at her. She was a tiny woman with white curly hair. She smiled when she saw us and began speaking, but it was all in Spanish so I couldn't understand her. My mom smiled back and said, "Your grandma says welcome home."

As I opened the screen door and went inside, I couldn't imagine this place being our home. The farmhouse was the only home within miles of anything. It was a dilapidated four-room shack that smelled of dust and mildew. Everything in the house was old, including our grandmother. We'd never met her before because we lived far away in the city. I didn't know how to feel about her.

My mom carried my youngest brother inside and put him on Grandma's bed. Grandma stood beside him and stroked his head, singing to him. Although I couldn't understand what she was saying, my brother seemed to like the song. She turned and gave each of us a hug. Her arms were thin and bony, and when she moved she moved slowly. I was afraid she'd break.

That night we lay on blankets on the cold wooden floor. I heard all kinds of noises I'd never heard in the city. Strange birds called out in the darkness. Crickets and frogs chirped and croaked. I heard sounds in the wall that I guessed were mice. I shivered under the blankets and moved closer to my brother. This was in no way the place I'd hoped to come home to.

That first week we all got a crash course in farm living. You get up early on the farm, and I mean early. Grandma showed my brother and me how to gather eggs from the chicken coops behind the kitchen porch. I got pecked by more than one angry hen. Mom and my sister helped Grandma in the kitchen, and as I stood throwing feed at a horde of clucking, scratching chickens, I shivered and wished I was anywhere but here.

Grandma showed us how to care for her kitchen garden. My hands got raw pulling weeds and hauling buckets of water to the screened-in garden. We finally got a break after lunch, and my brother, sister and I wandered around. We found a turtle in the grass, and built a house for it from scrap wood. When we showed it to Grandma she smiled and nodded. I was actually happy as I sat down to a great tasting chicken dinner that night. That is, until my sister leaned over and whispered, "This isn't chicken. Grandma took our turtle and fried it. Grandma told Mom it was nice of us to catch dinner."

Life went on like that. Since Grandma had no tub or shower, she, Mom, and my sister bathed in a big iron tub inside. When it was our turn, my brother and I had to take the tub outside and bathe under the trees while the chickens and goats looked on. When winter came we got to experience cold like we never had before.

But something funny happened along the way. I got really good at taking care of chickens and goats, and the vegetables my brother and I got from the garden that fall made everyone happy. Grandma showed us how to do a hundred different things with just our hands and some simple tools. Even though we couldn't talk to each other, smiling and hugging went a long way to showing how we felt.

Then one summer day, Mom told us she had found a job in the city and rented an apartment. We were going to leave for our new home the next day. That night, as we lay on our blankets and tapped on the wall to scare the mice away, I thought about all that had happened, and about the grandma I had come to know and love.

The next day, we said our goodbyes. I hugged Grandma tightly, feeling her small but strong arms hug me back. As we drove away from the farmhouse, I realized something. The place you live isn't really what makes any house a home; it's the people with whom you share it. Smiling and waving at the woman who had welcomed us with love and caring, I knew that no matter where I went there would always be a place for me here, a place that truly was, now and forever, my home.

~John P. Buentello

Art Lessons

He didn't tell me how to live; he lived, and let me watch him do it.
~Clarence Budington Kelland

s a child, I loved coming home from school in the afternoons. While I was the studious type from an early age, there was a different kind of world waiting for me at home that enthralled me even more.

After throwing my backpack down on the living room couch, I would help my mom prepare our afternoon tea, pouring the aromatic Persian blend into the little golden teacups my dad had brought back from his last trip to Iran. As the cups gently rattled on the tray I carried, I could hear the sound of a voice gradually growing louder as I approached the door to the studio. There before me was the moment I had envisioned since waking up that morning: the sight of my dad standing over his canvas completely absorbed in his painting, as Maria Callas greeted me with her lament over lost love.

I was in awe of my dad as I watched him paint. At first, he didn't even seem to notice that I had entered the room. He was in a world distinct from the one that encompassed him, fueled by his imagination and the tenderness of the soprano's voice as it resounded within the studio walls. As I saw how intensely he concentrated on his work, I often feared that my presence might disturb him. Sometimes I even felt compelled to leave before he could see that I was in the room. Yet, his delight at suddenly noticing me standing near his table always kept me by his side.

"Hi Golrizie! How was school?"

"It was really fun, Daddy! I wrote two poems today during writing time. And I got to paint, too!"

At the mention of painting, out came a small blank canvas from under his worktable.

"Then let's paint together."

For hours, we would work diligently, my dad with his large canvas at one end of the table, and me with my little one at the opposite end. As he worked, he told me stories. He told me how he first knew he wanted to be a painter when he was six years old and how his family never supported his passion for art. He told me how he used to draw on every surface he could find and often got into trouble for it, as pages of textbooks and the walls of his house were his early canvases. He told me how he designed my mother's wedding dress and ring and how their shared passion for art convinced them to come to America for a college education shortly after their marriage.

As I listened to his tales, I was not aware at the time that I was receiving an education I could never truly find in school. As a seven-year-old, I was mesmerized and entertained by his often humorous accounts of his childhood antics. I could not see back then, however, that his words were more than just a retelling of his personal history. He was not merely sharing his thoughts with me; he was showing me how to dare to dream, discover, explore, and become the closest thing to what you are. Passion, he would repeat, is what keeps you going in life. To settle for anything less than what it takes to fulfill your dreams is a disservice to yourself. As the hours passed by and we finished the cookies my mom had brought for us, I learned how to live.

These days, his words echo in my mind more vividly than ever as I try to navigate my way through the working world, through my dreams, through life. At every fork in the road I remember these words and feel a little less afraid of taking the journey. And whenever life becomes hazy, I know what to do.

I park my car, walk toward the house, and hear Plácido Domingo's voice soaring above the surrounding valley. I see a figure crouching over a table and another holding a little golden teacup. A smile spreads over my face. I am home.

~Golriz Golkar

Tables Turn

There are no seven wonders of the world in the eyes of a child.
There are seven million.
~Walt Streightiff

It starts with a table.

It's an old oak table, the strongest table I've ever known. Even though it stood only on one center post the table never, ever wobbled. Huge claw feet extend out from the center trunk, each one holding onto carved wooden balls with a visceral tenacity. This table is still my grandmother's, even if it is in my house now.

When I was a little girl I spent hours under that table, crawling around the feet of what I imagined were a pair of mated eagles, their big oaken wings a perfect circle over my head.

The table was huge in those days, and everyone I knew and loved in the world could sit around it. Their voices were distant as clouds, and as immutable. There were stories, murmurs, and many, many peals of laughter.

The table was in the middle of the biggest kitchen in the world, which was the center of my known universe. I'd guess ninety-five percent of our waking hours were spent in the kitchen, with light streaming in from every window, even on rainy days.

That was the magic of that kitchen at my grandmother's house.

The table held the best food in the world, all of it made from scratch, and the smell alone drew everyone in from outdoors no matter what they were doing. At each place setting was a cold Coca-Cola, the kind made with real sugar, sparkling tall glasses with condensation glistening on their sides like jewels. I dined below with ease, reaching up periodically for a few bits of flour tortillas and rice to hold me over until dinner.

The space under the table transformed so often that it surprised me that I was the only one who noticed. Some days it was a coral reef, with mermaids and neon colored fish swimming through. I'd swim through, sometimes quickly, as I evaded sharks, and sometimes just floating with graceful and gentle jellyfish.

Other times it was the front gate to the castle and was guarded by a beautiful white horse with a mane that nearly touched the ground. I'd hold court with salt and pepper shakers and potholders until someone needed to get some cooking done.

Sometimes, usually late in the day, it became a cave. Bystanders were often taken by surprise when bats would suddenly fly out from the cave, screeching and whirling around the kitchen right as the sun started to set outside and bedtime was announced.

I don't remember the day that I stopped spending most of my time below the table and began to sit in the chairs around it. But I do remember even then feeling those strong eagles' feet with my toes, my mind drifting back to oceans, castles, and caves.

Then, in a blink of an eye, the kitchen was gone, the table had to be moved and, with great anticipation and the help of many strong backs, it had come inside my house.

But something strange happened in transit. The oak table was much smaller. I looked at it in the corner of the room, not sure it was even the same table. I wondered if oak could shrink after thirty-five years. I theorized that when tables travel from cotton farms in El Paso to the Hill Country there was a miniaturizing effect.

The first day it was in our house I ran my hand over the golden wood, puzzled. Everyone I knew and loved in the world couldn't begin to sit around it. It hardly seemed big enough to serve a meal on. It stood in the corner of the room, dwarfed by everything around it.

Then, after a few weeks I spotted something from the corner of my eye. It was my child, crawling around the base, arranging stuffed animals and a few books around the eagles' claws. The next day there was a sign up next to the table, indicating when it was "open."

Right then, the table grew.

Today all I have to do is peek around it and I can see silvery mermaids jumping under the eagle's feet, a proud white horse galloping up the curved balls, and the bats hanging from underneath, blinking their eyes, waiting for dusk to fall.

There are new additions too—gallivanting snow leopards hunting in the mountains of Nepal, fashion divas working the runway in Paris, and a few artfully placed drawings in the Louvre.

It starts with a table. And from there it goes on—forever—making a kitchen into a magical home that will live forever in a child's mind.

~Winter D. Prosapio

House of Sunshine and Tears

Youth is a crown of roses, old age a crown of willows.
~Jewish Proverb

I pulled my 1959 Plymouth into the driveway, fairly sure that I had the correct address. The "for rent" sign was still hanging in the downstairs window along with the monthly rent listing of $125 a month. To a college sophomore who'd already spent a fortune on tuition and books, this was pretty steep, especially back in the mid-1960s. Additionally, it was in a rundown section of San Jose, California. Row upon row of aging, dilapidated Victorian homes lined the streets that paralleled my college. As I got out of the car I gazed at this once-elegant home, which I guessed had to have been built before the turn of the 20th century.

As I was about to knock, the door opened, and there stood a tiny, gray-haired woman of about seventy. She wore a pair of jeans and rain boots as well as a large apron, which covered her entire torso. She smiled and asked, "Are you here about the rent?"

Her accent was clearly Germanic but pleasant. "Yes, ma'am," I responded. She must have noticed that I was gawking at her outfit because she tittered, saying, "Oh, I was about to do some gardening in the front. After last night's rain, it can get pretty messy."

"I understand. My mother does pretty much the same thing." She smiled, her eyes squinting at the early morning sun.

"My name is Ester Levinsky, and whom do I have the pleasure of meeting?"

"Oh… I'm sorry, I'm Jody Chaney. Uh… I go to school here at San Jose State."

"That's wonderful. Without an education, the world can be pretty harsh." There was a momentary pause until she added, "Well, why don't we take a look at the room, yah?" I nodded, and together we went inside and up the polished staircase. My eyes darted everywhere, from the faded photos on the wall, to the two facing china cabinets on either side of the hallway, filled with glass crystals and vases of various sizes. Despite the bright morning, the house was dark, even with the flowered curtains that had been pulled back and tightened with bows. Everything seemed to be extremely tidy.

As we walked down the narrow hall, I couldn't help but notice a large portrait of a young man and woman in what appeared to be a wedding picture. "That was taken on my wedding day in the spring of 1917." She pointed to the man in the photo. "This was my husband, Isaac. He was a chemistry teacher." She spoke no further of him but continued to walk down the hall until we came upon the room at the far end of the house. As we entered I noticed it was a bit more modern than the rest. The paint on the walls appeared brighter, and light from the window shone down on a comfortable looking bed. Opposite the bed at the far end was an old writing desk and chair. Two rows of bookshelves hung over the desk.

"Be careful opening the door too wide. The radiator is right behind you. Now, let's see… oh, the bathroom is right across the hall and it has a full shower and bath. As far as meals are concerned, you're welcome to join me for dinner… that's included in the rent and you can keep your breakfast foods in the kitchen cupboard or refrigerator. I do require though that you wash your own dishes. Also, you can use the washer and dryer whenever you need it."

This is a great deal, I thought, especially with dinners thrown in. "I'll take the room," I said a bit too enthusiastically. "Would you like some references?"

Ester shook her head, her hair neatly pressed into a bun. "No, you seem like a good boy. My husband always told me sometimes instincts are more accurate than cold facts."

"Are there other rooms rented out here?" I queried.

"No, this is the first time I've ever rented out a room. I hope I'm doing the right thing you know, with all the crime going on. I think I'd feel safer knowing someone else was in the house, other than just myself."

The following week I moved in, bringing with me my little record player, clothes, lamp, 49ers poster, and my baseball glove and bat. Looking about the room with its oddly shaped trapezoidal window, I wondered who had lived here in the past, what they were like, and whether they were as content in this room as I seemed to be. Within an hour I'd set everything in place and was off to my afternoon class.

Returning to my newly rented room, I smelled the delicious aroma of chicken and rice being prepared. "Supper's on in thirty minutes," shouted Ester. I smiled to myself, and my stomach rumbled.

"Thank you ma'am. I'll be down shortly."

It was during our first evening together that she told me about herself and her husband. They'd both been raised in Frankfurt, Germany where they met at the university. She was beginning her studies in English literature while Isaac was doing graduate work in chemistry. Soon after graduating he got a job working as a chemist for an agricultural company, but was later forced to leave once Hitler came to power. She remained at home, raising their only daughter, Sarah, who died of polio at seven. Once it appeared that they would eventually be sent to a concentration camp, they arranged to leave, smuggling themselves out through Switzerland and eventually landing in New York in 1938. Isaac found work, not as a chemist but as an assistant researcher for a beverage company. In 1942 his company moved him to San Jose where they purchased the Victorian. They lived there together until 1962 when he died of cancer.

Day after day we'd sit together, discussing history, politics, religion, literature—anything that we fancied. Through the wisdom of Mrs. Levinsky, I gained insight into life that no teacher could ever have imparted on me. I no longer looked at her as my landlady but as a grandmother.

As a history major, I was fascinated with her understanding of Germany in the 1930s, and we ended up talking for hours on the subject late into the night. When we were done, I'd climb the stairs to my little corner room and study until overcome with exhaustion.

For three years I remained in that house, helping her with her chores while she regaled me with stories from her childhood. When I finally graduated, I was offered a job in Nevada. Although excited, I felt a certain sadness at having to leave. When the time came to say goodbye, we hugged tearfully, promising to keep in touch. For over a dozen years we did just that — until I received word from a neighbor that she had suffered a stroke and died a few months later.

I will always remember that house and the enchanting times spent with this most remarkable woman.

~J.D. Chaney

Home Sweet Home

You CAN Go Home Again

All in the Family

To know after absence the familiar street and road and village and house is
to know again the satisfaction of home.
~Hal Borland

he drive from Florida to New Jersey had been blessedly
uneventful—at least until now. As our Honda struggled through the last few miles of rush hour gridlock
on I-95, familiar sights and sounds poured through
the open window. It had been a little over a year since we'd moved,
and in that short time I'd begun to think of myself as a Floridian. But
as I inhaled the cool, exhaust-laden air, my inner Jersey Girl returned
with a vengeance. I turned on the radio and searched for my old
favorite station. A deejay whose voice I didn't recognize was doing
a commercial for Tastykakes. I could almost smell the Butterscotch
Krimpets.

"You've been pretty quiet," my husband said. "Anything wrong?"

I shrugged. "It's weird how everything seems different. Like
we've been gone for ages instead of just a year."

"Some things never change—like this traffic." My husband muttered a few expletives as he hit the brakes.

We were going back home—or rather, back to our old house,
where we had raised three children and transitioned from young par-
enthood through middle age to what I liked to think of as "active
retirement." My daughter and son-in-law were the owners now, having purchased the house from us when we moved on to our new

lives in the Sunshine State. Somehow, the thought of returning made me feel unsettled—as if I were trying to put on a timeworn coat that didn't quite fit anymore.

From somewhere up ahead came the sound of screeching brakes and a blaring horn. I rolled up the window and rested my head against the seat back. Then I closed my eyes and exhaled. The monotonous stop-and-go of the traffic was making me drowsy. I let my mind wander, picturing the house as it had been when we pulled out of the driveway a year and a lifetime ago.

"Honey, wake up. We're here." My husband gave my shoulder a gentle shake.

I opened my eyes as the car pulled to a stop in the driveway of a two-story white house on a quiet suburban cul-de-sac. Fat green buds covered the branches of the sugar maple tree, but the old tire swing that my three children had loved was gone. Under the tree that shaded the final resting place of Tweety the parakeet, Flopsy the rabbit, and a series of brown and white hamsters, there was a new wrought iron bench and a large terracotta planter overflowing with petunias.

My husband gave a low whistle. "The old place really looks spiffy," he said. "It definitely needed a facelift."

"It wasn't all that bad," I said.

The green trim that had once framed the garage door had been painted a trendy slate blue, as had the front door and the shutters on the three upstairs windows. I stared at the center window, picturing the chipmunk-cheeked face of my middle child pressed against the glass. That window looked out from his bedroom, and he loved being the first to spot and announce the arrival of visitors. "Com-pa-nee!" he would shout as he pounded down the stairs.

The flowerbeds were still there, but gone were the leggy irises and spicy pink carnations I had planted so many years ago. In their place were neatly trimmed azaleas, their masses of white flowers plumped like little pillows on the ground. The juniper bushes that shaded the bay window had been painstakingly pruned into precise cones, the blue-green berries nestled like tiny ornaments among the branches. The beginning of a smile twitched at my lips as I recalled how my sons would use those berry-missiles to pelt their little sister as she dashed up the walk, screaming protests.

The weeping cherry still graced the center of the front lawn, cascading its pink boas onto the grass. But now it was surrounded by nodding daffodils instead of my frilly purple hyacinths. I could remember the day my husband and I planted that tree; how I had laughed when he broke the shovel trying to pry loose a large rock and landed squarely on his behind. The tree, like my children, had been no more than a sapling then. And, with the passing of the seasons, it had grown tall and strong—just like my three babies.

I shook myself back into the moment, opened the car door, and stepped onto the familiar front walk. Then I pushed the doorbell by the strangely blue front door and heard Westminster chimes instead of the two-toned "Bing-bong" I was expecting. I listened for the ghostly echo of "Com-pa-nee!" but it never came. The feeling was eerie, like being in a dream where everything is slightly askew. Part of me itched to return to the reassuring sameness of the car.

Then the door opened. There was my daughter, tall, strong and smiling. She held out her hand.

"Mom! Dad! Come on in. I've missed you both so much."

I took her hand, crossed the threshold, and I was home again.

~Jackie Minniti

Where the Green Door Goes

Home is a place you grow up wanting to leave,
and grow old wanting to get back to.
~John Ed Pearce

When my wife Renee and I first met, we would sit on the porch of her childhood home sharing secrets, laughing and on occasion, crying. The dark green front door stood stoically behind us, sometimes looming but always welcoming. Secure and always there.

That home with the green door soon became my home too. I spent many days and nights in that house... dinners, birthday parties, holidays and garage sales. Church gatherings and meetings with neighbors. A friend here and family there. Moms and dads, brothers and uncles, aunts and cousins all helped to create a patina of experiences that could be felt seeping from the walls. Orange trees in the back yard and olive trees in the front. It sat along a quiet street covered and lined by shadowy trees that created a veil from the hot summer sun.

Years later with our own family, Renee and I would often visit Grandma Eunice for dinner at the house and help to build yet more memories. The same back yard... with our own kids, dogs and dreams.

And so it went as time marched on. Then one day those experiences ended when Eunice passed away. There were so many memories in that house that even when she was gone she was still there. After the shock, mementos were boxed, antiques were moved. More garage sales and more boxes. Picture frames were taken down: their bright markings remained on the walls like empty windows to the past. The house was sold for another family to carry on and create new memories.

A year or two later I drove by the house down the corridor of trees I knew so well. I drove by again. Then again. I circled around and parked. New paint, new plants, many new things, but the same feelings of that old house came back. I walked up the steps, the same steps I had walked up so many times in the past. And knocked.

I introduced myself to the new owners, a nice young family with kids. I told them of the memories past and the long story behind the house. The presence of Eunice could still be felt. Inspiration, a thought then occurred to me.

"I love what you have done with the house," I said. "You are going to think this is crazy, but, do you have anything left over from the remodel that you may want to part with?"

The gentleman pondered, then smiled, and asked me to follow him to the back of the garage. He climbed up a ladder and rustled around in the attic space as bits of dust fell. Then very slowly he lowered something from the shadows and asked me to grab a hold. It was the green door.

I said my thanks as I hefted it on top of my car, tied it down with great care and drove home. I took the green door, blemishes, peeling paint, scratches and all, and secured it to the wall at the top of the stairs in our own house. An opaque reflection of many years of happiness. The door to a home.

When Renee came home I covered her eyes and walked her up the stairs. I took my hands away as she stood in front of the door. At first she was not sure what she was looking at. She started to ask me… then the recognition set in. She was speechless at first; then the tears started. A spectrum of tears and emotions flooded forth. Melancholy and wistful, happy and joyful, they were all there.

It took her back, way back to a time of childhood memories, both good and bad. Memories of many years gone by. Memories of us watching television together as we sat on the couch next to her aging mom. It became a symbol—it was a symbol of days gone by and yet days to come with our own children. An embodiment of feelings and familiarities. It is just a door and yet it is so much more.

At the top of our stairs against the wall, the green door still stands. A constant reminder of memories going nowhere and yet everywhere at the same time. That's where the green door goes.

~Stan Holden

54

Chicken Soup for the Soul

Home to the B & B

What greater thing is there for human souls than to feel that they are joined for life—to be with each other in silent unspeakable memories.
~George Eliot

After my mother's death, I was sorting through her box of photos. I found assorted pictures of my sister Mary and me on our First Communion, peeking out of a tent, sitting with our then current pet, playing with cousins. Other pictures showed my brother alone by a Christmas tree, playing with toys, being held by my mother, wearing a little league uniform.

My sister was eight and I was six when our brother, Steve, was born. We were two different families. My sister and I went on hikes with Dad, tagged along with him while he worked at his electrical business, and pretended to drive while we sat on his lap and steered the 1936 Ford sedan. Since our mother kept Steve close to her side, he doesn't have the memories of a family unit that Mary and I share.

On Steve's third birthday, October 2, 1945, the family moved into a large 120-year-old two-story Victorian house sitting on a rise of terraced land at the top of a hill. The house was built in Golden, Colorado in the late 1800s by a prominent judge whose niece was a silent film star.

After high school graduation, I married and moved to California. Mom and Steve followed us the next year. Dad sold the house two years later. My sister, who owned a ranch in the mountains above

Golden, kept us informed each time the house sold, along with the ever-increasing price and finally its conversion to a bed and breakfast.

As we three went about our separate lives, the family ties stretched but we kept in touch on holidays, birthdays and an occasional family reunion. Nevertheless, with the exception of our parents' funerals, the three of us never spent time alone together.

When I found the website for The Silk Pincushion Bed & Breakfast and took a virtual tour of the rooms, I called my sister. "Wouldn't it fun to rent our bedrooms?"

"Absolutely," she cried. "You call Steve. I'll call the B&B and tell the owner who we are and set up the dates."

Before long all the plans were laid. Now, fifty years after the last of us left home, the oldest child, the middle child and the baby were making a pilgrimage back to their childhood home.

We parked on the side street and stood together looking up at our homestead. The lawn was manicured, but the large tree that shaded the front of the house was gone. The retaining wall that Dad built years before still held the front lawn in place but the brick side-walk was covered by dirt and grass. The shape of the house was the same but the white walls were painted gray. It was our house, but something was off.

"We're all here," my brother said. "Time starts now."

The owner answered our knock and handed Steve the house keys. "Welcome home," she said with a smile. "The house is yours. I'll be back to fix breakfast in the morning." We eagerly went inside.

The stairs to the second floor were in the same place, and we lugged our suitcases up to what were once our bedrooms. The room that my sister and I shared was in the front of the house. The walk-in closet had been converted into a bathroom and an air conditioning unit blocked part of the window. A large queen-size bed had replaced the twin beds.

Steve took the room over the dining room. It was small and had been remodeled, but his memories were there.

The big air return register at the bottom of the stairs, where we secretly swept the dirt from the stairs, was gone. The hall furnace register, where we warmed ourselves when we came in from the snow, was also gone—all replaced with a wooden floor.

The kitchen seemed smaller. The sink was in a different place and cabinets were on what had been a blank wall. It felt like I had been in a similar place, but the room didn't fit with my memories. The kitchen window was in the same place, and I could picture Steve's football sailing through the air and shattering the glass as it missed its target—my head.

We ventured into the dining room, which was just as I remembered it. If I closed my eyes, I could see the tracks of Dad's electric trains snaking around the floor in different configurations.

I walked to the middle of the living room and tried to dust off the memories, but I simply could not scrub away all the years that had distorted the view. It was like looking into a mirror that had lost its reflective ability—there was an image, but it was not clear.

Later we walked the two-block-long main street and argued over which store occupied what site, never entirely agreeing.

"This was the Red and White Grocery," recalled Steve.

"I think this was the hardware store," challenged Mary. "The next store was the Red and White."

We had coffee in the building that once housed the five and dime store where I worked when I was a student. We ate dinner at a restaurant that had been the home of our parents' friends.

Too soon our four days together were over. The memories were tucked back in their special places, the small hometown receded back into the fog and we stood in the driveway of "our house" surrounded by our luggage. One last kiss, a tight hug, a promise to meet next year and we went our separate ways again.

I felt a stronger connection to my siblings, and I wished I had known them better when we were children. Now we have decided to meet again, in a different place next year, to explore old memories and make new ones.

~Ruth Smith

My Parents' Pears

It is difficult to realize how great a part of all that is cheerful and delightful in the recollections of our own life is associated with trees.
~Wilson Flagg

I did not know what to expect when I knocked on the door of the house my parents had built in 1948. The door, now bright green, had a new brass knocker, although the old brass keyhole and doorknob were the original ones I remembered. This was no longer my home. I was just passing through town.

When a young man opened the door, I blurted out, "My mother and father built this house. It was their home for many years and mine when I was young. May I please have some of those pears on the ground and hanging heavy on the branches? My dad planted those trees—"

"Do you want a sack or a basket?" laughed the young man. "Take all you want. I'm a history major at the college here. My parents own the house. They were renting it, but now they let me live here. I'd like to know about the house."

So I stepped inside. "Those are the hardwood floors I knew. It was my job to paste wax and polish them, once a week." I looked and pointed. "That was my bedroom. That was…"

The young man listened. He showed me his choices of fresh paint, excellent colors for the house, this house no longer my home.

I myself had chosen blue wallpaper and a floral border for my room when I was young. I loved making choices then.

I stepped back outside, quickly. I clutched a strong bag. I filled it with pears from a tree in the front yard. Then, I walked back to a pear tree that had been special to my mother, the one just outside her kitchen window, which brought first blooms of spring to her, year after year. From that tree, I picked a few more pears.

Later on that rainy autumn day in 2010, I shared the pears with our daughter and grandson as my husband and I passed through their city on our 360-mile trip back to the place where we live now.

"These are pears from trees your great-grandfather planted," I said to my grandson. He remembers his great-grandfather, that house, those trees.

We ate the pears and decided they were the best we'd ever tasted.

Some of the remaining pears were soft and turning brown by the time I got home. I dug a hole and planted them. Who knows? The pears come from good stock. They may thrive here.

~Shirley P. Gumert

104

Peace—that was the other name for home.
~Kathleen Norris

When I met Tom he lived in a beautiful one-room apartment in Brentwood, California. His apartment was #104. It was small and there was nothing overtly special about it: cream carpet and white walls, a small kitchen, a small living room with a fireplace, a bedroom area, and a bathroom with one sink. But even though that description doesn't sound like anything special, it was gorgeous. Tom loved this apartment and everyone who saw it said, "How beautiful!" Maybe it was the way the light came into the apartment. Maybe it was the ergonomic layout of #104 that made it so appealing. Or maybe it was the antique furniture. I don't know what it was, but the apartment was peaceful.

I used to work in the entertainment business, and on one particularly tough assignment I collapsed. I'd been living in Las Vegas with the film crew and working on a 3D IMAX film called *Siegfried & Roy: The Magic Box*. Despite the fact that I loved Siegfried and Roy's incredible rags to riches story and I was fairly experienced in production, I couldn't keep up with the pace of this job. I was intrigued, but terrified, by the lions. I also wasn't comfortable living in a hotel, hours away from Tom and my cat, Spot. The pressure was enormous. Wild animals, the most famous magicians in the world, and long workdays that always turned into work nights.

One night in the production office I started sobbing around midnight and didn't stop for the next four hours. It was hard for me to even breathe. I alternated between calling Tom and my parents. They all tried to calm me down and assure me that I was just exhausted, but I felt sick. I was deliriously tired and decided I couldn't complete this shoot. I felt ashamed and defeated when I resigned that morning but I had no choice. I was emotionally and physically depleted.

Tom told me to catch a cab to the Las Vegas airport and he'd have a ticket waiting for me. I was so disoriented from stress and exhaustion that it was all I could do to find the right ticket counter and get on the airplane. Tom met me at the Los Angeles airport and took me to his apartment. I took a hot shower, got into bed and didn't get back up for the next two months. Tom went to my apartment and got Spot so I would have her with me at #104. We kept the lights low and the A/C high and Tom brought food into the bedroom for me as I recovered.

Once I recovered, I returned to being my normal sweet-but-kind-of-bossy-let's-call-it-persistent-self. We were going to live together now, and I insisted that #104 was too small. I argued that we needed a larger apartment, and preferably one near the beach since I "rollerbladed every day." Tom was hesitant—he loved #104, but wanted to make me happy, so we found what appeared to be a palace close to the beach in Playa del Rey. On moving day, I found Tom sitting in the now empty #104. He looked glum and said, "Sorry, I was just really happy here."

I hugged him and reminded him that our new place had two bedrooms, a loft, two bathrooms, marble counters, cathedral ceilings, and a fireplace. I assured Tom that we would be even happier at this larger apartment… but we weren't.

We were uncomfortable. Spot kept standing in the living room staring up at the tall ceilings as if to say, "What is this place?" Tom and I found it weird not to know what the other one was doing since we'd been used to living in closer quarters. We didn't like it there, so we moved to a smaller apartment even closer to the beach. We actually liked that place a lot and lived there for close to ten years.

On occasion, Tom would look at my rollerblades gathering dust in the garage and sarcastically say, "So, are you going to the beach to rollerblade today?" The first few years I'd say, "Soon, but not today—I'm really busy." Eventually, Tom and I would just laugh when we'd walk by my rollerblades. Tom and I loved living in Playa but on occasion he'd say, "I still miss #104. We really had a good thing going there."

After living by the beach for close to a decade, Tom and I decided to move back to Brentwood. He'd gotten a full-time job at the Getty Museum and we wanted him to be closer to work. Tom said, "Let's look in my old apartment building. Who knows, maybe all of the units are as great as #104." So, after dropping Tom off at work, I stopped by and the apartment manager showed me around. There were several units available. All of them were nice but none had the magic of #104.

As the apartment manager and I walked by #104 I said, "My husband and I actually used to live in #104, many years ago. It's where we first fell in love so that's the apartment we really want."

The apartment manager raised her eyebrows and practically yelled, "I didn't know you used to live in #104! You're not going to believe this! The tenant in #104 gave notice just forty-eight hours ago, which is why that unit isn't even being shown yet. The current tenant is sad to leave because she loves that apartment too, but this will make her feel much better knowing you guys are moving back in!"

When I told Tom we were going to move back into #104, he started yelling. "I get to go home! I get to go home! Put the deposit on it right now!"

#104 has less storage area than the apartment Tom and I'd been living in by the beach so we had a garage sale. My rollerblades were the first thing to go but we also sold books, clothes and CDs because we didn't want to bring any clutter to #104.

We didn't sell any of our furniture, though. As it turns out, we still had the same couch, bookshelf, and dining room table that Tom had bought when he first moved into #104, all those years ago. So when we arrived back at #104, we knew exactly where everything would go. The couch went where it had sat ten years ago. The bookshelf went where it'd always been and the dining room table went back to its rightful place. Our new bed went where Tom's old bed had been. And #104 felt exactly as it had always felt — fantastic!

It was an incredibly strange, but good, déjà vu sensation to wake up the next morning in the exact place we'd lived ten years prior.

"It seems like a dream that we lived at the beach for ten years," I said.

"This feels so right!" Tom replied.

Some say you can't go home again — but Tom and I did, and we've never been happier!

~Rebecca Hill

57

The Homestead

Where thou art, that is home.
~Emily Dickinson

My grandparents, Hervey and Ethel Parke, lived in the home that once belonged to the famous American poet Emily Dickinson in Amherst, Massachusetts. By the time they bought the house, the huge brick mansion at 280 Main Street was already over 100 years old. Emily's own grandfather built the house in 1813, and the poet was born within its walls. She and her sister Lavinia and brother Austin lived there for years after their parents passed on.

When my grandfather became pastor of the old Episcopal church just a few blocks away, he needed a place to raise his expanding family. He bought the homestead and its three acres of property from the Dickinson family in 1916. My father, the fourth of five children, was born there shortly after the family moved in.

As a young child, however, none of this history impressed me. To me, this was simply the home of Nai Nai and Yeh Yeh, the affectionate names we used for my grandmother and grandfather. My twelve cousins, three brothers and I descended on the home each summer and at holidays. We ran up and down the stairs, sometimes sliding down the bannister of the main staircase in the front hall. Excluded from the front parlor, we children played with our toys and enjoyed games in the library. As toddlers, we ate our meals in the kitchen. But as we grew older, we graduated to the formal dining room, sitting with bare legs on the itchy horsehair chairs. We climbed high up to the cupola, looked out the windows at a vista of rooftops and thumbed through stacks of old *National Geographic* magazines stored on the shelves.

The great rambling attic was a place of special delight. Large black trunks held treasures from earlier centuries. A dusty stereopticon and slides foreshadowed the 3D movies of today. Stiff top hats (still in their custom-fitted hat boxes) stirred up images of Abraham Lincoln, and yellowed lace dresses dated from the same period. Letters, brittle from age, gave accounts of the Civil War.

Outdoors we enjoyed a grass tennis court—albeit crowded with weeds—and a formal garden. A large lawn beckoned children to run to their hearts' content. Many afternoons, aunts and uncles set up a croquet set for us to use.

On summer evenings at exactly 9:00 p.m., Nai Nai would announce, "Time for bed!"

She would shoo us children upstairs, bid us a good night, and then retire to her own bedroom for the night. There she would let her silver hair down and brush it carefully before climbing into bed.

As soon as all was quiet, my brothers would sneak out of the Emily room, I would emerge from the Lavinia room and other cousins would join us from the Austin room. Together we would tiptoe down to the library and play cards until midnight.

Sprawled with our games on the floor around the fireplace, we listened as our aunts and uncles talked of growing up in the house. Uncle David, at age two, crawled up onto the roof of the garage with the help of his sister. His older brother Hervey straddled the flagpole sticking out from the third story window. Aunts Priscilla and Mary used to play "doorsie" in the scullery, a single room that had six doors leading to the basement, kitchen, dining room, backstairs, library, and hall. My uncle told us of the night when Yeh Yeh dreamed he was being chased by a crocodile and, in his sleep, climbed up a "tree" that happened to be one of the posts of their four poster bed. He screamed when his concerned wife reached over and grabbed his toe to wake him. We children loved all the family lore.

Tourists often stopped by to see the Homestead where the famous poet had lived. Some didn't even knock. They simply walked right in. My grandmother welcomed them all. She always offered a cup of tea and an opportunity to talk about their favorite poems. When such guests showed up, we grandchildren fled upstairs to be certain our beds were made. Nai Nai didn't mind showing complete strangers around the house! Rumors that Emily had stuffed poems in the walls of the house only added to their fascination with the house.

Then my parents moved across the country to California. Our visits to the Emily house stretched farther and farther apart. My brothers and I graduated from high school and headed off to college.

In 1965, shortly after the house was named a National Historical Landmark, my grandmother concluded the house was far too big for a widow in her late eighties to occupy alone. She sold it to Amherst College.

At first, a college professor and his family lived in the house. They agreed to open the public areas of the home to visitors on certain days of the week. Later the college trustees took steps to restore the home to look as it had in the time when Emily and her sister Lavinia occupied it. The college added wallpaper and collected furniture from the right historical period. Some of the pieces belonged to Emily herself. Eventually the Homestead became a museum. Only a few rooms were open to visitors.

Five years ago, the Parke clan gathered for a family funeral at the old Episcopal church where my grandfather had once pastored. After the service and a time of sharing memories, a caravan of family members, including my ninety-two-year-old father, drove around the corner and down the street to 280 Main Street. The sudden influx of guests filled the foyer, but when the museum guides learned that my father had been born in the house, they granted us permission to tour some of the private areas of the house no longer open to the public.

One of those rooms was my grandmother's former bedroom. The director of the museum now used it as her office. A large desk and several bookcases filled the area, but my mind could still envision Nai Nai seated there on the end of her heavy oak bed, brushing out her hair. Memories flooded back. My cousins and I scrambled up the stairs to the cupola for one more glimpse of the town's rooftops.

My parents and relatives referred to the home as "280." Tourists called it the Emily House. Today, museum volunteers call it the Homestead. But in my heart? It will forever be my grandmother's home.

~Emily Parke Chase

58

My Room With a View

Home is a shelter from storms—all sorts of storms.
~William J. Bennett

I stood by the open window, heart thudding as an October breeze sailed into the house. A shiver shook my body. How could something like this happen to me? It seemed surreal. This was my house, my favorite window, and my favorite room.

I had spent hours converting the dining room into a library and filled it with shelf after shelf of books. Glorious, happy books. Lazy Sunday afternoons were for lounging on the sofa, reading or daydreaming while I watched squirrels and birds play outside the window. Most of all, I loved listening to my mom's old records on my grandmother's record player that I proudly displayed on the library coffee table. My grandmother passed away two years before, and listening to records connected me to three generations of mothers and daughters. But at that particular moment, the window in front of me had changed—it held none of the magic and good feelings it always had before.

This window—my window—had been violated and hacked open with a crowbar. The sunny, little corner of books and happiness had been my sanctuary, and now it would never feel the same again.

On my way into the house that afternoon, I had turned the

burglar alarm off before I even opened the door, using a remote fob while juggling the mail and my oversized workday bag. I couldn't wait to change into my comfortable sweatpants and maybe listen to a few records in the library before dinner. But even though I'd turned off the alarm, it beeped, alerting me that something had tripped the alarm at the same moment I was walking in.

Once I connected the beeping to an open window straight ahead, terror struck. I ran to my car and locked the door, unable to think clearly. Were the burglars still in the house?

I frantically tried to verbalize to the police what happened. Although I was relieved to see two kind faces, their search through the house was another type of invasion. They clomped up the wooden stairs in heavy thick-soled shoes with guns drawn, as if danger was imminent.

After a thorough search, they decided the burglars had opened the window, set off the alarm, and run away. I breathed a sigh of relief, although I couldn't stop wondering what would have happened if I'd come home a few seconds earlier and met them face-to-face.

One of the officers handed me his card and said, "Please call us if you need anything. We'll increase patrols in your neighborhood." His smile was comforting. It filled the entire house like a protective shield. By then, my mom was there too, and she made me feel supported. I would be okay.

My mom and I added advanced security after a run to the home improvement store. Her strength encouraged me as she drilled holes with power tools and proved that we could take care of ourselves. My grandmother had been exactly the same, living through the Great Depression and World War II. The women in my family knew how to survive.

But when it was time for bed, I didn't feel strong. Rationally, I knew I was safe. Yet, the image of the forced-open window played in a loop in my head. I couldn't shake the feeling that my warm, familiar home had become an unfamiliar dwelling where I was forced to sleep.

"They know you have an alarm now, so they won't be back," a friend said, reassuring me the next day.

I knew she was right, but I was still uneasy.

After days stretched into weeks, I learned to sleep with less panic. Eventually, I stopped jumping every time fresh ice cubes clinked from the icemaker or tree branches tapped against the side of the house. But I still couldn't handle lingering in the library, let alone sitting by the window to listen to my favorite records. This had once been a ritual that helped me feel connected and strong. It was ruined now. The burglar hadn't stolen a physical object, but he had stolen my sense of peace in the very room that comforted me most when I was down.

I tried to find moments of bravery. I went into the library to grab a book, but then convinced myself I'd enjoy it more if I lounged upstairs in bed. Another time, I pulled up the blinds, but I was unable to appreciate the view. Each time I tried to remain in the room images of the invader flashed into my imagination. I had created a monster in my mind worse than any hairy, grotesque boogieman hiding under a three-year-old's bed. I wasn't brave enough to fight my imagination or the memory of what happened.

Months after the break-in, I decided to journal in my favorite pink glitter notebook. But for me, reflecting on the significant and insignificant details of my life wasn't possible without a soundtrack. And I needed something more alive than an MP3 on a computer so I could feel connected to my mom and my grandmother. I needed the sound of my mom's old records that had comforted me while we had listened to them together when I was a child. I needed the shine of the wooden finish on the old-fashioned player that my grandmother kept in perfect condition. The record player still sat on the coffee table in front of the library window, heavy and awkward. Moving it to another room wasn't an option.

I selected a Cream album and placed it carefully on the player. The needle dropped with a hint of static before "Sunshine Of Your Love" filled the library. My tense shoulders relaxed as my mom's music surrounded me with childhood memories that felt safe, then and now. I ran a few fingers along the wooden edges of the player, remembering how happy my grandmother had been listening to her polka records through these speakers.

I cautiously raised the blinds to see magnolia and cherry blossoms swaying in the breeze. Squirrels and birds darted through the branches—the transformation from fall to spring that I had missed in the past few months while I was bound by fear. I had felt as if I hadn't lived up to the standards of the strong women in my family. They didn't flinch when faced with a hardship. This musical reminder of those women who had come before me was what I had needed all along to face my own fears. Unexpectedly, the house felt like my home again. Nothing could take that away.

~Ann Thurber

59

Becoming a Home Again

Be grateful for the home you have, knowing that at this moment, all you have is all you need.

~Sarah Ban Breathnach

We bought our home thirteen years ago. It took a lot to get us into our little beach cottage. We had to scrimp and save and beg and borrow, but we did it. We bought our own home even though it started as the worst place I'd ever set foot in. It was so bad when we bought it that my foot went through the floor the first time I walked around inside.

But we fixed it. Lots of hard work, time, money, blood, sweat and tears, but we made it exactly the way we wanted it. I could tell you where every light switch and outlet is. The name of the store where we purchased the tile. The name of the paint color on the walls. The first three things we planted in the garden (three palm trees, which is why we call the house Tres Palmas). Our house became part of my identity.

We had people over constantly. We had dinners, parties, holidays, hosted family and friends from all over the world. A niece and a nephew lived with us for a few years. The house was always full of people and fun.

Then, life started to change. My niece and nephew moved out.

We didn't entertain as much. Mike and I started to work more. We didn't eat at home as often. We began to neglect the house a little. An old beach cottage built in 1910 needs constant TLC.

Gradually, I decided I no longer liked our house. I hated that it was so small. It made me angry that the house required so much maintenance. I loathed summertime because the fog is notoriously bad for weeks at a time. I couldn't stand our large yard because it took so much work. I wished the kids at the school next to our house would stop making so much noise. The house that had been my dream home became the house I didn't want to go home to.

Then, life changed. My husband and I had a son. I focused, as new mothers do, only on my son. I didn't put any time or energy into the house. I sort of forgot about it. I had bigger, well technically a smaller, fish to fry. A six-pound, five-ounce fish to be exact. I worked less, stayed home more, started having family and friends over again. We almost always ate at home as a family. I even started hosting parties again. Over the course of about a year, I realized I was once again enjoying our home.

Now that we are a little family, I realize that many of the reasons I didn't like our house are now the same reasons I love it all over again. It is small, but it's cozy. I like that the fog keeps the summers from being too hot, so my son and I can walk to the beach and play in the sand or look for beach glass. I love the big yard because it's a great place for my son and his friends to play. I love hearing the laughter coming from the kids at the school next door and feel lucky that when my son is old enough, he will be attending that school and that I'll be able to peek through our fence and watch him while he plays on that playground.

Home isn't about the physical space or the location. It's about what goes on inside. The people, the fun, the happiness, and mostly, the love. It took a big change in my life to make me fall in love with my house all over again. But I did, because this little house has become a home again.

~Crescent LoMonaco

Dad's House

*Home is the place where, when you have to go there,
they have to take you in.*

~Robert Frost

After my parents separated when I was seven and my brother was three, my dad moved into a series of small apartments, none of which felt like home to us. The first, in the basement of a family house, was sparse and sad, save for the huge trampoline in the back yard we got to jump around on. The second was in an actual apartment building. We had friends from school staying with their divorced dad on a different floor so we could scamper down the hallways whenever we felt restless. Of course, it being Dad's house, we had an abundance of sugary cereal, pizza, and TV shows we probably shouldn't have been watching. But after a night or two, we always headed back to Mom's house, and the strangeness of being in Dad's apartment would wear off.

The third apartment my dad rented had two extra occupants — my future stepmom and her Pug, named Hercules. My brother and I adored Hercules, with his squished-in face and his loud snoring, but we slept on couches in a room together and were always forgetting something or other at Mom's house. That place wasn't home either.

Soon after my dad and my stepmom got married, they bought a house together. It was big — big enough for the two little kids who were still to come — but nothing particularly fancy. It was a bit of a fixer-upper, but it had lots of land for Hercules to roam and it was down the street from some of my friends. It was a step up from the apartment, but it still didn't feel warm.

Truthfully, we hated going to Dad's house. My brother would throw tantrums the minute we got home after a weekend at Dad's, taking his anger and discomfort out on both me and my mom. As for me, I just bided my time at Dad's house, sitting quietly until the days passed and I could go back to my real room and my clothes and everything I couldn't carry back and forth in my little bag.

I had a friend at the time, Ally, whose parents were also divorced. Her dad had a big, beautiful house not far from ours, and in it she had a room with a duplicate of everything she owned at her mom's. She had a second wardrobe, a bed she picked out, and a rosy pink paint color she'd chosen. My room was blue—a color my brother had chosen before we found out my stepmom was pregnant and we were going to have to switch rooms. Mine was supposed to be the bigger room, but it would soon house my brother and the new baby boy as well.

There in my blue room I would sit, avoiding my parents. Dad's house always felt oppressive. There were things I wasn't allowed to wear or do, and never with a rational reason. I was a fifteen-year-old straight-A student who had never lied to her parents and yet I wasn't even allowed to have sleepovers. And with the new baby on the way, I was feeling more and more like an unwanted houseguest.

When I turned eighteen, I was no longer required by law to go to my dad's house—so I hardly did. In turn, my dad and I started fighting frequently. The summer before my sophomore year of college we barely spoke, and we were on such bad terms before I left that I didn't say goodbye before packing the car and driving to my second dorm room in New York City. He didn't even know I had left.

But somehow we started to get back together again, my dad and I. We would have dinner in the city and talk about nothing too serious. I figured that if I saw him on my own terms, in a restaurant in midtown, I could escape if I needed to. There we'd sit, with chopsticks or pizza or whatever the dinner entailed, tentatively getting to know each other. I was surprised to find that when I left the restaurant, I didn't feel like I'd escaped. I felt like a load had been lifted.

Eventually, I went back to my dad's house. Two of the biggest reasons were my little brothers, who needed to see their big sister. And I wasn't rebellious enough to protest Christmas—I had to make the pilgrimage to Dad's. It began with holidays and easygoing visits, until slowly, over years, my dad and my stepmom became my friends and my support.

Now that I am out of college and making my own home, I often take a weekend to head back to my dad's house. My mom has since moved out of her house, my childhood home, but Dad's house remains. I am tentative—afraid to touch things, to take food, to linger too long—because I am reminded of the days when I felt like a teenage houseguest and a burden who needed too many rides back and forth from the movie theater or track practice and could never do anything quite right.

But whenever I ask my stepmom for a bite to eat or a couch to sleep on, she laughs at me. "Take whatever you want! This is your home too," she says, as if I never should have doubted it. And as I pull the blankets up to my chin and sleepily read a magazine with my youngest brother at the other end of the couch, I believe her.

Dad's house feels like home.

~Madison James

Coming Home

Having a place to go — is a home. Having someone to love — is a family.
Having both — is a blessing.
~Donna Hedges

A vibrant blaze of autumn colors swept by my window as we drove down the road. My grandpa, hands tight on the steering wheel, was telling me a story about his childhood. I smiled, but as hard as I tried to pay attention, my mind was on other things. This was my first trip home as a college freshman. My grandparents had made the two-hour drive to my school so that I could come home for fall break. I should have felt relaxed and free from my heavy class load, but instead I was weighed down by a different burden. What if home didn't feel like home anymore? I had only been away for a couple of months, but my whole world had changed. Most of them were good changes, but I needed home to be somewhere familiar, a solid foundation to anchor myself. What if this part of my life had changed too?

"Are you okay, honey?" My grandma patted my arm. "You seem quiet."

"I'm fine, just tired from late-night studying," I said.

"Well you should get plenty of time to rest soon. We're just about at your house," she said.

We rounded the last corner and I could see our big house peeking around the maple tree in the front yard. Everything looked exactly as it should. The fence my dad and I had built wrapped around the lawn. I could see the worn picnic table and my childhood swing set in the yard. My brothers' bikes were abandoned on the driveway. It all looked the same. It should have felt the same too. It didn't.

For some reason I felt like I was looking at somebody else's home. It seemed like the life I had lived in that house belonged to another person. Everything was so different now. How had that happened in such a short time?

Before the van was even in park, a jumble of blond heads raced across the driveway. I opened the car door and scooped up my two smallest brothers. We passed around hugs and smiles as my parents came out to join us.

"It's good to see you," my dad said as he laid his hand on my shoulder.

My mom had tears in her eyes. "We're so happy that you're back," she said. "Let's head inside. I have some homemade chocolate chip cookies fresh out of the oven."

As we moved into the house I tried to shake off my unease. It was silly for me to feel this way. I didn't want these doubts to ruin my time with my family, so I pushed them as far back in my mind as I could. We gathered around the dining room table. The boys hit me with a barrage of excited questions.

"What kind of food do you eat at college?"

"What does your dorm room look like?"

"Do you have to make your bed?"

I shot back answers to all of their questions, but I couldn't help but feel strange about it. Like I was a visitor sharing about my life somewhere else. I felt even more disconnected when I heard about all of the things I had missed in the last two months. They talked about new family friends whom I hadn't met and new activities they were involved in. Things I hadn't heard in our phone calls and read in e-mails.

The afternoon slipped by as we swapped stories. When the darkness started to sneak in through the picture window my grandparents decided they should head home. We walked them to their car.

"It's such a blessing to have you back for the weekend," my mom shared quietly.

"I'm so glad to be here," I replied. Silently, I wondered if my family saw me as a guest for the weekend. I just wanted this place to still be my home.

My mom had made my favorite dinner. We ate it together and then watched a movie in the living room. Then it was time to go to bed, and the lights flipped off one by one while I heard as many "goodnights" as John-Boy Walton.

I brushed my teeth and got a drink of water before I headed to my room. When I opened the door, I found everything where it should be. Which was weird. Because nothing was ever where it should be in my room. Tonight, it looked so nice and tidy. I knew right away that my mom had straightened up, and I was grateful. But it still felt like somebody else's room. I walked over to my bed. The sheets were crisply folded and the comforter smooth. The kind of smooth that belonged in a movie or a magazine. Something else stood out as unusual. A simple brown envelope propped against my pillow. I carefully broke the seal and slid out a note that said:

Logan,
I'm so happy for where you've been, but I am so glad to have you home.
Love,
Mom

And suddenly, the doubt was gone. I knew I was home. It didn't matter how much time I spent here. It didn't matter what things I missed out on. As long as I was part of this family, I knew this house would be my home. No matter what had changed or would change in my life, this was a constant. Something that I could always count on. So, as I stood there in my room, holding that handwritten note, I let go of my fear and confusion. Then I mussed up my bed sheets just for good measure.

~Logan Eliasen

Chapter 7

Home Sweet Home

Unwanted Guests

Holiday Harpooning

Decorate your home. It gives the illusion that
your life is more interesting than it really is.
~Charles M. Schulz

Early morning phone calls on a holiday weekend are always cause for alarm. When I saw that it was my neighbor on the caller ID I feared the worst.

"Cathi," she said, "I hate to bother you this early, but I wanted to apologize for trashing the side of your house."

"Wait. Trashing our house?"

"You mean you don't know?"

"Know what?"

"Go outside and take a look."

I hopped out of bed and walked out the front door. My neighbor called me to the side yard, where she held up the twisted and tattered canvas of her patio umbrella.

"Wow. Where's the rest of it?" I asked.

She pointed above my head. I turned to find the umbrella pole lodged in the side of the house with the accuracy of an Olympic javelin. "What on earth?" I asked.

"Remember the big wind gusts last night?"

I recalled the fierce howling of the wind before bed. "Yeah."

"Well, we ran out to grab the patio furniture before it blew off the deck, but we were too late. The wind picked up the pole, and it shot through the air like a missile."

"Obviously." I looked at the pole's location in relation to the inside of my bedroom. "Uh, that's awfully close to our bed." I cringed. "And it's my side, too."

"We thought your bed might be along that wall, but we figured you were okay because we didn't hear a scream."

"I hate to point this out, but if it had impaled me in my sleep, I wouldn't have had time to scream."

"Good point." She winced.

We stood there a moment, taking in the sight of the pole suspended from the siding. "I suppose I'll call my insurance company to file a claim."

"Do you want us to help you remove the pole today?" she asked.

"I think we'll leave it there because they'll have to assess the damage. But thanks."

"We're so sorry," she offered.

I wagged my finger at her. "It's because our dogs bark early in the morning that you're trying to kill us, isn't it?"

"No, actually, it's because you accidentally set off your house alarm one too many times."

I looked toward the death spear. "Well, the alarm certainly didn't go off when this thing came barging into the house unannounced."

My neighbor and I parted on amicable terms, and I went back inside to find my husband standing in the kitchen. "What's all the commotion?" he asked.

I motioned for him to follow me. We walked into the bedroom, and I pointed to the visible drywall chips on the floor by the bedside. On further inspection, we saw that my nightstand had cracked in half. The pole had sliced though the siding, the wall, and the piece of furniture.

"What the heck is that?" Michael asked, pointing to the pole's end, which protruded a good ten inches through the bedroom wall.

I nodded toward the neighbor's house. "Their patio umbrella."

He stood for a moment trying to comprehend what happened. I explained the wind gust and my near harpooning while we slept. "I don't know what disturbs me more," he said, "the fact that a pole came slicing through the side of our house, or that we failed to notice."

"If it had sounded like one of the kids sneaking in after curfew, or one of the dogs barfing on the bedroom carpet, I would've shot right up in bed," I offered.

Later that day Michael called the insurance agent to report the incident, but due to the holiday weekend it would be a few days before an adjuster could come out.

"A few days?' I said. "What do we do in the meantime?"

"Just ignore it."

It seemed like we could ignore it, but others had a more difficult time. When I went back outside, a woman walking her dog stopped on the sidewalk and called out, "What happened there?" Then a few phone calls from neighbors came in, followed by cars stopping curbside. It appeared the pole had become a public spectacle of sorts, so I decided to make the most of our newfound celebrity status.

I hung an American flag on the pole. It was, after all, Memorial Day weekend. After a day of stares, snickers, and headshakes from passersby, I decided to try a new décor—hanging planters—petunias, impatiens, ferns, and moss roses, which caused more cars to slow and take a gander. People hung out of their car windows, pointing and laughing.

Two days later, our son Holden came home from his friend's house and asked, "Mom, why are there bras and underwear hanging from the pole on the side of the house?"

"Because they can," I replied, smiling at my creativity.

Piper, our daughter, laughed and said, "What the heck, Mom? Cars are stopping in front of the house. Can't we have a little privacy around here?"

"Privacy?" Michael chuckled. "We no longer have privacy since your mother decided to air our dirty laundry in front of the neighbors."

"Can't we just go back to normal?" Holden asked, tired of the parade of people.

"Normal? Oh, you mean just the pole jutting from the side of the house?"

"Exactly," he said.

Fearing the display of intimate apparel might eventually cause a traffic accident, I removed the garments from the makeshift clothesline.

By the end of the week, the adjuster arrived at the house. He stood, shielding his eyes from the sun while peering at the now barren pole. "Isn't this the strangest thing you've ever seen?"

Michael glanced at me and smiled. "Close."

~Cathi LaMarche

Lizard in the House

For a man's house is his castle.
~Lord Edward Coke

"**R**ay, come here." My wife, Quyen, called out to me from the house as I was pulling clover out of the ice plant in the front yard. Her use of my first name and not the customary "Honey" told me this was a serious matter.

I dropped the garden shovel into the plastic container of uprooted clover and went directly through the garage into the laundry room.

"Daddy, there's a lizard in the house!" Our seven-year-old, Kristie, conveyed this with the excitement of a child announcing her birthday to arriving guests.

"Yeah, Daddy, it's huge." Our ten-year-old, Kevin, chimed in exuberantly.

Quyen, in the kitchen, spread her hands apart to indicate the length of a large-mouthed bass. Then she pointed to the loveseat in the family room and said, "It's behind there."

I went into the garage to put on my work gloves and retrieve the stick I carried on family walks around the neighborhood to protect us from mountain lions and coyotes in the surrounding canyons. Then I armed my wife with a broom and Kevin with a plastic yellow Wiffle ball bat.

"What about me? How come I don't get a weapon, Daddy?" Kristie said.

I went back into the laundry room and brought Kristie a short-handled whisk broom. Our family was now prepared to do battle with the marauding invader.

I opened the sliding door in the family room. Next, I pulled the loveseat away from the wall and stepped gingerly onto the cushions to peek over the back.

"Be careful, honey," Quyen said.

I gave her a thumb's up to indicate her husband had matters well in hand. I peered over the loveseat and spotted the creature crouched against the wall. It was chubby, with scaly desert-dry skin, and large, black zigzags along its back.

I reached over the loveseat with my walking stick and touched the lizard's tail with the tip. Instead of escaping through the door opening, the pesky reptile scurried under the loveseat and through the other side to scamper along the rug in a twisty, jerky jaunt to hide beneath the stuffed Winnie the Pooh in the middle of the family room.

Kristie screamed and Quyen hurdled onto the sofa to safety. Kevin stood with his feet rooted to the ground, mouth agape.

I descended from the loveseat wielding the stick and was about to lift Pooh to get at the enemy when Quyen said, "Wait!"

My hand froze in mid-extension.

She stepped over the arm of the sofa onto the floor and went into the garage. She brought back the now empty plastic container I had been using for clover and handed it to me.

I gave my stick to Quyen and positioned my family in a defensive perimeter around the denizen's hideout. Slowly, carefully, I raised Winnie the Pooh, and the lizard monster stayed still. Fast as a sprung trap, I dropped the container over the reptile.

"Yeah, you got him, Daddy!" Kristie said.

Quyen let out a long, relieved sigh.

Kevin said, "Now what, Daddy?"

I looked at him, then at my wife and Kristie, and tried to hide my uncertainty. Finally, I tossed Pooh onto the couch, his mission complete, and knelt on the carpet with both hands around the container.

I pushed the container toward the sliding door and heard the riled inmate thrashing in its moving prison.

At the lip of the door track, I gestured for my family to be ready with their weapons in case the unwelcomed guest tried to dash back into the house. Then I lifted the container's edge, and the lizard wasted no time hightailing it over the track onto the patio and through the back yard.

I hurriedly slid the glass door closed and was mobbed by my family for the courageous and heroic efforts to save them from the dire threat of the wayward lizard.

~Raymond M. Wong

The Home Invasion

Hospitality is making your guests feel at home, even if you wish they were.
~Author Unknown

We finally did it! After years of saving and planning, the real estate market plummeted and we were able to buy our dream home. The house was everything we wanted: situated in the perfect school district for our son, with a swimming pool, granite counter tops, walk-in closet and even an extra room for guests.

Aside from my best friend living out of town, I wasn't sure who would ever need to stay over in a guest room. But we set up the room just in case. The room sat empty for a few months, but at some point our dog began to sleep in there and it became know as Pepper's room. We often joked as we watched him leave the TV room to head upstairs to bed that he would use his hind leg to shut the door. On one occasion I even received a call from a neighbor asking if Pepper was having a hard night or up reading a book since his room light was on late into the night.

Pepper became more and more comfortable in his surroundings, until one day the call came. It was from a former colleague who I hadn't seen in years or known other than through her work as a tele-commuter. She and her family were going to be traveling and while "passing through" my town asked if they could "bunk" at our place. She took me by surprise, but I figured it would be okay to host them for one night, so I said yes.

The day they were to arrive, we moved Pepper's bed to our room. They weren't sure when they would arrive so I prepared dinner in the Crock-Pot. I shopped for breakfast items and filled the refrigerator with things I hoped would make them feel welcome.

As the car pulled up around 7 p.m. we greeted them with open arms. Thank God our arms were open as the items that they unloaded kept coming. Suitcase after suitcase, video games, a guitar, blankets, pillows, computers—you name it, and it was entering my house. I couldn't help but wonder why they needed so much stuff.

We graciously showed them around and they immediately announced that "little" Jonnie, who by the way was thirteen, the same age as my son and not so little, would not want to sleep on the couch in the family room but on the floor in my son's room. As you can imagine, my thirteen-year-old son was not too keen on a stranger sleeping in his room. But I gave my son the "let's be polite" look and little Jonnie set up shop and made himself comfortable. Apparently while "on vacation," he's allowed to sleep with candy on his pillow and any other food item he wants. I explained that we don't have food in our bedrooms... for obvious reasons, I think. They disagreed and allowed it anyway since when on vacation little Jonnie always gets his way.

Once they were settled, dinner was served. Over dinner we visited and learned more about their trip. It all sounded very vague, with no real plans for where they were headed and what they were doing. After dinner they felt so at home they sprawled on the couch, turned on the TV and announced: "Since we are on vacation, we are going to let you do the dishes and clean up after dinner." Anyone who knows me knows I would have declined their offer for help and told them to relax, but the fact that they declared they were "on vacation" and I was the hostess made me question what was still to come.

I was excited when they said they had brought wine from a vineyard in their area that they knew I loved, until they brought out the invoice and asked me to make the check out directly to them. Maybe I was crazy to think this was a hostess gift but I was raised to bring something when I am a guest in someone's home.

We got through the evening and headed to bed. As we lay in bed, I kept thinking, "Just one night… I can do this." That was, of course, until 2 a.m. when the knock at our bedroom door came from the husband saying they heard a loud crash and thought a plane hit our house! A plane? We were in the next room and had fallen asleep with the window open. Besides the obvious fact that there was no way a plane could have hit our house, I think we would have heard something.

Being good hosts and worried about this strange occurrence, we bolted from bed and my husband surveyed the back yard and perimeter of the house to see if there was anything that could have made a loud noise. Keep in mind it was 2 a.m. As he walked the yard he was startled when he turned around to see her husband right behind him, creeping along timidly behind him! While the men were outside, I went to the guest room to check on my "friend." To my amazement she was sitting up in bed and throwing up in my son's bathroom trashcan, her pajama top barely hanging on. Apparently, she was upset about the imaginary plane crash. It was something I am not sure I can even explain.

After a little while I noticed my husband was missing and went into our room. He was back in bed, stating this was all too crazy for him and he was going back to sleep. He had to leave for work in a few hours. Once we knew we were safe from crashing airplanes and the trashcan was hosed out, we all went back to sleep.

Morning arrived all too soon. It couldn't have been 5 a.m. before the sounds of music filled the house. "What is that?" I said out loud. As I went downstairs, following the noise, I found the husband playing his guitar. Apparently this was part of his morning routine. I acted interested as he shared their morning rituals. It went something like this: He gets up at 5 a.m. and plays guitar for a few hours. His wife sleeps until 8 a.m. or so, then gets up to read the newspaper—by the way, I don't get the paper—and rub little Jonnie's back for thirty minutes. Then they start their day. I realized that meant it would be 10 a.m. or so before they were on the road. I had errands to do in the morning and since I wasn't "on vacation," I had a full day of work ahead of me, too.

Since I clearly had until 8 a.m. before the others would wake up, I got my son up and off to school and ran a few errands. When I returned home I was greeted at the garage door with, "Where were you? We have been calling your cell phone but you left it on the counter."

"Is everything okay?" I asked.

Their reply was, "Well, we needed ice for our coolers, and we needed you to get us ice and... where is the newspaper?"

I was dumbfounded as I calmly and politely gave them directions to the store at the end of the street. When I asked what was in the cooler, they told me their coolers had food for the days at my house when I would not be serving them meals. What? Days? Then they emptied my refrigerator and made the largest breakfast I have ever seen. After that, the coolers were brought in and ice added, and I saw they had many of the same items in their coolers that I had previously had in my refrigerator.

They then informed me that they decided to go to an amusement park for the day and would return again in time for dinner. I was not sure how to respond except with an "okay" and a silent prayer of gratitude that my husband was working overnight and not returning until the next day.

The family returned right at dinnertime, and I had purposefully not made a plan. When they announced they were hungry I asked what they had in mind. I suggested a pizza or going out. Their response was, "We will do pizza and even pay if you allow us to take the leftovers when we leave." Again dumbfounded, I agreed although I no longer even wanted a slice.

The rest of the evening was fine, as my son and I made a plan to go to bed early. I promised that the next morning I would be more assertive in sending them on their way. Once again 5 a.m. came all too soon, and once the guitar was played and my refrigerator was cleaned out and little Jonnie's back was rubbed I asked about their plans for the rest of their trip. With no destination in mind they got out the

AAA travel guide and started asking about places. I was very enthusiastic about each place they mentioned, selling hard, even though I'd never been to most of them! They indicated that they might need a key because my son had soccer practice that night. What? They were planning to stay again? I had had enough. I explained that we had too much going on that evening and they would need to set out on the rest of their trip. They still didn't get the hint and indicated that they would check in later that day....

As they refilled the coolers with ice once again, I helped load all their items into their car... including the two slices of leftover pizza.

Once they pulled away, I locked the door, got in my car, and headed to The Home Depot to look for dog border wallpaper. I even thought about removing the bed and building a doghouse coming out of the wall. A few months passed before I heard from my guests again. I was able to state without guilt that we no longer had a guest room.

~Cassidy Sanchez

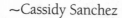

65

Chicken Soup
for the Soul

Masked Bandit

Nothing ever goes away until it has taught us what we need to know.
~Pema Chödrön

$\mathcal{I}$ rolled off our makeshift bed one Saturday morning and tiptoed around the two twin mattresses that lay side by side next to ours. We had just completed phase one of a planned three-phase renovation of our new home. The family was camping in what was to be our home office. The kids thought it was cool that the four of us, our eight-year-old Lab Sam, and the three black bear hamsters were camping in such a tight spot for a much longer-than-expected period of time. Truth be told, I loved it too.

Hoping to steal a few quiet moments, I silently crossed the room, opened the door and had just about left the room when Sam jumped up and nudged past me, running like the wind.

The promise of coffee and blueberry muffins guided me down the dark hallway. I was careful not to trip over the sixty feet of extension cords stretching from one level of the house to the next. That cord ran the refrigerator and coffeemaker and was the only power we had for the other side of the house. When I reached the empty space that was to be our new kitchen, I felt something was wrong. Then I saw it. The muffins that had been stored on top of the refrigerator were gone.

Muffin crumbs and the remnants of a cardboard box were scattered all over the floor. Instinctively I turned toward Sam and read him the riot act.

"How could you do that? Those were MY muffins!"

We kept such a small supply of food in the house that everything was rationed. I continued to rant at poor Sam until it occurred to me that Sam had been locked in the office with us all night.

After apologizing to my bewildered pup, I took him out for a walk and picked up the newspaper waiting for me at the end of the driveway. If I wasn't going to have a muffin at least I could relax with my coffee and the paper.

The next night I was the last one to go to bed. I went up to our makeshift bedroom, shut the door and crawled onto our mattress. Immediately after I turned off the lights, I heard a light tapping sound in the hallway. It seemed to be pacing up and down.

My husband Jack and I grabbed a flashlight and crept down the hall to the kitchen area. Two glowing eyes peered back at us in the flashlight's beam. Rocky the raccoon was dining on top of the refrigerator.

We both gasped as the raccoon stopped munching on our bread. I was at a loss. What do you do? Jack shouted for them to stay in the office, shut the door and keep Sam in there with them. We knew we could control the kids but not Sam if he got a whiff of the raccoon.

Jack told me to open the front door and go to the stair landing. He grabbed a broom and pushed at the raccoon, trying to coax it to leave. But it just snarled and screeched at us. I was terrified. Then it occurred to me to call my friend who was the director of the local nature center.

The phone rang and rang. The minute she answered I could tell we weren't going to get much assistance from her. Loud music and people singing in the background clued me in to the fact that she was having a party. The second clue was her loud hey-come-over-and-have-a-drink voice.

I explained about the raccoon perched on our refrigerator. She listened, let a minute go by and then let out a loud roar, which was followed by her repeating the story to the entire party. In unison everyone howled!

Finally, she got control of herself and realized we were seriously frightened. She came up with a credible solution. Take bread and leave a trail from the fridge to the door and then throw the rest of the bread outside. Then, turn off the lights and go back upstairs.

We did as she said and then shut ourselves in the office with the kids, Sam, and the black bear hamsters. After twenty minutes we crept back downstairs, and to our surprise the raccoon was gone. Two minutes after we were back in the safety of our office the phone rang.

"Hello?" I answered, wondering who would be calling that late at night.

"Hello, this is Bambi. Rocky told us you were having a party and wanted to know if Thumper and I could come over." You could hear the entire group laughing hysterically in the background.

"Very funny," I replied. "You will be happy to know that Rocky has left the building."

The next night I calmly tucked the kids in their beds and then climbed onto our mattress. I reached over to turn out the light and gave Jack a kiss goodnight, letting out a long sigh as I prepared for some much-needed sleep.

Within minutes, I heard it. That little bandit was back in the house. How was he getting in? I decided there was nothing I could do that night so I made sure the door was secure and went back to sleep.

The next night, after everyone had gone up to the office, I went downstairs with a Coleman lantern, my files and my computer. Sitting at a card table, I began to work on our taxes. Jack called down that he was going to sleep and turned out the light upstairs. Within a matter of minutes I heard it. The scratching of something trying to get into the house.

Then I saw him. A paw slowly appeared under our staircase. Then another paw. Rocky was back for an encore. He flexed his claws as if he were preparing to play the piano. Finally his face appeared.

I must have startled him as I let out a scream and he retreated back into the dark hole. Quickly I picked up a board and some nails that were lying around and covered the hole.

I wish I could say that was the last of our nighttime visitor but it wasn't. Rocky kept returning. I tried to board up all the holes on the outside of the house with discarded shingles I found lying around the construction site, leaving the outside somewhat of an eyesore for our neighbors. Somehow, that midnight marauder kept finding his way back in anyway. The day our contractor finished the outside siding Jack and I let out a sigh of relief. I'm sure our neighbors were happy too!

~Jeanne Blandford

66

The Zookeeper's Mother

May your home always be too small to hold all of your friends.
~Author Unknown

I surveyed my handiwork with the hands-on-hips satisfaction of a woman who had restored peace, order and good government to her home. The unruly cast of stuffed animals that had been roaming wild around my house—toucans, lizards, turtles, squirrels, kangaroos—were now safely back in their enclosures. My family room no longer looked as though Noah's Ark had docked for shore leave.

I hadn't managed to thin the herd—the culling had been thwarted by the Zookeeper. But having narrowly escaped the ruthless downsizing that reduced the ranks of their plastic comrades, all of the soft, plush critters in my house had a newfound respect for the Zookeeper's Mother.

The smell of fear was still in the air when the phone rang. "Hi, it's Miriam," said my son's babysitter. "I've been going through some of my old things, and I know Joe loves stuffy toys and I have one... which is very special to me... and I want it to go to a good home."

Her timing was uncanny. It's as if she knew on a subatomic level that I'd been purging. (Had the inanimate animals sent out a distress signal of some kind?)

Part of me wanted to be cold and practical, to say, "There's no room at the inn!" But in spite of Miriam's adolescent nonchalance, I heard the faintest trace of the little girl I once knew. I figured any toy she'd hung onto through the tumultuous transition from tween to teen must, indeed, be something very special. How could I deprive this vestige of her childhood from finding a loving home?

"Bring him over," I said. "The Zookeeper will always make room for one more."

Joseph, the Zookeeper, had proved his loyalty to his collection of stuffed animals during the clear out. He'd made tough sacrifices with many of his other toys in order to keep the whole plush gang together. (So long Mr. Potato Head, may you rest in peace. Too bad you weren't stuffed.) Earlier that day all the soft toys had been laid out, sacrificially, at the foot of my son's bed. "You can't keep them all," I said.

But who would stay, and who was to go?

Joseph made a compelling case for why each and every one must be saved. With gravity-defying tears clinging to his lower eyelids he pleaded with me: "You can't break up the family!" And just so you don't mistake me for a heartless witch, I too had trouble saying good-bye to some of these fine fellows. In no time at all I'd assembled my own class of untouchables in the safety zone at the head of the bed.

"Not the Wolfe Island bunny," I said. He is one of my nearest and dearest. "Not Doggy!" I plucked him off the pile right away. To other people, he is a speckled dog of no great importance, but in his glassy eyes I see the reflection of my Uncle Adrian buying him in the nursing home's gift shop—a present for the baby boy I was bringing for a first, and final, visit.

Between Joe's favourites and mine, pretty soon the whole rag-tag circus had simply migrated from the footboard to the headboard. With two sentimentalists like us, there would be no letting go. These animals were connected to memories that neither of us was ready to toss in a green garbage bag.

Not long after the great purge the Zookeeper quickly began forgetting to corral his stuffed animals at day's end. Within a few days I found New Leopard (Miriam's beloved for whom we haven't settled on a name) sitting on the floor of my closet with one of my bras strapped to his chest. It got me thinking about my first screenplay: *Toy Story 4*, starring a rogue, cross-dressing leopard having some fun in Andy's mom's closet.

I try not to be annoyed by the shenanigans, though. The truth is it will be a sad day when the Zookeeper is no longer devoted to his synthetic menagerie.

While the Zookeeper is at school, sometimes I gather up the wayward troupe and arrange them on his bed, mixing and matching animals that don't really belong together. There is no lion and no lamb, but the bunny and the tiger do well as stand-ins for my new world order: Where foe becomes friend and we all live together like one big, happy family.

~Michelle Hauser

67

Itsy Bitsy Spider

We hope that, when the insects take over the world, they will remember with gratitude how we took them along on all our picnics.
~Bill Vaughan

One good thing about being disorganized is that one is always making exciting discoveries. Our little log home is full of odd storage spaces so during my occasional housecleaning excavations, I can come across some real treasures from my past. One day, I had such an encounter, with a plastic tub of vacation clothes from the era when the kids were small and we went on Disney vacations. My daughter's little Princess Jasmine swimsuit emerged from the box along with one of my husband's flowered Big Dog shirts.

Unfortunately, these odd storage spaces and charming nooks and crannies make wonderful homes for squatters too, as I discovered when I was clasping my daughter's Princess Jasmine swimsuit to my bosom in a fit of nostalgia and saw something fuzzy moving in the bottom of the tub.

If you've spent any time in the woods, you learn that spiders live there too. Fundamentally, I don't have a problem with that, because technically we are invading their space. I'm proud to report that a kinder, gentler me has evolved over the past few decades. There was a time that I would have thought nothing of dropping an encyclopedia on the hairy little creepy crawlies with the intention of breaking all eight of their legs. In truth, I always took that coward's way out because I could never squash them with my foot. I thought a plummeting encyclopedia seemed forgivable, something more like an accident.

By the time my babies came along, my intellectual self had come to accept what beneficial neighbors spiders really are. I've even read that they are excellent indicators of the absence of radon. Got spiders? No radon! Between that left brain data and my right brain's endless viewings of *Charlotte's Web*, by 1989 I could no longer squash them at all. At that point, my weapon of choice became a vacuum cleaner with a very long extension tube.

Fast forward twenty-two years. I was in my flip-flops, rummaging alone in the bedroom when I found myself out-gunned four-to-one by a wood spider and with no vacuum cleaner in sight. For those of you who don't know, a wood spider is not the itsy, bitsy spider of fairytale fame. A wood spider is a spider on steroids, a large brown obviously crunchy thing—absolutely terrifying.

I did the only rational thing; I backed away quietly, being careful not to make contact with any of its four pairs of eyes, and closed the door, a symbolic gesture only. An hour later, when my son arrived, I put on my snowboots and welder's gloves. He armed himself with a paper plate and the glass dome to my cheese tray. He and I have honed our teamwork skills over the years and we've wrangled our fair share of renegade chickens and the occasional errant black snake. A wood spider is simply no match for the two of us.

We knew the plan. I held the flashlight while he goosed the spider from the back so it scooted onto the paper plate held strategically against the side of the tub. The cheese dome came down on top and presto! We had spider under glass. The tricky part is always keeping a tight seal between the plate and lid, and I wisely left that up to my younger, nimbler offspring.

My husband has always said that fear is simply a lack of knowledge, so in an effort to give my fearlessness a booster shot, the three of us—my son, the spider and I—sat down at the kitchen island and chatted a bit with a layer of protective glass between us. When we had exhausted all conversation that could have been of any possible interest to a spider, my son secured the bottom of the plate against the glass once again and escorted the spider to the far side of the driveway and set him free.

By evening, the spider was on the outside of the back porch. By morning he was on the inside of the torn porch screen. By the next evening, he was peering in the bathroom window. I know it was the same spider; we had a moment of connection as I saw a look of gratitude in his eyes, all eight of them. In that special moment that only manifests when Homo sapiens and an arachnid have truly found their truth, it occurred to me that he had been living the good life in my closet before I had invaded his privacy. He was simply on a mission to get home and I felt a tiny pang of regret as I watched him entreat me with his outstretched little arms — or first pair of legs, whichever.

Our minds melded and we sealed an unspoken pact. It was our own "don't ask, don't tell" policy. He promised not to show himself again and I promised not to go looking. And so we agreed we could share the space and both call the same location home sweet home. But that doesn't mean my vacuum won't be locked and loaded, just in case.

~Mitchell Kyd

68

The Indecorous Friend

I would be most content if my children grew up to be the kind of people who think decorating consists mostly of building enough bookshelves.
~Anna Quindlen

Interior decorating is the art of changing what already exists into something better. That means redoing my entire house. I never thought anything was wrong with my home until my friend, Arlene, an interior designer, stopped by for an unannounced visit.

"May I speak frankly?" Arlene asked. For years, "frankly" meant telling me exactly what I was doing wrong in all areas of my life: marriage, child rearing, investments, and now, home remodeling. What I wanted to say was, "Of course I mind if you speak frankly, you critical little wench!" Instead, I smiled and gave her my pat answer: "Your opinion means the world to me."

"Good," she said, dragging me into my living room, "because I've wanted to tell you this for ages, but never had the heart to hurt your feelings."

"Don't let that stop you."

"It's this room: it's got to go."

"Where should I put it?"

"What I mean to say," she said, strutting about, "is that this house needs some work. Your home doesn't reflect your personality. You need to emerge. You're projecting the wrong statement."

"Get to the point," I implored.

"Do you want to be a beige person all your life? Your interior complexion is a bit pale."

"Shall I consult a physician?"

"If it were only that simple," she sighed. "You need to liven things up a little. Smear on some terra cotta—a touch of salmon perhaps. A smidge of café au lait. It will brighten up your furniture, not to mention add some excitement to your marriage."

"Mort is already overly-excited," I said.

She looked me straight in the eye and got serious. "Decorating is good for your sex life," she whispered.

I stood there wondering why, with all the friends in the world, did I happen to get this one?

I looked around. "Where do you get off telling me that my living room is pale? And what's wrong with beige? It blends."

"Darling," she said, "beige is so yesterday. It gives off the wrong aura. The walls resemble Muenster cheese. You need a complete face-lift—an overhaul."

"Maybe just the jowls," I said.

"A window treatment, sweetheart. Get rid of those things that hang down. They're getting stale."

"You mean the draperies?"

"Draperies are a word you're better off dropping from your vocabulary. The buzzword today is 'window treatment.' You want the room to scream 'You.' The décor must harmonize with your persona. It must create an effective design element that expresses your meaning of life."

She picked up a piece of artificial fruit and bit into it, nearly cracking her porcelain laminates.

"For example, who puts fake fruit in a bowl?"

"That way it always stays fresh," I said.

"You want to make order out of chaos. You need to think functional. Feng shui."

"Perhaps, I should stack up the old pizza boxes and use them as an end table," I suggested.

"Very funny," she said. "Look, I'm here to save your marriage. A man's home is his parking lot. There should always be an available spot or he'll look for another place to park his car, if you catch my drift. It's the special little touches that men find comforting. Let's start with the basics. What is Mort's favorite accessory?"

"The remote control," I said.

"Darling," she said, "I'm offering my advice for free. Don't you want my acumen?"

Acumen, hell. What I wanted was to punch her in the mouth and tell her to go home to her color-coordinated, antiseptic, politically correct palace and leave me to my eclectic abode that defined my own style of personality: disarray.

"Your homework is to go out and buy all the home design magazines you can find," she said. "And I'll return with the swatches."

"I don't do swatches."

"Oh-My-Gawd! You don't swatch?"

"Is that bad?"

"Swatches can make or break a room," she said. "You've simply got to develop a decorating attitude. Your home is a shrine, not a warehouse of inappropriate miscellaneous bric-a-brac. It needs organization. It needs élan."

"Perhaps, you're right," I said, surreptitiously kicking a Häagen-Dazs container under a chair.

For the next several weeks I became the Decorating Queen of Westport. I poured through magazines and visited designer showrooms. I decided to discard the old and bring in the new.

"We'll start with the bare essentials," the saleswoman at the D&D building said.

"What is it that's been sitting around for years, serving no purpose?"

"My husband," I said.

She handed me swatches and told me to come back when I had a developed a better handle on home improvement.

In the end, I decided to stay with the look I love most: clutter.

When Arlene arrived on my doorstep a month later, I let her in with some trepidation. She surveyed my interior landscape and came out of the upstairs bathroom, beaming.

"I didn't know you faux marbled the bathroom walls. They look marvelous."

In her house, they may call it faux marble. At my place, we call it mold.

~Judith Marks-White

Trench Warfare

There is no gardening without humility…
~Alfred Austin

O ur children were grown and on their own. My husband Chris and I had finally realized a long-awaited dream and moved to a cottage in the country. Now we could wake up each morning and look forward to watching an occasional deer meander through the yard, spot squirrels scrambling up trees with their acorns, and observe the social order of birds at the feeder. Blue jays first, unless a bully of a redheaded woodpecker lurks on a tall tree trunk nearby.

Life in our new home would have been grand if it hadn't been for those unseen critters waging war with this pair of country newbies. My love and respect for the animal kingdom was about to be sorely tested. For those of us who feel a kinship with animals, occasionally there comes a time when an earth-shattering upheaval, so to speak, separates theory from practice.

During that first summer in our new domicile, my mettle was tested by a platoon of voles. They are the insidious little critters that hide in the dark netherworld of our yards. They stealthily slide along their well-crafted underground tunnels, munching on tender plant roots they view as a well-stocked salad bar.

They're probably held in high regard among their animal friends since they believe in sharing the wealth. Voles act as company commanders forging the way for other tunnelers, like chipmunks and field mice. Our back yard had become one big garden party down there at our expense.

Ferreting out this destructive militia became our summertime obsession. We had called upon our animal-friendly arsenal of weapons but were failing to reclaim our territory.

Over breakfast one morning, I'd said to my husband, "I've been getting neighborly advice about ways to send those critters packing."

Chris was immediately interested, if somewhat reluctant to look like a country bumpkin, when I suggested theory number one—human hair as repellent.

Undaunted, I continued, "The next time you go to the barber shop ask for a bag of hair." I related the theory that the voles would be scared off by the scent of big, bad Homo sapiens.

Reluctantly, Chris marched off to the barber shop, collected several large paper bags of hair, spread it around the garden, wet it down, and waited for the motley crew to turn tail and head for the hills. It didn't work. The voles must have had a good laugh at that over lunch.

It was time for theory number two. Someone suggested rolling up several sticks of chewing gum and shoving them down the vole hole. Allegedly, the voles would get a fat wad of gum in their jaws making it impossible for them to munch on plant life—at least for a while. Hah! The Juicy Fruit turned out to be nothing more than a pre-lunch appetizer.

Theory number three: the high-tech approach. A sympathetic friend bought us a sonic tube that you insert into the ground. It is battery-operated by a small fortune's worth of D-sized batteries. This theory purports that the underground tremors created by the sonic tube would drive the voles and their party animal friends away. Mission unaccomplished.

Then the nasty little critters began taunting us. Yes, they really did. One day, Chris was in the back vegetable garden with our yellow Labrador Retriever, Savannah, who was on a leash. He watched in utter disbelief as a budding pepper plant was pulled underground right before his eyes. He was quite sure those criminal masterminds knew he wouldn't let go of the leash long enough to save his new sprout.

We stopped relating that episode to our friends when they began comparing us to Bill Murray's character in the movie *Caddyshack*.

The war took an ugly turn about midsummer. By then, at least half our prize hostas were chewed off at their base. Our lush borders of variegated greens along pathways and around thick tree trunks looked barren. Little did we know that the final defeat in our battle was imminent.

We had received a beautiful, young Japanese red maple tree as a gift. It was both sentimental and valuable. Its feathery, deep red leaves graced a small garden by our front porch. One day I saw Chris holding what was left of the tree in his hands. It literally had been chewed off at the base. He cradled the poor, dead tree in his arms, took it out back, and laid it to rest. I could see the crushed spirit written on his face. Then he got mad.

"We'll fix those nasty little creatures," Chris said through gritted teeth. He called our local Cooperative Extension Service. One of their master gardeners mailed us a brochure full of tips for getting rid of voles.

When the brochure arrived, our hearts sank. Short of using pesticides (which we preferred not to do), we'd already tried every recommended remedy. After having lost each skirmish in our battle of wills, we surrendered. The underground army had been triumphant. It was time for compromise.

These days, every plant we hope to harvest lives in containers, above ground. Peace reigns. The salad bar crowd has moved to a new neighborhood.

~Judy Harch

Home Sweet Home

Do-It-Yourself Disasters

70

Out of the Mouths of Babes

If we would listen to our kids,
we'd discover that they are largely self-explanatory.
~Robert Brault, www.robertbrault.com

"Poo!" I stopped short at the bathroom door. Peering in, I saw my two-year-old daughter pointing excitedly at the toilet. Seeing me, she grew more animated and jabbed her pudgy little finger toward the bowl.

"Poo!"

Aw, wasn't that cute. After what seemed like a lifetime of noxious diapers, baby wipes, and sheets, my little girl was starting to get that whole potty thing down.

"That's right, sweetie," I said, smiling, "that's where you go 'poo.'"

Ignoring the bewildered look on my daughter's face, I scooped her up and went off in search of my wife. "Honey!" I cried. "You can throw away those Pampers!"

Lost in my enthusiasm, I ignored my daughter's continued cries.

"Poo! Poo!"

The following week my wife stormed into the family room.

"The toilet's still stopped up. You really have to do something about it this time."

Reluctant to pull my eyes from the game, I shot back, "I took care of it!"

"Jiggling the handle doesn't count."

Of course she was right. When it came to home repair, I wasn't exactly Bob Vila. Don't get me wrong, I enjoy strapping on a tool belt and launching into do-it-yourself projects. Yep, I can fix everything from a broken heart to the crack of dawn with my bare hands.

And, with those same bare hands, dial the phone for an actual repairman.

That said, I confidently took on the task of fixing our only toilet. I ignored the fact that one small slip would place the family's entire lavatorial capability in the, no pun intended, dumper.

Hoping to achieve maximum success with minimal effort, I pulled the flush lever. Watching the water slowly swirl down the drain, I jiggled the handle, hoping for the best.

As I watched the water leave the bowl about as slowly as in-laws go home after Thanksgiving, I knew this was going to take much longer than I feared. Grabbing the plumber's helper, I commenced to violently plunge up and down like some manic Dutch milkmaid assaulting a butter churn.

Water flew everywhere. I jammed the plunger in as far as it could go before yanking it free in the hope that whatever was impeding the flow would be thrust onto the floor.

Out of breath, I ceased my exertions. Easing the plunger out of the way, I peered into the bowl. All I saw though were tiny, rusty flakes that no doubt had been violently ripped from the pipes by my efforts.

Time to give my original trick another shot. Maybe the clog had been loosened down the line and all it needed was another flush.

This time, the water went nowhere. Instead, it rose menacingly to the lip of the bowl. Frantically grabbing towels, dirty laundry, and anything else I could lay my hands on, I prepared for the flood.

Luckily, the water stopped just short of the rim.

At this point, I knew the problem couldn't be solved by an amateur. A clog of this nature cried out for an expert who was highly skilled in the plumbing arts. Only a professional could get to the bottom—no pun intended—of this situation before my family was left without the means to flush away their problems—okay, pun intended.

In other words, time for me to tinker some more with it. Like a master hydraulic surgeon, I knew I'd have to remove the bowl.

Dutifully securing the valve feeding water into the tank, I checked to see what kind of wrench I'd need. Normally vise grips or channel locks with a rubber band would do the trick, but I knew it was critical that I not just guess. A wrong wrench thingie could shatter the fragile porcelain into a million pieces.

Passing my wife on the way to the garage, I assured her there was nothing to fear.

"You mean like that time you cleaned the fireplace and set the house on fire?"

Ignoring her, I kept on going.

"Or the time our furnace fell out of your truck and into the middle of Main Street?"

Finding what I needed, I returned to the family room. "Completely different situation," I said, and headed toward our bathroom.

"You're right," she called after me. "This time you're working on our only toilet. Want me to call the plumber now?"

She was just a Nervous Nelly, I groused, as I prepared to remove the bowl.

I gently removed the porcelain caps atop rusty anchor bolts. Better be extra careful. My wife was right about one thing. This was our only toilet.

I gently eased the wrench onto one of the bolts and paused. Now, which was it again? Righty-Tighty? Lefty-Loosey?

Suddenly, it came to me. If I'm looking down at a bolt, it's the exact opposite. So, I have to go right to loosen a bolt!

Confident, I pushed at the nut. But, instead of watching it ease off its bolt, all I heard was a barely discernible crack.

Half a second later the entire toilet exploded, leaving me only with a rusty nut gripped firmly by a Sears Craftsman 1/2" combination wrench.

"What was that?" I heard my wife from the family room. Her cries were shortly followed by the stumbling footsteps of my daughter.

I'd done it again. I had written another chapter in the annals of my do-it-yourself disasters.

My daughter peeked in. Her eyes grew wide as she took in the devastation that littered the floor, the walls, and even the bathtub where she kept hundreds of Disney toys.

As I peered into the empty maw of the toilet outflow pipe, I saw the source of the clog. Nestled among the porcelain shards was a toothbrush, baby's comb, half a wad of Kleenex, what looked like a bag of Twizzlers, and, grinning insanely up at me, a little plastic Winnie the…

My daughter clapped her hands and excitedly squealed, "Pooh!"

Yes, out of the mouths of babes…

~Ken Lynch

71

My Downfall

If men can quilt and take over the kitchen,
then women can pick up a wrench and fix a leaky pipe.
~Hanna Rosin

I have always been the one to figure out where the leak or squeak is coming from in our home. I help my friends with their projects, too. I don't see why an able-bodied woman has to rely on the man of the house to do everything. I have fixed plumbing, replaced light fixtures, changed HVAC filters, repaired appliances, and put furniture together. No pink tools for me, either.

So I was supremely confident that I could fix a damaged piece of my garage door mechanism all by myself. My teenage daughter had put a large dent in a section of the metal runner that guides the wheels on the door as it rises. I made an expedition to the scary industrial area where the garage-door-opener-parts place squatted among all the other boxy buildings. I had the dented piece of metal with me, since I didn't know what it was called. I received a few skeptical looks from the guys behind the counter, but I'm used to that when I venture into "man territory." I don't know what I was thinking, but when I got home with the replacement piece, I pushed the small red button that started the door on its journey to the ceiling of the garage. As the door rose, its mounted wheels were supposed to roll up the track, the one that I was holding in my hand! At that moment, I noticed that the missing piece of metal track, the one I had just bought a replacement for, and now held in my hand, served a very important function. Without this piece of track, the door started to sway, which started a catastrophic series of events in slow motion, resulting in the wheels popping out of the track.

I had managed to create a mess now, with the door hanging like a hammock from the garage's ceiling by two strands of terrifyingly thin wire. I was in big trouble. Would the door fall down? My garage has two stories of house above it. Would the whole thing collapse like a house of cards? And what was I thinking when I took on this project? I should have realized I was not invincible.

I ran upstairs and called the guy who had installed the garage door in the first place. I agreed to pay time-and-a-half so that he would come right away. I went back downstairs to the garage to keep an eye on the swaying door and just then my son came home from school, a witness to my humiliation. His jaw dropped, first when he saw the garage door, and then when he saw me, pacing in front of the garage. He stood there for a moment, and I knew he wanted an explanation.

But instead, I barked an order: "Just go inside… go!" He scurried inside. Meanwhile, a couple of my neighbors drove by, waved and pointed at my obviously broken garage door. "Something wrong?" they shouted.

Time crept by. The other two kids came home. Finally, the garage door repairman arrived, not exactly rushing despite the time-and-a-half. He was a titan with muscular arms, long curly black hair and a neat goatee. I asked him, "Is this the stupidest thing you've ever seen?" and, without waiting for an answer, "Can you fix this?"

"I can fix it," he said.

He lifted the door with his bare hands. His grease-covered fingertips made a dainty border up the sides of the white garage door as he put the wheels back on the track and secured the new piece of metal to the doorframe.

He pushed the red button; the door went up and down. Perfectly.

I paid him gratefully.

I left his fingerprints there, though—a reminder that some things are harder than they look.

~Risa Nye

The Color of Joy

Color is my day-long obsession, joy and torment.
~Claude Monet

Soon after we bought our first home, an older row home, I discovered that my husband Larry and I had different decorating styles. Once the movers left, I explored the rooms, ready to make changes. I found Larry sitting amongst the packing boxes thumbing through a Star Trek novel.

"I see sky blue or pale green. Which one?" I flicked a disapproving glance at the beige living room walls. Beige couldn't describe the color. More like sad tan. It had to go.

"Neither. Everything's fine." He continued to read.

I scooted a box over. Obviously, he'd misunderstood the question.

"Honey, look around you. The whole house is beige."

He closed the book. One of his strengths is that Larry really listens. He also lectures like he's facing a roomful of disinterested college students sneaking looks at their phones. He cleared his throat. Straightened his shoulders. Shuffled through mental notes.

I felt a lecture coming on and resisted the urge to duck under a desk.

"Beige equates to cleanliness, simplicity and order. Without beige, the color spectrum would be thrown into chaos. I prefer a life without chaos." Lecture over, he kissed me and re-opened his book.

As much I enjoyed reading, there were clearly issues at stake. "What are you really saying?"

"Beige is dependable. Sensible. Utilitarian."

Women have to frequently ignore comments that are clearly insane. Words couldn't describe my horror at the thought of living in a house decorated in manly utilitarian. One of my strengths is that I do pretty much whatever I want. Beige was boring. Sensible wasn't fun. That left me with only one alternative.

I needed to show my husband the joy of color.

I started in small ways. A red bedspread. Floral kitchen curtains. A year later, still drowning in utilitarian beige-land, I staged a revolt.

I called in sick. My sympathetic husband brought me a cup of tea, advised me to get plenty of rest and left for work. I sprang out of bed, retrieved the painting gear stashed in the basement, a roll of fabric and my staple gun. I planned to transform the middle bedroom into a writing sanctuary. A horrible orange and brown mural covered one wall; I couldn't wait to hide it.

Our cat, Tiger, reclined on the bed, watching as I removed the paint-encrusted antique doorknob, covered it with goo and laid it in the bathroom. While the first coat of primer was drying, I stapled swaths of a gorgeous French print over the mural. It took a little longer than I'd counted on. I gobbled a PB&J sandwich and kept working. I wanted Larry to be dazzled by the change.

It was fine until I tapped in the last staple and did a dance of joy.

Tiger must have stepped out for a bite and a wee, because I didn't know that he was behind me. I accidentally stepped on his tail. He yowled, swiped my legs and ran out of the room. I fell against the door.

It clicked shut.

I rubbed my scratches, only thinking of making peace with my beloved cat.

"Tiger, I'm sorry." I reached for the doorknob. My voice trailed off. A gaping hole jeered at me where the glass knob usually resided. I stuck my finger inside, trying to snag the catch. The lock didn't tumble open. Disaster! For the next twenty minutes I tried bobby pins, a pen and a nail. Nothing worked.

I was locked in.

"Okay. Don't get upset. Call someone. Tell them to hurry up home and let you out." I grabbed my phone. Disaster number two stared at me. The phone was dead and it was my own fault. I truly hate cell phones. Anyone can find you at any time. Period. Larry always recharged it for me, but I guess he'd forgotten to.

I don't wear a watch, so I flicked on the TV. 1:08. Larry usually got home around 6:30 or 7:00.

I gave myself a pep talk. "You have paint, entertainment and a few hours of alone time. Get busy."

I did. I hung lace curtains, got dizzy from paint fumes and decided to re-read a book. I found a dusty mint in a jacket pocket, but I could've eaten a whole pizza. Three hours later, I was starving, thirsty and needed to go to the bathroom. As an added perk, Tiger alternated between howling and sticking his paws under the door just in case I'd gone deaf and hadn't heard his pleas to enter.

I was beginning to hate decorating. Normal women go shopping, visit the nail salon or hit the movies when they play hooky. I had to stage my own HGTV intervention. Maybe I'd start watching sports.

The phone rang periodically; half the time I was sure that it was my husband. By the eighth time, I was sure of it. I stopped envying all the skinny actors torturing me with food commercials. Maybe he'd come home early and rescue me.

Tiger and I wailed in unison when we finally heard the front door open at 7:12.

"Up here! I'm locked in, honey!"

"Meooooow!"

"What did you do? Where's the rest of the door?" He banged on the door.

I glared. Did he really think that I'd deliberately lock myself in a room?

Larry must have sensed the death rays hurtling at the speed of exhausted, annoyed woman, ready to gag him.

"Just a minute."

He ran downstairs, and returned with the magic that opened the door.

I flicked the knife sticking out. "Clever. Thanks, love." I wrapped my arms around my big, handsome husband and squeezed hard. "It's been quite a day."

Larry took in the splendor and blinked. "Uh… guess you're making a stand. It's nice."

Nice wasn't exactly the word I wanted, but, hey, he's a guy. I'll take it.

"Yup. Let's sand the kitchen cabinets next weekend."

He hauled me downstairs. "Let's not. How about some pizza?" He pulled out his cell and placed the order.

I smiled and let myself be hauled. "Fine. But, you've got to admit, a little bit of color is exciting."

He shook his head. "Paint whatever colors you want, honey. You're exciting enough for the both of us."

~Karla Brown

As Seen on TV

The plumber came by this morning and the painter is due on Monday,
My checkbook's open and ready, for I "did it myself" just last Sunday.
~Amy Newmark

The TV commercial made it look easy. All you had to do was use this product and your tired, old, worn-out deck would look like a brand new deck. No more splinters. No more cracks. No rotten boards to replace. This miracle product would take care of everything. You just painted it over the old wood and your deck was as good as new. And the people in the TV commercial, walking on their refurbished deck, looked so happy. My deck was old and I was sold. I don't like to think of myself as cheap but I do like to save money when I can. And not having to replace the deck sounded great.

Now, I must tell you, I am not a handy kind of person. I had refinished redwood patio furniture when I was a teenager and I had helped my friend paint a picket fence, but I have never taken on a project like this. But how hard could it be? I mean you just open the can of deck paint and roll it on. I was ready.

I went to the hardware store and found the product I had seen on TV. I read the instructions and calculated that I would need two gallons. I showed my measurements to the man behind the counter and he confirmed—yes, two gallons would do it. "But what about the primer?" What did he mean... primer? Why would you need primer? He explained that I would need to prepare the deck for the miracle product so I would need a coat of primer first. Okay, that sounded reasonable. After all, when I do my nails I always use a base coat. Must be the same idea. So I added two gallons of primer to my order. And some rollers and a roller handle. Now I was ready.

Well, maybe not quite. He asked me if I wanted to rent a power washer? A power washer? What for? He explained that I would need to remove as much dirt and old varnish from the wood as possible so that the new deck paint would stick. The easiest way to do it was with a power washer. I was beginning to have doubts. This was a little more complicated than I thought it was going to be. They didn't mention power washing the deck in the TV commercial. They just opened the can, rolled the paint on and invited their friends over for wine and cheese the next afternoon.

My car was loaded down with supplies and the power washer, but I got everything home and unloaded without incident. I followed the instructions on the power washer. I filled the tank up with water, and turned it on. Whooooosh! Water everywhere!! The hose had disconnected from the washer and the spray went everywhere! Finally I pulled the plug but everything was soaking wet… except the deck. None of the water had even gotten close to the wood but I was very clean after my shower.

I tried again. This time I turned the pressure down and was actually able to power wash the entire deck. I was pleased. Now I had to let it dry before I put on the primer. The next morning I started rolling primer. This went pretty well too. It only took me a few hours to complete the job. Now I had to let it dry.

The next morning I was ready to use the miracle product that would make my deck look like new. I was excited. I started planning the party I would throw to show off my accomplishment. I opened one of the gallon cans. But it was so thick. How would I pour it out into the roller pan? The product wouldn't budge. I reread the instructions and it said you had to warm the product to get it to pour. How do you warm a can of paint? In the oven? In the microwave? Who knew? I finally put some towels in the dryer, heated them and then wrapped the can.

Rolling the stuff was a nightmare. It clumped, it dripped, it smelled, and it didn't cover very well at all. The only thing it really covered was me. I could still see all of the cracks and splinters on the deck. I had to roll the same area over and over again. This was really stupid. I was sore, tired, angry, and covered in paint, but I was determined to finish. And hours later I was done. The damn deck looked awful but at least it was all the same color. Now I had to let it dry. Maybe it would look better then.

The next morning I opened the drapes to check out how things looked. Then I opened the patio door and put my hand down on the deck to see if the paint had dried. It was a little tacky in places but it looked like most places were dry. But something was weird. What was I seeing? Prints. Footprints. Not human footprints, but something had walked all over the deck during the night. And not just one something. That something had brought a whole bunch of friends along. It was raccoons! A gang of raccoons had invaded my deck, had a party, danced until dawn, and ruined my paint job. Paw prints were all over the place. The deck was a disaster.

Forget about the plans I had for that deck party. I threw all my painting supplies in the trash. How could I have believed that a paint product would make my deck new again? The only thing that would make my deck new again was a new deck. I called a deck building company. They came out and tried not to laugh when they saw my disaster. They took measurements, destroyed the old deck and built a beautiful new deck.

I wish I could say that was the last time I tried to "do it myself."

~Leticia Madison

On a Clear Day

Cleanliness is next to impossible.
~Author Unknown

It was the first week of May and one of those clear-blue-sky, smell-of-freshly-mown-grass days. With average annual snowfall of 125 inches, we Central New Yorkers tend to go a little crazy on a spring day like this, and I was no exception. I had inherited the do-it-yourself gene... sometimes successful, sometimes not. And it was time to execute the brilliant plan I had conceived during those long winter months.

The double-pane thermal picture window in our living room had been getting progressively cloudier. Evidently, the thermal seal had leaked, allowing moisture to collect between the two panes of glass, ruining the view. My plan was to break just one pane, thereby allowing me to clean both sides of the remaining windowpane! As far as the thermal window feature being lost, I'd just buy a really nice pair of insulating drapes.

Steffy, five, and Chip, three, didn't know what to think as I assembled my "tools." They sat on the floor, saucer-eyed and uncharacteristically quiet. After moving the furniture aside, I spread an old paint-speckled canvas drop cloth under the window and anchored it with the large metal trashcan from the garage. I peeled open the new package of masking tape and taped the window so that it would break into manageable pieces rather than tiny splinters. Next, I pulled on a pair of my husband Charlie's heavy-duty work boots, his thick protective fireman's gloves and jacket, and a pair of safety glasses from the toolbox. By now, the kids were rolling around on the floor, hysterical with laughter. I must admit I did look ridiculous! Finally, I told the kids to leave the room so Mommy could break the window! Really! I said that!

I was ready. I picked up the hammer and based on no scientific theory whatsoever, mentally calculated how hard to swing it; too hard and both panes would shatter, not hard enough and neither would break. I took a deep breath and swung! Nothing happened. I'd been too tentative. I mustered up the determination to break it this time, and swung again. Again, nothing! I tried a different area of the window. Wham! Nothing!

"Mommy, how ya doin?" little Steffy yelled from the kitchen.

"Mommy's fine, honey! You guys just stay there!"

As I stood looking at the window thinking, I heard little giggles coming from the kitchen. Then it hit me! The reason the window wasn't breaking was because I'd taped it too well! Just like I'd seen people do on The Weather Channel when a hurricane was threatening… they taped so their windows wouldn't break!

I peeled off a few strips and went to the garage to find our aluminum baseball bat. I planted my feet before an imaginary home plate and swung for the top of the bleachers! Yes! Home run! The glass finally broke! Some glass ended up on the drop cloth, but most of the window hadn't fallen. It was cracked in a million places but the tape had done its job. I carefully pried the rest of the window out, piece by piece, smug with my accomplishment of breaking just the one pane. That done, I swept the glass onto the drop cloth, into the dustpan, and into the trashcan. Eager to clean my "new" window, I tore off the gloves, jacket, and safety glasses. The only thing left to do was to return the trashcan to the garage. Grabbing the handles I went to lift it. Oops! I had no idea how heavy glass could be! I might as well have been trying to pull a fire hydrant out of the ground.

"Oh well," I thought. "Charlie can do this when he gets home."

My moment had arrived! In just a few minutes, I'd have a beautiful, clear view! Armed with a new bottle of window cleaner and a full roll of paper towels, I began to spray. And wipe. And spray. And wipe.

"What the heck?"

A little knot started to tighten in my stomach. I tried a different spot. Nothing. Another spot. No luck. I slumped into Charlie's favorite chair and stared at the window in sheer disbelief!

"What's wrong, Mommy?" asked Steffy.

Only minutes before, they'd been sitting on the couch clapping and cheering: "Mommy broke the window! Yay! Mommy broke the window! Yay!"

Undaunted, I went through the house and gathered up every conceivable cleanser and chemical I could find. First I tried good old-fashioned vinegar. It didn't touch it. Powdered cleanser. Nope. Turpentine. Nail-polish remover. Oven cleaner! Absolutely nothing worked. The moisture that had crept in between the panes had actually etched itself into the window, creating "frosted" glass. A single-edge razor scraped away some of the cloudiness but left little scratches at the same time. I stepped back, staring and hating the still-hazy window, when suddenly something became crystal clear: Charlie had just pulled in and was about to become a very unhappy husband. (Did I mention that I'd kept this idea to myself?) As soon as they heard the door open, the kids raced to their daddy, virtually exploding with their mommy-broke-the-window-on-purpose story! Suffice it to say he was not amused.

"Okay, let me get this straight," Charlie said. "You decided to clean the window by swinging a baseball bat at it?"

"Well, actually," I replied, "I tried it with a hammer first."

Okay. Maybe that wasn't the best time to joke.

He just stood there shaking his head while looking at me, then the window, then again at me. I asked him if he would do me a big favor and take the trashcan back into the garage. When he came back in, he was still shaking his head.

"Do you have any idea, any idea at all what it's like being married to you?"

I detected a slight smile.

"Full of surprises?" I ventured.

"Ha!" was his very loud reply.

Then he started laughing, so of course I started crying.

The following week we had a brand new picture window professionally installed!

~Pamela Kae Bender

Beam Me Up

Humor is merely tragedy standing on its head with its pants torn.
~Irvin S. Cobb

*J*ust do it! That's my husband's mantra when it comes to doing someone a favor. So when his boss asked him to install flat screen TVs in his new McMansion, he agreed to do it. After all, he was the new guy and still on the clock.

"I'm going to need some help with this," Prospero said to the manager. Word in the office was that the last guy who went out to do some electrical work in the boss's house never came back. "Send someone who knows what they're doing, like J.R." Prospero knew that the young fellow who worked at assembling the copiers had the strength and smarts to be useful to him.

The next day Prospero had done as much as he could on his own, but it was late morning and no one had shown up to help. Knowing he would need an extra set of hands to run the wiring through the walls, he phoned the office. "Sorry, we can't spare J.R. today," said the manager, "but we're making a few calls and we'll get someone over to you shortly."

A while later Izzy, another technician, arrived. "They sent you?" my husband asked incredulously. He had a sinking feeling this was not going to work out well. Prospero led him up to the attic. "Alright, just stand behind me on those beams and hold the flashlight over my shoulder so I can see."

Prospero went to work snaking the wires through the walls when suddenly he found himself working in the dark. "Hold the light still," he barked, but he was still in the dark. "Izzy?" He turned around to tell the guy to focus the light. No Izzy. Where the heck did he go?

"Help!" cried a small voice.

Prospero looked down to where the voice was coming from and there was Izzy, spreadeagle with a beam up his crotch, and in Prospero's words, "crying like a little girl."

"Are you okay?" Prospero asked, trying unsuccessfully to stifle a laugh. Izzy looked like a gymnast whose balance beam stunt had gone horribly wrong.

"No, I'm not okay," snapped Izzy. "And stop laughing at me!"

Prospero tried to pull him up but it was useless. Izzy was wedged in the insulation. "I told you to stand on the beams," Prospero told him, now laughing out right and adding insult to injury. "Wait there," he added needlessly, "I have an idea."

Prospero went down to the balcony that ran across the center entrance hall, and sure enough there was the bottom half of Izzy dangling through the ceiling, those slippery leather shoes flailing every which way.

"Hey, Izzy," shouted Prospero, "if you know the name of a good sheet rock guy, this would be the time to give him a call."

With that the front door opens and in walked the boss.

"What the hell is going on here?" he demanded.

Prospero held up his hand. "Boss, don't worry. There's no extra charge for the skylight."

You know I've heard this story a million times but never did hear how they got Izzy out of the ceiling. Forever he remains etched in my memory, a living mobile swaying to and fro.

The boss was very good about the damage to his home. Not only did both men keep their jobs, but at the company Christmas party when the boss played his traditional game of *Let's Make a Deal*, Prospero won a big screen TV. Personally I think it was fixed, but we've been enjoying the TV all the same.

And another holiday tradition began that year—the telling of the tale about how the boss got the skylight in his ceiling. And like all good traditions that have predictable outcomes, the retelling of the story always ends with Izzy jumping up from the table and storming out of the party in a rage.

Honestly, some people have no sense of humor.

~Lynn Maddalena Menna

76

Number Two

You can learn many things from children.
How much patience you have, for instance.
~Franklin P. Jones

Our fixer-upper was in need of repair to various parts of its concrete construction. With each cement job, my husband Larry would smooth out a nice, even finish. We would walk away with pride.

We would return later to admire our work, only to find a "Z" etched into the cement. One of our many children had become a Zorro fan and was leaving Z's everywhere possible. We would question the children as to who had left their mark, but, as any true Zorro knows, anonymity is of utmost importance.

One day after smoothing out a new step in front of the bathroom, Larry pleaded with me to guard the step while he went after more supplies. He then asked that the children not etch any Z's in the new step. When he left I set up a chair and grabbed a book to pass the time while I kept watch.

But I was called away from my post—probably to break up a wrestling match turned rough. And when I returned there was something new in the cement. Not a Z; a 2.

I wanted to make sure that I wouldn't mess up the step, so I called Larry's cell phone to ask him what tool to use to make the cement perfectly smooth again. The conversation went something like this:

Me: Hi, babe. Sorry to interrupt your shopping, but I need to know how to fix the cement. One of the kids made a number two in it.

Him: WHAT? Why would they do such a thing?

Me: Oh, you know how kids are… So how do I go about fixing it?

Him: I just don't understand kids sometimes. What on earth were they thinking?

Me: Listen, babe, it's no big deal. I can just smooth it out.

Him: SMOOTH IT OUT? You can't just smooth it out. That's disgusting! Why didn't they just use the toilet for the number two? The bathroom is right there!

I don't know why it took me so long to catch the obvious miscommunication, but when I did, I couldn't contain the laughter. It must have been contagious because he began to chuckle too.

Finally I was able to compose myself and explain that is was a numeral two that someone had drawn in the cement.

To this day, this is not only our funniest adventures in miscommunication, it is our favorite home renovation story.

~Carrie M. Leach

77

Everything Including the Kitchen Sink

You don't get anything clean without getting something else dirty.
~Cecil Baxter

ave you noticed when one thing breaks in your house, it's as if an airborne virus slinks into everything breakable and infects them too?

The latest was the kitchen sink. It wasn't draining. My husband, Bob, went to The Home Depot. (Trip #1.) He bought a plunger and unclogged the sink... he thought. After he washed the four cats' bowls, containing majorly icky "by-product" of tuna, the sink was once again filled. Bob used his chainsaw, also broken but just repaired, and cut plywood to cover the sink so the swarming cats wouldn't drink the putrid tuna-ish water.

Then he opened the cabinet underneath and removed the pipe, expecting that the clog would simply drop into his cute little bucket. He forgot the covered sink was full. What came out was a deluge of fluids that made a beeline to the living room. With no time to mop, we used every towel we had.

"Sweetheart?" I said, while he was under the sink putting the pipe back. "Let's call a plumber."

Smashing his head on the counter, he came out from under and snarled, "I can do it myself!" Drano was nixed because of chemicals. He got the garden hose, snaked it through a window, put it into the drain and turned it on. Not only did the pipe underneath burst, a geyser blasted from the sink.

"Sweetheart?" I said gently. "How about going back to The Home Depot and buying something that unclogs drains?"

He did. (Trip #2.) He bought a five-inch-long rubber balloon that's flat. You connect it to your garden hose, insert it into the drain and turn on the water full force. Then the balloon expands. The description: "Powerful pulsating jets of water will loosen and flush blockage down the drain."

It was such a "dirty" shame that Bob didn't read the instructions. Had he read them, he would have known to insert it way down the drain—as in, near the clog. Instead, he stuck it in an inch. What do you think happened when he turned on the water full force? It backed up with amazing velocity and we had another ferocious geyser of water that rapidly proceeded on its already established route to the living room. In attempting to remove the now-damaged balloon, he broke the pipe under the sink again.

"Sweetheart?" I said, even gentler than before. "Why don't you go back to The Home Depot, get another pipe and another sink unclogger?" He did. (Trip #3.)

Unfortunately, the night before we had pork chops. We had stored the dirty plates in the oven, which now emitted quite an aroma. Trust me. It wasn't like the fragrantly rich autumn scent of smoke from wood-burning fires. It was more like summer-hot dead meat.

I felt sorry for him so I figured the least I could do was wash dishes. Would you have remembered there was nothing to hold water, like a pipe, under the sink? I didn't. I was breathing through my mouth while rinsing the rancid roast pan when I felt my slippers getting drenched.

Bob came home with the pipe, but he was bowled over in hysterics. His laughter had such a maniacal tone, I was scared he had gone nuts. Trying to get the words out while gasping for breath, he said, "I left the thing that unclogs drains on the checkout counter!" Now we were both out of control attempting to catch our breath in side-splitting manic laughter.

(Trip #4.) I drove, as Bob sat next to me, trying to stop some weird gag reflex while laughing like a lunatic.

Here's what I learned, and therefore suggest, when it comes to clogged sinks:

1. Don't take a working sink for granted.

2. There are 100 more plumbers in the Yellow Pages than there are psychiatrists.

3. Call one.

4. If you're married to someone like Bob, call both.

~Saralee Perel

The Outhouse

Today you can go to a gas station and find the cash register open and the toilets locked. They must think toilet paper is worth more than money.
~Joey Bishop

stood at the end of the driveway waiting to cross the street one night in January. Once the coast was clear, I walked over to the Mobil station directly across from our house. "Hi Ryan," I said to the cashier. "Can I have the bathroom key?" Our only bathroom at home was getting remodeled and the toilet was currently out of commission. I'm a roughing-it type of girl, thanks to many years of camping in the woods. However I refused to use those skills in the middle of winter. In New England. And at night.

Thankfully I could go to the Mobil station — until it closed at 10 p.m. — because my husband Steve is the owner. But when it looked like our toilet would be on extended leave, I put my foot down. I was not going to go across the street every time I had to pee. And what about the middle of the night? We got a bucket.

The guy remodeling our bathroom was a friend who worked as a contractor part-time. By part-time I don't mean he had a full-time job and did this on the side. Part-time because he only seemed to work part of the time. I was not a happy woman. But he cost significantly less than a professional, even if he took longer.

Sometimes when I got home from work I would be pleasantly surprised by a functioning toilet. Our contractor friend would take pity on me and temporarily hook up the toilet. But over the course of several weeks, it was more often than not the bucket. Sometimes the bucket was actually in the bathroom. Other times it was in the hallway. This went on for weeks.

So I was thankful to have the station across the street. I was also thankful to have my mother-in-law living nearby. I drove to her house for two months straight to shower. Every. Single. Morning. I did, though, enjoy our morning chats. And I missed that part of the routine when I could shower at home again.

However, I did not miss going over to the Mobil station when our bathroom construction (finally) finished. Or that bucket.

~Kristiana Pastir

Decorating Dilemma

The most elegant interiors are just slightly tatty.
~David Netto

"What happened to your sofa?" a good friend asked one morning while unexpectedly visiting. "The side is all ripped and torn."

"I know. I usually have a blanket thrown over it, but it's in the wash," I answered.

"Did your cats do that?"

"No, I did."

"You?"

"It's a long story," I said.

"I have time. Tell me," she said and plunked herself down on the sofa in my little home office and curled her feet under her.

I hesitated. It wouldn't be easy to admit the stupid thing I did. "All right, I'll tell you. If you promise not to laugh."

"I promise."

"Well, you know I love my house. I love each room in it, how it is decorated, how comfortable everything is."

"Right," my friend said and drew out the word. "But?"

"There was just one thing I didn't like. It was the couch I used to have in here. So one weekend when I was home by myself, I decided to make a change. This couch was in the living room, remember?"

"I remember. It looked okay in there."

"Yeah, but I wanted it in here."

"Okay. So what did you do with the one you had in here?"

"I gave it away. I stood it up on its side and shimmied it through the doorframe and down the hallway into the garage. Goodwill picked it up that same day."

"So you had an empty spot in here."

"Yup, and I wanted that sofa from the living room."

I took a deep breath and thought back to that weekend. I was so excited. I had rearranged the entire room. I put the desk in front of the window and a great side table to the right. I stacked my files on top of that and hooked up my computer and fax machine and printer. Everything was set and ready for the sofa. It would be just perfect after I got that baby in there.

"This room used to be a bedroom, right?" my friend asked, bringing me back from my memories.

"Right, it's only 10 feet by 10 feet, but I wanted another sofa in here. I like having a place for friends to visit with me while I'm in my office, just like you're doing now."

"So what happened?"

"Well, I went into the living room, took the cushions off and stood the sofa up on its end. Then I wiggle-walked it through the family room and over to the doorway to my office. That's when I realized my mistake."

"What?"

"It wouldn't fit through the doorframe."

"You're kidding."

"Nope. It was too wide and too tall. I crammed it, I shoved it, I pushed and heaved. But it would not go through the door."

"How did you get it into the house in the first place?" she asked.

"Through the double front doors. And it went directly into the living room, so it didn't have to pass through any doorframes."

"So you wiggled it back into the living room and gave up on the idea?" she asked with a wry grin.

"Have you ever known me to give up on something?" I said.

She smiled. A best friend kind of smile. "No, so how did you get it in here?"

"Through the window."

"What?"

"I popped the screen off and then I finally got some smarts and dug out a tape measure. The width of the sofa was the exact width of the window opening. I sashayed it back through the family room, through the sliding door, and then around the back of the house to the outside of my office window."

"You are one crazy lady," she said, "and stubborn."

"Good thing it was dark and the neighbors couldn't see. Probably would have thought someone was robbing the place."

"And I'd have had to bail you out of jail!"

I had to laugh at the thought of that.

"So how did you do it all by yourself?" she asked.

"I propped it up on the windowsill and pushed. But it got stuck. So I went inside and pulled, and it got stuck again. I finally got it through the window, onto the top of my desk, then down onto the floor. I stood it up on its end, moved it over to the wall where it was going to go, then dropped it down with a thud."

"Why didn't you wait for someone to help you?"

"I wanted to get the room set up that night. It was all done except for the couch. I was determined to get it in."

"Well, it looks like you did. But what happened to the side?" she asked as she fingered the shredded material.

"I didn't think to lay something on the windowsill. As I pushed and pulled, the windowsill and side of the window frame ripped the material down the side and along the whole back."

"You could have left this sofa in the living room where it was," my good friend said with a snicker.

"Nope, not an option. The shredded back and side are a casualty of the move. Couldn't be helped."

"So now you put a blanket over it?" she said, holding back a giggle. "How is that for fitting in with the room?"

"Just great. I bought new curtains to match the blanket, and an area rug in the same shade of blue."

"What are you going to do when you want to get rid of this sofa? Are you going to pull it through the window again?" she said.

"No way. I'm going to chop it up into little pieces and carry it out of the room bit by bit."

"That'll make you feel better, right?" she asked, this time almost doubled over trying to hold back her laughter.

"Definitely. And I can't wait for that day. In the meantime, excuse me while I go get the blanket out of the dryer."

~B.J. Taylor

80

Watts My Line?

We now know a thousand ways not to build a light bulb.
~Thomas Edison

lectricity and I don't mix. For some reason, when I turn my mind to electrical repairs, my mind turns to mush. So I was surprised to find myself tackling a problem with an overhead recessed light fixture in our basement rec room.

For years, there had been a loose connection with an occasional annoying flickering from the light bulb. But recently, the flickering had turned to darkness and I began to attempt rudimentary repairs.

For the first few days, I periodically pushed the glass plate covering the recessed bulb, hoping that this would restore the connection. Sometimes it did, much in the way that a random kick will occasionally fix a malfunctioning vending machine.

But after a while, my taps on the plate failed to elicit a luminous response. So I bravely stepped into uncharted territory and actually removed the plate covering the bulb. I pushed the bulb up; I pushed the bulb down. I partially unscrewed the bulb and then screwed it in tighter. Sometimes the light came on and sometimes it didn't.

My past history with electricity should have dictated that I stop there and call in someone who might know what to do—someone, say, like an electrician. But faced with an electrical quandary, the logical synapses in my brain once again gave out.

If there was a loose connection, I reasoned, then it must have been in the socket and all I needed to do was put something in there to tighten things up. As my left brain struggled weakly to object, the right side boldly insisted that I put a small piece of foil next to the base of the bulb to create a snugger connection with the socket.

Even my three-year-old daughter knows that she isn't supposed to put anything into a light socket. But something told me that this little piece of foil would do the trick.

So I screwed the foil-encapsulated bulb into the socket and was greeted by a loud "Poof!" and instant darkness throughout the basement. Something had obviously gone wrong.

I admitted defeat and groped my way up the basement stairs to the cordless phone and called an electrician. I explained what had happened and he gently reminded me that it was not a good idea to put anything in a light socket other than a light bulb.

After he had me confirm that the bulb went "poof," he directed me back to the basement to the circuit panel, with flashlight and cordless phone in hand. After banging my head on the furnace and my knee on a stray bicycle, I located the panel.

The electrician asked me to push each breaker switch all the way to the off position and then back to the on position. I diligently moved each switch right and left until I was greeted with a loud static noise on the cordless phone.

Once I finally realized that I had disconnected the circuit for the phone base upstairs, I hung up the phone, reset the breaker and waited for the electrician to call back. He soon did, and after he stopped laughing he suggested that we wait until the next morning to continue our investigations. I readily agreed.

Having suffered enough humiliation for one week, I decided to get an early start for work the next day. Just to be safe, I exited the house at 6 a.m. and left my wife to deal with the electrician.

~David Martin

Chapter 9

Home Sweet Home

Downsizing and Retiring

81

Under a Lucky Star

Be glad of life because it gives you the chance to love,
to work, to play, and to look up at the stars.
~Henry van Dyke

My husband Richard startled me while I day-dreamed on the patio of our new home. He stood in front of me holding his cellphone, the color drained from his face.

"It's Bob," he said handing me the phone.

I thought it odd that Bob, the real estate agent we'd enlisted to sell the home we'd recently moved out of, would be calling. A few weeks ago he'd brought us a buyer and we signed a contract. We were three days from the closing. With such a short window of time, Richard and I had agreed we were comfortable moving to a new home a few hundred miles away.

"Hello," I croaked.

"I have some bad news. The sale is off. The buyer lost his job."

My knees buckled. I slipped down into the one chair that had found its way outside. With the phone still to my ear, I looked through the window to see Richard standing among the bustle of moving men and boxes. Stunned, he could no longer give them directions.

One of the moving men placed his hand on Richard's shoulder.

"Don't worry, man. It'll all work out. Where do you want this picture?"

Speechless, Richard pointed to the last empty spot in the corner of the living room.

The timing had seemed perfect to make a move to a calmer, less stressful place for the next phase of our lives. My job of fifteen years had been eliminated and Richard had decided to retire. Our move to the Space Coast of Florida, however, had suddenly turned into the most impulsive decision of our married life. We had been here less than twenty-four hours and suddenly found ourselves in the center of a crisis.

During the next week Richard and I emptied the moving boxes and tried to get the house in order. We barely spoke except to remind each other of the new phone number or ask for directions to the grocery store. Our dream had quickly turned into an emotional and financial drain. Nothing about this new place brought us any comfort.

One night, my mind racing with worry, I'd only just fallen asleep. A roaring, thunderous noise jolted me awake. The house shook. The windows rattled. The clock read 4:34 a.m. Scared half out of my mind, I had no idea what could possibly be happening. I elbowed Richard and urged him to go check all the doors while I tried to calm our barking dog. Richard reported nothing was out of place and crawled back under the covers. The noise faded. I slept fitfully the rest of the night.

In the morning, I ate breakfast in front of the television, watching the morning news.

"Last night a Delta II rocket carrying a military satellite successfully launched from the Cape Canaveral Air Force Station," the newscaster reported.

"So that's what woke us up," I commented.

"Does that happen a lot?" Richard asked. "Did you know about this before we decided to move here?"

"I guess the shuttle isn't the only thing that gets sent up into space," I replied through a mouthful of cereal. "Satellites have to get up there somehow."

Richard handed me the front page of the morning paper.

"If we can hear it, do you think we can see it?" he asked.

A picture of the rocket at the moment of liftoff took up more than half the page. A column to the left of it was headlined "Upcoming Space Missions."

"Look, Richard. The paper tells when the next launch is."

"Really?" He grabbed the paper back from me.

He had a smile on his face for the first time since the devastating phone call from Bob.

"Mark it on the calendar. I want to see it," he said.

A few weeks later, I struggled to stay awake for the midnight launch of an Atlas V rocket. My eyelids refused to stay open while Richard snored on the sofa. When the earth-shattering rattle began, I nudged him awake before racing outside. A bright orange ball blazed up from the horizon, lighting up the black of night.

"Richard! Come quick!" I shouted.

We stood side by side, our mouths hanging open, watching the puffy white plume race across the dark sky.

My pride in our nation and our ability to explore space had been instilled in me from an early age. While in elementary school, when space flight was still new, I remember my class being ushered into the auditorium to watch the Mercury rocket launches on a tiny black and white television. As a child, the liftoff was incredibly exciting even though I was too young to understand the magnitude of its importance.

But watching it live from my back yard sent me over the moon, no pun intended! My pride in America and its accomplishments in space flooded through me. Unable to take my eyes off the sky, I followed the ball of light high into the atmosphere until it finally disappeared.

A few weeks later, the Space Shuttle Atlantis was scheduled to go up in the afternoon. I poured a glass of wine and made a plate of cheese and crackers. Richard and I settled on the patio to watch. With our eyes fixed on the general area of the launch, we waited.

The rumble started. The ground began to shake. The roar of the engines grew louder and louder, reaching a fevered pitch. In the distance a brilliant, bright ball of light appeared over the tops of the palm trees. The two of us sat in silence absorbing the fascinating spectacle of light and sound.

"Amazing! What a way to spend an afternoon." I raised my glass in a toast toward the sky.

The only word Richard could say was, "Incredible."

All things space became a part of our lives. We never missed a launch no matter the hour of day or night. I'd let out a sigh of relief when a sonic boom announced a shuttle returning to earth. At dusk, we once caught a glimpse of the International Space Station passing overhead. And when the shuttle program ended, we waved goodbye as the plane transporting it to a new home flew low along the coastline.

Space flight uncovered a deep sense of pride in our country. It allowed us to find contentment in a community full of people committed to American technology. And most importantly we realized we had found a home in a place that presented us with new and extraordinary experiences unlike anywhere else.

Our old house finally sold to a new buyer. I found a great job I enjoyed. Richard settled into a peaceful retirement riding his bike and walking the dog. And every time a rocket launched into space, we watched in awe, never missing the chance to thank our lucky stars for finding such an inspiring new home in which to live and dream.

~Linda C. Wright

Upsized View

Just because you're miserable doesn't mean you can't enjoy your life.
~Annette Goodheart

"'m not cleaning my room. I don't care. I'm not helping you sell this house," said Zoe as she slammed the front door and screeched down the driveway.

Selling our house was a sudden decision that had been brewing for four years. When the financial world "collapsed" and my husband's management job was "downsized," I got that crushing feeling that life was about to radically change.

"We have money in savings," said my stoic financial-advisor husband. "We're going to be okay; we can ride this out for a while." And so we did. We told Zoe we'd have to make changes and be more conscious about spending, but she didn't have to worry. We had it handled.

I loved our house especially since the renovation. I had spent a year with a designer reconfiguring the space and picking every detail down to the distressed bronze knobs and hand-scraped floors. We converted the odd alienating spaces into open welcoming areas, allowing family and friends to gather for meals and parties, and to dance to the most amazing jazz jams we held in our back yard. We had infused our home with love, life and laughter, and the money and time we had spent on the renovation was worth the outcome. It wasn't that it was just beautiful, it was as if a cold lifeless house now had a soul and was alive.

My husband started his own business, and as expected there was more outgo than income. About halfway into the fourth year of tightening our budget we sat down to re-evaluate things.

"We still have equity in our house, but every month we hold on it lessens," my husband said. "Besides, I'm ready for a change; it's too dead here. It's a smart financial decision; we don't want to dip into our retirement in our fifties."

"What about Zoe and school? She's going to be a junior. We have to let her complete high school here." My stomach knotted in anticipation of telling her.

I don't remember how I told her, but I do remember the tears, the screaming, the doors slamming, the reeling away from me as I tried to comfort her. She was having none of it. She refused to accompany me on searches to look for a rental and chose to deny the inevitability of the move. Boxes mounted, reams of clothes, books, furniture and knickknacks were given away or trashed. I titled this new phase my "En-Lightenment" period and had "en-lightening" sales to further shed stuff. There were days I was in tears myself, especially on the days I'd come back from looking at rental properties.

Amazingly, we got an offer the day before the broker's open house. Never having sold a home, and of course thinking mine was so desirable, I was none too excited when my agent called to tell me the "great news" about how far below our asking price the "extraordinary" offer was.

"Well that's just the first offer," I smugly replied. I was reminded that the buyer was putting seventy-seven percent down and had a pre-qualified loan. There is an adage in the business, "the first offer is the best offer," and as much as my heart said no, I had to be realistic. The market was tumultuous and prices were dropping rapidly. We wanted to sell, and the sooner we did, the more equity we would keep. We accepted the offer and immediately launched into the grueling details of escrow. I opened myself to the good house karma with rentals I'd always had in the past. I set harp-sound phone alarms reminding me to breathe as I juggled contract details and my daughter's demons. I was desperate to find a place and the newest one on the MLS listing looked promising.

"The front looks like a prison," I said to the agent.

"Wait till you see the view," she said.

The house was a lot smaller, with funky cheap patch up jobs meant to modernize it, but I was drawn to the sunroom, an illegal addition that overlooked a 180-degree unobstructed view of the ocean. It was breathtaking. We were down to the wire as it was almost Christmas. Our move-in date was set for January 2nd. This was the best of what I'd seen. It was far from perfect, but the view seemed to compensate. I took Paul and Zoe to see it. Zoe finally evolved from angry and sullen to sad and weepy. I bandied around phrases like, "Your home isn't about stuff, it's where your heart is. Stuff is like air—it's always there. This change will add depth and complexity to your character." To which Zoe responded, "I'd settle for shallow."

A tiny glimmer of hope appeared as we showed her the bedroom that would be hers. "It's not bad," she said, concealing any enthusiasm.

Moving day arrived with three movers, Paul and me working non-stop. Zoe returned home to a made-up room. "Oh my God," she said in the flickering candlelight, "it's actually cute and cozy." We were beat and longed for a shower. I flipped the hot water on and waited. Nothing. It ran for five minutes ice cold. "Oh great, no hot water." We still had access to our old home, as the new owners weren't moving in for a few days. We gathered towels and soap and crept into the vacant home. It was familiar but oddly empty. It no longer was ours. We dashed out and returned to spend our first night in our new place. The moon was full and hung low over the ocean. The house was full of boxes, but the moment was magical. The next morning I called the gas company to service the water heater, dryer and stove that weren't working.

"Good thing the water heater didn't work," the gas man said. "It's hooked up illegally and could either start a fire or send carbon monoxide right to that bedroom."

Then he checked the stove and looked underneath to see if there was any obstruction. "Ma'am, you've got rodents," he said. "I don't see any bodies, just droppings." Zoe found the situation both disgusting and amusing.

The next morning, my husband woke early to let the dogs out. He bent down to pick them up when his elbow tapped the plate glass sliding door and it shattered into razor-sharp shards. Then, as the repairman was replacing the glass door later that day, and I was washing dishes, I heard the sound of water gushing. Sure enough, the kitchen sink was draining outside through a large hole in the exterior wall.

"We are living in Clampettville," I cried on the phone to my husband.

"We'll get it all fixed," he soothed me.

It was sunset when he arrived home. Our sunroom had turned into an IMAX theater. We sat in utter amazement as the sky unfolded in a thirty-minute display of changing color and cloud formations. We were speechless in the presence of this majesty. Our lives had changed, our views had changed, and Zoe was happily giggling with her girlfriends in her new room.

~Tsgoyna Tanzman

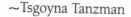

Our Mayberry

Don't buy the house, buy the neighborhood.
~Russian Proverb

My husband was raised in a small town that had changed very little in the last hundred years. And he never quite embraced living in a city of over four million people.

When the last of our children left home, he was ready to move someplace with a slower pace and maybe a little acreage. In my mind this was a three-acre mini estate in the suburbs. But after three and half years of searching, I came to realize that my husband's idea and mine were vastly different.

One evening he called to me, saying he had found the perfect place. "Wonderful!" I exclaimed. "Where?"

"Right here," he said, pointing his finger to a dot on a Georgia map.

"Are you serious? We have looked in a dozen counties for over three years and you have found the 'perfect place' on a map?"

My husband reads maps with the same zeal the average person would a Pulitzer Prize-winning novel.

"See right here; it is the perfect area. It is within fifty miles of Atlanta so we can still commute to work. There is a divided highway all the way and very few roads, so obviously it's not very populated."

"Not very populated—what makes you think we can even find a house in an area you are calling 'not very populated'?"

"It won't hurt to look. Let's just ride out there Sunday and check it out—what do you say?"

I agreed and we planned a trip out the following weekend. And as crazy as it sounds, after three long years of searching, he found our dream home—on a Georgia map. It was not the mini estate in the suburbs that I had envisioned, but instead twenty-six acres in a rural farming community. I knew it would be an adjustment, but it wasn't like we were moving to a mud hut in the Yukon. So I agreed.

My husband was ecstatic. I heard him happily mumbling as he wandered off to the garage: "I can have a little garden and grow my own food... of course I will need a tractor... I can deer hunt on my own land... fish in my own front yard. We can literally live off the land. It will be like paradise...."

It was a quaint little town with a kind of a Mayberry feel to it. And I actually began to look forward to it as I remembered scenes of Andy Griffith picking "Church in the Wildwood" on the porch swing. I envisioned a neighborhood Welcoming Committee, and I could almost smell the homemade cookies and hear the crickets chirping as I began to pack.

However, my fantasy quickly faded as I realized it was forty-five miles to the nearest mall. Seven miles to a tiny grocery store. And the only place to eat within fifteen miles was a Dairy Queen. There was no cable TV; no trash pickup; and we had to use propane and well water. And the community's idea of animal control was a twelve-gauge shotgun! Oh my gosh—we were moving to 1962!

So as visions of dead animals floating in my water supply played out in my head, I packed up a case of Clorox and reluctantly headed for "paradise."

We moved in early September. Shortly before Christmas, we were sitting down to dinner when the doorbell rang. I thought back to my Mayberry fantasy. As it turned out the "Welcoming Committee" was wearing a badge and carrying a summons—a boundary dispute that had begun twenty years earlier had just landed in our laps.

Many tears and many thousands of dollars later, our "dream" home on Maple Springs seemed a lot more like A Nightmare on Elm Street.

And so began the first year in our new home.

The following spring, my son, his wife and nineteen-month-old son came to spend the weekend. We awoke Saturday morning to fifteen inches of snow—fifty miles from Atlanta, Georgia. Snowdrifts were up to the tops of our windows!

I had never seen that much snow. I was so excited... for about fifteen minutes. Until the power went out. We had no lights, no heat and no water! Then one of our neighbors called with a comforting word: "Well usually when we get snow up here we don't have power for about two weeks, but we've never seen anything like this!"

I sat in silent disbelief, my throat tightening as the full impact of that statement sank in. And then I remembered—we had a baby here.

My husband had figured out how to pull the concrete cap off our well and get water with a rope and bucket, and he had gathered plenty of firewood, but he couldn't help us with the diaper situation.

The second day of the blizzard the neighbor across the road called to check on us "city folks." I told her we were fine, our only problem was we had a baby with us and were about to run out of diapers. About two hours later there was a knock at the door and there she stood. She had walked over two miles in fifteen inches of snow and ice from house to house to gather a supply of diapers, milk and baby clothes for us.

I was speechless.

The next day there was another neighbor at the door asking if we had a grill or a camp stove he could borrow—not for himself but for another neighbor with three children who had no way to prepare food. The third day we looked out and the neighbor involved in the lawsuit, his teenage son and two other people we did not know were shoveling snow and ice from our 650-foot-long driveway!

I sat in total disbelief as I saw my vision of Mayberry come to life.

Over the years, we have come in from work to find: one of our neighbors waving happily as he mowed our lawn; a little windmill fashioned from an old bicycle wheel—spinning around—in my flower bed; a warm pound cake anonymously stuck inside my door; a basket of fresh homegrown tomatoes sitting in our porch swing; and a dozen white irises planted by my fence!

Our neighbors have taken in our dog during a storm; came while we were on vacation to pick up tree limbs, lawn chairs and our trash cans after high winds scattered them over the yard. They have brought us apples from their trees, fried pies from the Amish country, fresh vegetables from their garden, and even once a puppy after our dog died.

It has been twenty years since that first rocky year. Looking back today, I think everyone should be so lucky as to be able to move to 1962. After all, it was a really great year!

~Andrea Peebles

The Greatest Show on Earth

The real safety net of life is community, family and nature.
~Bryant McGill

A clown on stilts walked down the main street of the small New England town where I live. He was stopped short by a telephone wire strung between two low-lying buildings, which blocked his passage. The bystanders quieted, all eyes glued to the towering jester who then dipped at his waist, tipped his neck sideways and maneuvered underneath. Those gathered for the parade, one to honor hometown hero P.T. Barnum, burst into applause and appreciative hoots.

Tears welled in my eyes and caught me off guard. I instantly recovered but knew my emotional response wasn't over the clown's success. It was about the camaraderie of the crowd, the enthusiasm for our community, and the delight in sharing this celebration. At that exact moment I saw how this town was the first place I'd ever lived where I truly felt like I belonged, where I truly felt at home.

Fifteen years earlier, the loss of my job had forced my husband and me to move here with our two children. There was nothing scientific about our selection. We drew a bull's-eye on a map and found a house we could afford on a single salary. The main street was quaint. The schools were adequate. We packed our belongings and prayed for the best.

Within a month of living here, however, a pattern emerged.

During a stop at the local children's haircut salon my first week, I struck up a conversation with a mother waiting for her son. We discovered a mutual connection. She knew my neighbor, we had two acquaintances in common, and her son was in the same grade as my daughter.

A week later, as I waited for my daughter's gymnastics class to end, I met another waiting mom. When she learned I was a newcomer to the area, she offered to show me around town. With our spare forty-five minutes until class ended, we loaded in her minivan and I got a tour. During the car ride, I learned her friend's daughter was in the same first grade class as mine.

The next afternoon I registered for a library card. When I announced my address, the librarian happily informed me she and her husband had built the house back in the 1960s. In case I didn't think the world I now existed in was small enough, two weeks later at a PTO meeting the library connection resurfaced. Introduced to another parent, she asked where I lived, then replied, "Oh, I grew up in that house. My parents built it."

"That's funny," I said. "The woman at the library told me she'd built it."

"Yup. That's my mom."

Every single one of these conversations made me feel surprisingly comfortable and connected in this new place… a necessary bolt in the cog of the community. I battled the coincidence versus destiny theory. It felt like destiny. My life here had snapped together as easily as two Lego pieces.

Over time, the pattern continued. Every corner I rounded, a simple hello would unveil a thin thread connecting me in some way to a person I'd never met before. How was it possible to land someplace quite at random and then feel more at home than in the place I was raised? Or, for that matter, any other place I'd ever lived before.

For the past fifteen years, I've witnessed as friends and neighbors gather to support one another with the enthusiasm of the citizens of Whoville on Christmas morning. We beam with pride for each other's successes, whether it's to witness the annual high school homecoming parade or to honor a two-hundred-year-old hero. We join together for support, whether for the tragedy of September 11th or the annual fundraiser honoring the legacy of a three-year-old resident who lost his life to cancer. We form a united front. We are there for our neighbors. We greet each other with smiles.

Moving here, I learned the meaning of the word community. It defined the difference between having a place to live versus what it means to truly be at home.

The tears in my eyes during the parade were really about what I'd gained in the years I've lived here. From day one, this town has embraced me as if I'd returned from a long journey. The feeling came full circle the night of the parade when my teenage daughter turned to me and said, "Mom, I hope someday I can raise my kids in a place like this."

My town is set amidst other communities of more affluence. We often feel like a bit of an underdog. But its people are proud, salt-of-the-earth New Englanders who understand that our outreach to each other makes us stronger.

Earlier that same day, a bronze statue was dedicated to P.T. Barnum. An impersonator re-enacted the original speech the great showman had made at the age of seventy-one during his dedication of a bronze fountain he'd donated to the town in 1881. In the final words of Barnum's speech, he offered his gift "as a small evidence of the love which I bear them and the respect which I feel for my successors, the present and future citizens of my native village."

I'll bet P.T. Barnum never dreamed that close to 130 years later his words would be recalled by the townsfolk or that the love he felt for this small place on our large planet would reach someone who shared his appreciation... me.

~Sharon Struth

Mom's New Home

A little girl, asked where her home was, replied, "where mother is."
~Keith L. Brooks

I remember being so excited to move into my own place at age twenty. I was nervous and couldn't wait to take on the challenge of managing my own life. I thought it a bit of an overreaction when it took my mother months to come see my new place. When I'd asked her for the hundredth time to come over, she looked at me seriously, holding back tears and said, "Give me some time to come to terms with the fact that you don't live at home anymore. I can't imagine you living somewhere else right now." I'd laughed, thinking she was overreacting, but later it resonated with me.

Ten years later, I found myself in her shoes. I was newly married but lived only a short drive from my mother and her new husband. All my sisters had moved out by then, but we would still descend on my mother's house on the weekends and cook and talk and live for a few hours as if we'd never left. We all still had stuff there, our old rooms were there, our memories, but most of all, our mother was there, the same as she'd always been.

Then, as if overnight, she decided to retire and move to Florida. It was as if she'd decided to leave the planet. At first, I was excited for her and behaved as if she were going on vacation. Florida had been her constant vacation spot throughout the years and she'd always had a good time. She always spoke of it with fondness but never did I think she'd move there permanently.

I came over to help her pack, and we talked about how excited she was and how she would enjoy the more hospitable weather. It hit me while wrapping my baby pictures in bubble wrap that something greater was happening. I looked through a box or two while my mother went to get more things from another room. My handprint mold from kindergarten, a framed picture of a childhood vacation with all of our faces painted at a downtown festival, my mother's large can of random buttons that she would keep in her sewing room. We'd learned to count with those buttons, used them to decorate our Barbie doll clothes we'd made from scraps of fabric she had, and finally sifted through them to fasten our own clothes she'd taught us to make when we got older. Suddenly it seemed as if she wasn't going on an extended vacation. She was moving our home away, with her in it, to some strange, faraway place that I didn't know.

I tried to talk her out of it, but just as that hadn't worked with me when I moved out, it didn't work with her as she enthusiastically moved into the next phase of her life. After she moved, I'd visit her periodically but her new house never really seemed like home. My sisters and I had never written on the walls or had our own room. We'd never sat down as a family to dinner after a long day at school, or snuck in the back door past curfew. We hadn't argued and fought over the use of the bathroom or done our hair and make-up in the one mirror. It was my mother's house, not the family's.

For a long while, it was like visiting a stranger. I had to ask where things were, if I could go in certain areas, what certain things were for. I actually noticed when something was new and I noticed how many pictures of me were around and when they were moved or replaced.

My mother was different too at first. She reveled in revealing personal things about herself, now that she had a new home in a new city—it was like a new chapter in her life. I found out that she loved flowers everywhere—paintings of them, figurines, silk ones and fresh ones. She arranged her house to reflect her interests and desires — not to raise a family. Her sewing room was in the center of the house and everything else was arranged around that.

It was difficult at first, and on more than one occasion I told her that I did not like her house or visiting her. Every time I left to return home, I cried. But eventually, over the years, her home became more familiar. Maybe it was because I started leaving some of my things there. Or that as my sisters and I visited more often, we were sometimes together and then had to share a room or fight over the bathroom. Whatever the case, we began to have memories in my mother's new house and at the center of those new memories was the same person — my mother. She was older, and more rounded as a person to us, and a bit more self-centered than we remembered as children, but she was the same loving, magnetic, energetic person we rallied behind to grow up into fine, adult women. And eventually I realized that wherever she was, was home.

~Audra Easley

86

Time to Let Go

To look backward for a while is to refresh the eye, to restore it, and to render it the more fit for its prime function of looking forward.

~Margaret Fairless Barber

Ginny and I prepared for our move from New Jersey to Idaho. We assessed the basement and then the garage. Twenty-four years of my stuff stared back at us.

"Mike, if we're going to move ourselves to Idaho, we need to get rid of a lot of this."

"Gin, this is my stuff." I turned to her. "I don't want to get rid of my stuff."

"Mike, look at all these books. We don't need them. When was the last time you read these Reader's Digest Condensed Books? You never read them." We walked into the garage. "That ladder!" She pointed to my twenty-foot aluminum extension ladder. "When was the last time you used that?"

"Well…" I scratched my balding head. "I guess it was about ten years ago."

"What about the crib? We aren't going to have a baby. It's old and unsafe. Michael, it's time to let go."

"But, Gin …"

"Michael!"

I relented. "You're right, hon. There's a lot that needs to go."

We had a twenty-seven foot truck to move 2,500 miles to Idaho.

Our three-bedroom home would never fit in the truck. I had decisions to make.

I spent a week going through the things I'd accumulated. We sold a few things, including the ladder. A lot of things we gave away. In the back corner of the garage was the box I dreaded. After Georgia died, I tried to go through it, but failed. The memories it contained and the raw pain it inflicted were too much for me to handle. At the time, I closed it up and put it in the corner.

Ginny was upstairs. It was a task I needed to confront alone.

I lifted the box, sat it in the center of the garage, and opened it. It held cards my children made for me and my first wife. Crayon drawings from the past stared back at me. I found cards Georgia gave me for Christmases and birthdays and cards I gave her.

Tears spilled down my cheeks, but they were tears of joy. I lost her, but I still had the memories. Things change, but memories keep the past alive.

I grabbed two empty boxes and filled them with memories to give my son and daughter. All the drawings, cards and ornaments they created for us were distributed between them. When they gave them to us twenty years ago, I made a point to write their names and dates on them.

On the two boxes, I wrote their names and put them aside.

Before we left for Idaho, my daughter drove from Ohio to see us in New Jersey.

We'd already planned for Vanessa to take many of her mom's things back to Ohio with her. She took the dishes that belonged to her grandmother, pictures, and anything else she wanted.

Vanessa and I sat on my deck one night. "Dad?"

I looked up. Her eyes had the sparkle of fresh tears. "Yes?"

She reached out and held my hand. "Dad, would you mind if I took Mom home with me?" She was referring to her mother's urn. "I'm happy to have her dishes, but I want her to come home with me too."

I thought about the little shrine I'd created for Georgia—my first wife. Her urn sat on the credenza, surrounded by the little teddy bears I bought her when she was in the hospital. They've been there for five years. On special occasions, I'd pour a glass of wine and toast her memory.

Vanessa stared at me, waiting for an answer. "Vanessa, you're right. Georgia should be with you." I held her hand. "I have Ginny in my life now. It's time I focused on the present and not the past. It's time to let go."

A few days later, we pulled away from the curb with everything we owned in the back of the truck. I looked back as my home of five years faded from view.

We turned the corner. It was gone. Ginny grabbed my hand. "Look, hon!" She pointed forward.

"What? I don't see anything."

"Mike, it's the future. It's ahead."

I put my arm around her. "You're right, Gin. I see it. It's time to stop looking back—time to move forward—time to let go."

~Michael T. Smith

87

It's a Stretch

Bitter or sweet, we don't want any part of life to be really over.
~Marjorie Holmes

I eye the contents of my life—spread across the lawn and driveway—and the people milling among my own aged bridal presents. There's someone taking the wooden lazy Susan for a spin. Someone else eyes the plastic salad set, tangerine orange, a shower gift from Aunt Helen. A lady gives me five dollars for another wedding relic: the electric deep fryer, still in its original yellowing box.

How can I do this? Toss the jetsam overboard to lighten our cargo? It's a hard-hearted action on my part, something I've been doing a lot of lately as I close the door on one era and open it to another.

You see, we're moving, my husband and I, after almost a quarter of a century in this homey, elastic house that stretched with the arrival of each child and now hangs loose from their departures, slack at the waist. It's time to sort and crate our history, to discard our surplus, to move our memories.

You might say we're downsizing, as so many people do at this stage. Although the actual square footage isn't changing so much as are our needs. We're trading five bedrooms for two, three bathrooms for one and a half, a dim family room for a window-banked home office, a wrecked rec room for a fine photographic studio.

It would be stretching the truth to say I'm totally ready.

After all, this is the spacious two-story that grew our marriage, built our children, and sheltered our dreams. Yet, here I stand, nodding at neighbors, shaking my head at my husband's quirky jokes as he pawns our past.

"What?" Norm's voice is incredulous. "You want this fine canteen for a dollar? Why it's worth at least seventy-five cents." His eyelid drops in a slow wink. "And I won't take a penny less than fifty."

The customer crows and hands over two quarters. Like magnets drawn to iron, others swarm to the table Norm is manning and reach for bedrolls, scout tents, stakes, and mess kits.

Someone buys the redwood picnic table with the attached benches, so solid it takes two muscular men — or one husky teenage boy — to move it each time we mow, no longer practical for people facing both retirement and dwindling upper body strength. The site of hundreds of meals under the proud ponderosa pine, that table greeted scads of vacationers come to frolic in the Rockies. It played host to childhood birthday parties and teen tantrums; it welcomed new sons-in-law; it witnessed the seasons of our parenting.

My eyes widen as women snatch the kitchen items. Really? Who would've guessed! Do people even cook anymore? The mountain of rusty cookie tins, gone. Harvest-gold measuring set, minus the 2/3 cup, taken. Three stranded relatives of the Anchor Hocking goblets. Stained bread pans. Aprons and platters and vases and spatulas. Corningware casseroles and lidless stockpots. They buy everything, these bargain hunters, picking apart the expanse of our yesteryears like beachcombers scouring for seashells.

All our stuff. Going. Walking away to live in other homes. Kind of like Norm and I.

"This house has treated you well," says the dear neighbor across the street, substitute grandma to our youngest child.

I hug her frail shoulders and agree.

Sidling to the shade of the towering blue spruce that anchors the neighborhood and our family nest, I scan the wedge of front lawn where yellow tulips bob in their beds. I pluck a few weeds and think about the gardens in back that need tending.

I turn to wave Godspeed to the matching camelback loveseats. Flexsteel. No place for them in the century-old Italianate we've chosen to begin our life-without-kids. I've already found a Victorian settee to replace them. The sofas, not the kids.

"Finally. A place for all your antiques," our children said when they saw the house we bought. None of them expressed regret at the sale of their childhood home and the memories it cradled. Each of them had already stretched out, left home, moved on, and never looked back.

I think of the ancient apple trees waiting in full bloom, the white picket fence, the gracious high ceilings, the spacious office I will call my own. It's time for us to leave, too.

I'll try not to look back.

~Carol McAdoo Rehme

A Shelter, Indeed

Home is where the heart can laugh without shyness. Home is where the heart's tears can dry at their own pace.

~Vernon Baker

"Go ahead, Mom, read yours," I said, as the *Boggle* game timer dinged. Our separate lists of words competed with each other.

"Shelter," she said. "That's four points."

"How'd you get 'shelter'?" I challenged, looking across the kitchen table at the scrambled vowels and consonants.

Bent fingers glided across the letters. She was right and her list of words trumped mine once again.

In my mother's kitchen, it wasn't just about the food—it was about the words. Words spoken around this small table where secrets were whispered, good news shared, wisdom imparted. The table holds within it memories of a lifetime of visits, of family, of broken hearts, of friends. New babies bouncing on laps, children kneeling on chairs dropping cinnamon hearts into warm applesauce as it squished through the strainer. Widows trying to find their way. Teenagers attempting to do the same. All of us digging our toes in the proverbial sand, finding our place, murmuring the word "home." If I'm quiet enough and I gently rest my ear upon the table, I can almost hear the voices.

I long for those voices as I sort through cabinets, clearing them out for the next family destined to fill this kitchen with their own words. Newlyweds whispering of want. Babies babbling. Teenagers voicing rebellion. Word games played, vocabulary lists reviewed, letters written.

I have dreams for this kitchen, for this home. My life has, in one way or another, revolved around this place. My words were born here—some mimicked and some surely my own. I learned to speak here, to spell, to write. My first poem was written at this table when I was barely old enough to put words to paper.

My father, gone for over thirty years now, left his impact in this house through the words he'd spoken. Sometimes, they were stern, reproving. Other times, instructive. Often, they swelled with forgiveness and grace. His words resound as I whip up an omelet.

"It's in the wrist," he taught me. Every time, whether here or across the state in my adult home, I hear his words as I twirl the fork swiftly through the yellow foam, and I'm transported, with regret, to a time and place when my younger mind quickly rejected many of his words.

Now, with my mother gone, it's time to part with her house—the childhood home I never outgrew, the walls ever expanding to welcome new folks into the fold. Even as I look out the front door, the street calls to me with memories of bicycle rides and walks in the rain; of running to the corner to meet my best friend. There were birthday parties and sleepovers. Missed curfews and subsequent groundings.

I look out the kitchen window and see my prepubescent cousin and me crossing the back yard in our pajamas midday, the summer breeze carrying our giggles ahead of us. I remember my mother's words as she phoned my aunt for an explanation. In that same back yard, I see picnics and badminton games, croquet and cookouts. I see my mother lounging in the sun, the newest bestseller on her lap, bed sheets flapping in the wind. I hear laughter, conversation, and storytelling. All around me I see and hear home.

It is said that once a house is vacated by the people who lived there, it becomes merely a shell. I have to disagree, for this house whispers of tender moments and resounds with joyous laughter... a communion of those who were fortunate enough to spend time here within these precious walls.

Now I sit here alone, remembering. I shake the *Boggle* cube and place it on the kitchen table, lifting the lid. Blinking away tears, I start to write on my lone list: S-H-E-L-T-E-R.

"That's four points, Mom," I say. And just like that, I feel a warm embrace. A shelter indeed.

~Hana Haatainen-Caye

Down the Garden Path

Where we love is home,
Home that our feet may leave, but not our hearts.
~Oliver Wendell Holmes, Sr.

It was a wildly impractical house for a young couple with kids. But the moment the Realtor opened the front door to this old Jacobean (not Tudor, she had emphasized, but Jacobean) rotting before our eyes, we knew we had to own it.

So we hadn't evaluated things like traffic patterns, insulation, wiring or that wonderful catchall—"low maintenance"—when we joyfully signed on the dotted line. So overpowering was our lust that nothing but an agreement of sale could put out the fire. For us, the house's imperfection was, itself, a kind of wonderful perfection.

We spent twenty-eight years in that house, and left with the kind of sadness that marks significant endings. But our three daughters had had the audacity to grow up and leave. In their wake, there were three empty upstairs bedrooms, vast closet space and an almost solemn stillness.

So we did the sensible thing and downsized. Moved one-half mile—and an emotional continent—away into a sleek condominium with a sensible floor plan and modern conveniences. I still keep wondering when it will feel like home.

Fast-forward several years.

Our town's garden club had our former home on its annual tour. The new owners had brought the place back to its earlier glory, something we'd had neither energy nor the resources to do.

Two tickets for the tour had been tacked onto the kitchen bulletin board for weeks. I would glance at them occasionally, and then walk away. They made my heart lurch.

The big question: How would we summon up the courage to go back to our old house? Could we actually return to the yard where each of our daughters had been married, each joining her groom near the giant beech tree in the side yard?

And could we ever, ever endure handing over our $20 tickets at the door just to see our old house again?

I'd been back just once since we'd pulled out of the driveway. That visit was to allow my aging and infirm mother one last look at the place she too had loved. The new owners had been extraordinarily gracious, realizing how urgent that last visit was. My husband, however, had not set foot in the place after we moved.

The day of the garden club tour dawned as one of those rare, golden spring days, the kind on which our former dining room, with its creamy walls, would blush—and yes, this was a house in which rooms could—and did—blush.

So we went on the garden club tour, arriving at our old house with hordes of other "tourists." All of us were asked to remove our shoes in the front foyer so as not to disturb the floors. That was probably the strangest moment of all.

We wandered the first floor rooms, dazed and disoriented. The bones of the house were the same. The wonderful chestnut paneling in the foyer was polished to a gleam but was otherwise basically unchanged. The den still had its wonderful old bookshelves.

It was all so familiar that for one weird moment I wondered why the photographs on those shelves were of some other family, not ours.

There were even a few remnants of us…

The wall sconces made by a local artisan to replicate the 1929 era when the house was built were in place on the living room wall. The wallpaper we'd picked for the downstairs powder room—the source of some spirited arguments, as I recall—also had survived.

Upstairs, in the space we'd used as our family room, the crazy-patterned carpeting that we'd let our daughters select in a moment of folly was gone. But the sweeping views of the yard were as magical as ever, and the softer wall color was definitely better than our strange choice of refrigerator white.

Many of the other garden club wanderers recognized us—ours is a small town. Was it pity I read in their faces? Curiosity? Or just those nods of recognition that this must be bittersweet for us?

In the end, it was the kitchen that left us speechless. Ours was gone. In its place was a magnificent, modern, tasteful, perfect kitchen, the kind we'd dreamt about… Everything familiar had been swept away in a major, marvelous renovation.

Except—could it be? The old light fixture with its amber globe and sassy red ironwork was hanging where it always had. How many times that fixture had illuminated our kitchen life.

My daughters and I would sprawl on the kitchen floor, never on chairs, sorting out our lives, singing, bingeing on pretzels and peanuts too easily retrievable from the pantry closet nearby.

It was the one place in the house where I had to blink back tears.

It was almost dusk when we reclaimed our shoes and went outside to walk the grounds. The new owners are superb gardeners, and we marveled at the improvements. They had gotten it right. Their flowers and shrubs thrived—ours had too often withered. The grass was that green of magazine ads.

And yes, the wedding tree was still there. It was the one each daughter circled with her parents before she met her waiting groom.

We left our old house as some new arrivals walked up the path. This time, we looked back every few steps. Chances are, it would be our last visit ever.

At one point, my husband reached for my hand.

And without words, we walked away from our old home.

~Sally Friedman

We Can't Move

The home should be the treasure chest of living.
~Le Corbusier

"Mom, Dad, no! You can't do that!"

"You can't move!"

"Why not?" I asked, wondering at our daughters' strong reaction to our desire to downsize.

"This is HOME! We grew up here," Heather cried.

"How can we bring our children to show them our rooms, where we learned to ride our bikes, where we swam and partied with our friends, where we left for college and dressed for our weddings?" Jennifer circled and pointed with outstretched arms as she pleaded.

"We can show them videos." I watched their eyes widen as I said that. I could see they felt I was being flippant. Actually, I was just stunned at their response and continued, "Besides, YOU left. You have new homes, new lives. Why not Daddy and I?"

"You… you, uh…" Jen struggled to speak and Heather completed her sentence, a typical twin reaction. "You're just supposed to stay here at home, that's all."

"Honey, isn't home where Daddy and I are, wherever we live?"

"NO," they cried in unison. "Home is here!"

I looked at Bill and muttered, "We should have moved every few years so they wouldn't be so attached."

"Too late now," he shook his head as he answered.

I tried a different approach. "We need a one-story house. You know we have arthritis, especially in our knees. I stand at the bottom of the stairs every night trying to muster enough nerve to start climbing up to bed and I'm tempted to sleep in my chair in the family room."

Bill stepped in. "We're getting older. We need a downstairs master suite."

"So add one to this house," Jennifer said, her eyes gleaming as she contemplated the changes. "You can fill in the pool and build a great suite out there."

"And your upstairs bedroom will make a perfect guest room, Mom," Heather added.

"Good grief, we could buy a whole new house for what that would cost!" I countered. "So what do you want us to do? Stay here until you have to drag us out feet first?"

"You do realize, don't you," their father continued, "that you'd have to do all the cleanup and packing and sell the house yourselves?"

They both grinned and nodded, seeming to feel they'd won a battle. I shook my head, knowing that the battle had only been delayed. We'd just have to approach it in a gentler manner. Our daughters married, packed and left this house; wasn't it now our turn?

I looked at them again and headed to the kitchen to cook dinner for us all. As I pulled out the mixing bowl I could suddenly see the girls making chocolate chip cookies and buttermilk biscuits. I smiled at the memories that our daughters' despair had brought back to me.

Yes, I really would love a ranch-style house. But perhaps we can wait a while, a year or so, or longer. We'll talk about it some more, gradually easing our daughters into acceptance, waiting for the right time. For now, it's a discussion that will be put off—while we gather around the table to share yet another meal in this house, our home.

~Jean Haynie Stewart

Bloom Where You Are Planted

Wherever you go, no matter what the weather,
always bring your own sunshine.
~Anthony J. D'Angelo

ose had lived her entire life in the Midwest. Grew up, married her high school sweetheart, raised two sons, and was blessed with several grandchildren. She lived in the same house for over sixty years. She took pride in her vegetable gardens and many a neighbor envied her flowers. She painfully watched her husband slip from a strong, hard-working man to a frail, helpless one. And she wept as he was buried in the family plot by the old oak tree.

Years passed by ever so quickly. Her memory wasn't as sharp as it used to be. She didn't realize she had left the stove on again. She didn't see the extra step going down to the basement. And then, before she knew it, her two sons were taking her on a tour of an assisted living facility. Yes, it was a beautiful place. So many nice people. So many nice activities to keep the residents busy. Nurses smiling as they met you in the hallway. And even someone to clean the apartments and help with the laundry. That was all fine and dandy! But Rose loved her home and that was that! If her sons liked this place so much, then they could move in.

A few weeks later, her suitcases were packed, some of her favorite furniture was loaded in a moving van and many of her antiques were divided among family. She turned around one last time, with tears in her eyes, as she said goodbye to her home. Despite her wonderful memories, she was moving into a "new" home. That assisted living place her sons liked so well. How could this be? How would she ever adjust?

This is when I entered Rose's life. I fell in love with her the minute I met her. She looked exactly like my own grandmother, who had passed away several years earlier. I was the Activity Director at the assisted living facility that Rose was now going to call "home." I could tell she wasn't happy about the move. We saw each other several times that first week and somehow we started talking about our bucket lists. Truthfully, I was amazed that she even knew what a bucket list was. I shared with her that I hoped I could go up in a hot-air balloon someday. Without any hesitation whatsoever, she told me she had always wanted to ride in an eighteen-wheeler. She had that twinkle in her eye that made me almost think she was teasing me. So I asked her if she really meant that.

"Why, yes," she said. She had always wanted to get inside that big cab, roll down the highway, and have the ride of her life.

Going home that day, I couldn't get her off my mind. How hard could it be to find a truck driver who would be willing to take a little old lady for a short drive around the block? And besides, it might take her mind off leaving her home. I made several calls and finally settled on a co-worker's brother. We arranged to meet him in the parking lot of the truck stop across the river. I wanted so badly to help Rose accept her new home. Maybe this would help.

A couple of days before her ninety-third birthday, I told her I had a surprise for her. It would be an "early" birthday gift from me to her. I assured her that she was going to like it, grabbed her hand and walked her to my car. It wasn't long before she glanced to the left and saw a huge coffeepot structure that said Sapp Brothers on it. She obviously recognized the local truck stop because she touched my arm and said, "Are we going to do what I think we're going to do?" Tears had already filled her eyes.

"I think so, Rose!" I drove into the parking lot and there sat twenty or more eighteen-wheelers. I parked my car and we watched a young man climb out of his rig and walk toward us. I got out, opened Rose's door, and made the introduction.

We walked over to the semi and the driver placed a set of steps up to the passenger side. We helped Rose up and into the cab and shut the door. Her grin covered her entire face! I grabbed my camera and snapped a few shots as she waved goodbye. Twenty minutes later, the eighteen-wheeler pulled back into the parking lot and the smile was still on her face. The driver came around to her side, but she had slid over to the driver's seat and had the walkie-talkie in her hand. Talk about a Kodak moment!

It wasn't just the ride she had wanted. Rose had so many questions to ask the driver: How much does it cost to fill this thing up? What do you do when you have a flat tire? How much does this semi weigh? Don't you get lonely being on the road all the time? How much does a truck like this cost? After chatting for over an hour with the young man, it was time to go. She shook his hand, thanked him for taking the time to entertain an old lady, stood on tiptoe and kissed him on the cheek.

On the way back, she looked at me, smiled, and said with a twinkle in her eye, "If I hadn't moved to my new home, I would probably never have had the chance to cross this off my bucket list, would I?"

It was like a light bulb had just come on in her head. She saw that good things do happen in life, even when you have to leave something as special as your home. You either get bitter about the changes or you get better and adapt.

I'm so happy Rose chose "better." She was able to accept the change with time, and be an inspiration to all of us in the process. No one can take away precious memories we have built in our homes throughout the years. They are tucked away safely in our hearts forever. Rose showed us how we can bloom where we are planted, even if it does happen late in life!

~Judi Hockabout-Martin

Home Sweet Home

What Makes a Home

It's Just a Starter House

My whinstone house my castle is, I have my own four walls.
~Thomas Carlyle

"Have you actually seen the house?" the bank officer asked me as she studied the appraiser's photos.

"Yes, I've seen it."

"And you still want to buy it?"

"It's all we can afford," I replied sheepishly.

"And you plan to occupy this dwelling?"

"As soon as we fix it up," I said. "It's just a starter house."

My wife Christine and I were trying to purchase a small cape on the south shore of Long Island. We yearned for our young son Patrick to have a back yard to play in, rather than the confines of the sidewalk in front of our apartment building.

I understood the banker's concern. The house was built in 1949 and had suffered years of neglect. To call it a "fixer-upper" would be an understatement. Nevertheless, the bank reluctantly approved our mortgage application.

We couldn't even move in after the closing. We had to stay with family while we cleaned the house and made some of the most urgent repairs.

Christine enrolled Patrick in kindergarten at the local elementary school, with every intention he would graduate somewhere else. As soon as our finances permitted, we would move to a bigger house that could accommodate our plans for a larger family.

I continued to make inexpensive, cosmetic improvements to the house—not wanting to invest a lot of money in a place that was just a stop along the way to our permanent home.

During the next few years, my career advanced as we had hoped, so we put the house on the market. We were also expecting our second child. It was time to move on.

"The people we showed your house to yesterday made an offer," my real estate agent had advised me at the time.

"Let me talk it over with my wife, and I'll get back to you tomorrow."

I hung up with my agent and called Christine.

"Oh, really? That's great... I guess," she said.

"What do you mean 'you guess'?" I asked. "They came pretty close to our asking price."

"I know."

"Then, what's the problem?"

"Well, we have made some really good friends here over the past couple of years, and so has Patrick. He loves his school."

"Yeah, I know what you mean. But we decided moving to Connecticut was the best thing for the children. If we are going to do this, it's better to do it while the kids are still young."

"I guess so. We'll talk about it some more when you get home."

I was starting to share Christine's trepidation, but I didn't understand why. We had never planned on staying more than a few years.

Our doubts notwithstanding, I called the real estate agent the next day and accepted the offer.

"That's great news," my agent said. "I'll contact the buyers and let them know."

If this was such great news, why did I feel like I was going to throw up?

"The house is sold," I said to Christine when I returned from work that evening.

"That's great, honey," she said. "I guess this is really happening."

"I guess so."

"By the way, I have a PTA meeting tomorrow night, and you have to take Patrick to his baseball game," she reminded me. "And Eddie called. He wants to know if you can play softball on Sunday. It's fine with me if you want to play, because I am going to drop Patrick at my mother's and meet the girls for lunch."

Before I could answer, the phone rang. It was the real estate agent.

"They want to do what?" I yelled into the phone. "We had a deal. Now, they want us to accept less?"

"No way," Christine whispered. I nodded my head in agreement.

"I'm sorry, but we are sticking with the agreed upon price," I told my agent. "We have already come down twenty thousand dollars."

"They say it's all they can afford, Mr. Geelan. Are you really going to let this deal fall through over ten thousand dollars?"

My agent could not have known what my wife and I had just realized when we looked in each other's eyes. We wanted this deal to fall through. The community we were so anxious to flee had embraced us, and didn't want us to leave. As it turned out, we didn't want to go either.

"The deal is off," I advised my agent, "and the house is officially off the market."

Christine exhaled a sigh of relief, and the enormous weight I had been carrying around rapidly dissipated. We were so preoccupied planning where we wanted to live, that we almost overlooked the wonderful life unfolding before us.

We have been in our starter house over twelve years now. But we don't call it that anymore. Now, we just call it home.

~Ron Geelan

The Velvet Bench

The trouble with simple living is that, though it can be joyful,
rich, and creative, it isn't simple.
~Doris Janzen Longacre

I was nervous when my goddaughter, Wendy, got engaged to Matthew. He had two young children from his first marriage, and Wendy was only twenty-two and taking on a lot of responsibility.

They both worked full-time, but neither was particularly well paid. Matthew saw a fair bit of his two boys, every second weekend and sometimes during the week as well. He paid his ex-wife maintenance for the boys, but also spent money on them when they were with him. Wendy was so blissfully happy that, to begin with, I was just happy for her.

They were only engaged a week when she announced they were moving out of their rented apartment and buying a small house. I voiced my fears about taking on a mortgage but Wendy had it all organized; she had been to see a financial advisor and knew exactly what it would cost her.

With their salaries, they got the mortgage, but it left them little other money to spend on the house itself. Matthew's parents and my husband and I helped them decorate, and friends donated pieces of furniture here and there. Throughout it all Matthew worked all day and decorated well into the evenings, and he never once got bad tempered or complained. Wendy helped decorate, looked after the boys, and worked out all the bills. It amazed me how calmly she approached the whole thing.

The house was quite old and in time would need quite a bit of renovation. New paint and drapes made a big difference, and we helped Matthew floor the huge attic so the boys could play up there. Wendy was so happy to have a house of her own, a garden to themselves, and no noisy neighbors above and below them.

It worried me she would want to keep up with her friends who had higher paying jobs, and would rush out to buy things. Instead, she hunted through secondhand shops and yard sales. She bought some material at sale price and had a friend make her drapes.

They both had the house looking lovely on such a small budget that it brought a lump to my throat. I knew that the sofa didn't match the drapes, and a couple of the chairs had faded a little. Here and there, a carpet would need to be replaced fairly soon. Wendy's view was: "All in good time; we are in our own home now and that's all that matters!"

Ten years down the road, they had restored that old house bit by bit, and replaced the worn carpets and older furniture.

I mentioned to Wendy how much I admired what she and Matthew had done. I knew that some of her friends had big new houses with up-to-date furniture. I told her I admired the way she had not tried to compete with them.

Wendy shrugged and said, "Just as we were thinking about buying a house, I read an old French proverb and it hit me like a ton of bricks. It was as if it was talking to me," she explained. "It said, 'A throne is only a bench covered with velvet.'

"Matthew and I often used to joke when we were up to our knees in old floorboards, or up to our elbows in paint — one day we will wrap that old bench in the garage in velvet," she said, smiling.

"About a year after we had moved in, we had this awful row, mainly my fault. It was the pressure of working all day and decorating all the time with so little money. The boys had been difficult. I just kind of exploded and I took it out on Matthew, blaming him for everything.

"He went out and I couldn't find him. I was scared I'd driven him away. I finally found him in the garage. He was sitting on our bench, and he was in tears. I felt so terrible I just threw myself at him and told him how much I loved him. He was upset because he wanted to give me so much and he couldn't afford it. He felt guilty that I didn't have the things other girls my age had and he was so afraid I would leave him. We both sat and cried on that old bench and we have never argued like that again.

"We still have the old bench in the garage and sometimes we both sit down on it and take stock of how lucky we are. To me, it is covered in velvet because it's where we both found out how much we loved each other. I don't ever want to move out of this house, it's as if Matthew and I are part of it and it is part of us!"

~Joyce Stark

My Perfectly Decorated Apartment

The ornaments of your house will be the guests who frequent it.
~Author Unknown

"It's perfect!" I told the landlord. "When can I sign the lease?" It was a chilly April afternoon in the small college town of West Lafayette, Indiana. I had just been accepted to graduate school at Purdue University and, after three whirlwind days of sitting in on classes and meeting professors, I had decided that this was the program for me. West Lafayette would be my new home for the next three years. I was nervous, but also very excited.

Before catching my flight back to my California hometown, I drove around looking at apartments. The second place I visited was part of an old Victorian-style house that had been sectioned off into four separate apartments. As I drove through the shaded tree-lined neighborhood, the stress and frantic pace of the last three days ebbed away into a calm tranquility. Yes, I thought. This feels right.

The apartment was charming. Bay windows, hardwood floors, a wide front porch. It was the ground floor unit, which meant the front door was the original front door of the house. How neat it would be to walk through that beautiful front door every day! And the porch would be the perfect place to write or do homework when the weather was nice.

I signed the lease right then and there.

The rest of that spring into summer, whenever I felt nervous about packing up my life and moving halfway across the country, I would think of that apartment. I'd never had my own place before, and it felt like a milestone on the path to adulthood. In college I'd not only shared an apartment with three other girls, I'd even shared a bedroom with a roommate because living costs were so high. Now, I'd finally have a place of my own that I could decorate however I wanted. I explored websites and daydreamed about curtains and dishes, rugs and duvets.

On moving day, I crammed my car with clothing and books and drove for five days along Interstate 70, from the Southern California beaches into the heart of the Indiana cornfields. I walked up the stairs onto my new front porch, unlocked the giant glass-paned front door, and strolled around the empty rooms with a huge smile on my face. It was all mine! I was officially a grown-up, living on my own!

I immediately threw myself into turning my empty apartment into a home. I scoured Craigslist, wandered the aisles of flea markets and used furniture shops, and dipped into my savings account to buy kitchen supplies and dishes. I was a giddy, energetic decorating fiend. Before long my apartment looked like the apartment I had been dreaming about for months. Red accent pillows on the couch matched the red cushions on the kitchen chairs. Sunlight shone through the gauzy white curtains, warming up the rooms. Prints of my favorite Impressionist paintings hung on the walls. The book-shelves were filled with books I loved and photographs of my friends and family. I looked around and was filled with contentment. It was perfect.

Except… something felt a little off. I had carefully decorated and cozied-up my apartment, but somehow it still didn't feel like home. I would come back from class and sit on my comfortable couch, the pillows perfectly fluffed, the coffee table free of dirty dishes, the TV remote exactly where I had left it—and loneliness would flow through me in gigantic crashing waves. My friends and family were two thousand miles away, and I ached with homesickness. I tried to fill the emptiness with more decorating: a pretty embroidered tablecloth for the kitchen table, a bright rug for the bathroom, a congregation of houseplants under the bay windows. But nothing quite worked. My apartment still didn't feel like a real home to me.

One evening in mid-October I was eating dinner alone at my kitchen table, feeling nostalgic for my old cramped, but lively, apartment and my three roommates. My new apartment was too small for more than one person to live comfortably. Maybe my mistake had been thinking I could live alone?

As I washed my dinner dishes at the sink, I thought about the parties my roommates and I hosted in college, celebrating a holiday or someone's birthday. Those were my favorite memories from that time in my life: all of my closest friends together in one place, laughing and telling stories and sharing food.

Suddenly, I had an idea: What if I threw a party in my new apartment?

I sent out invitations for an autumn potluck to everyone in my graduate program and spent the entire day before the party cleaning my already-clean apartment from top to bottom. I bought autumn-themed paper bowls and napkins and made two big pots of chili. I arranged pumpkin centerpieces for the kitchen table and coffee table. Everything looked perfect. But I was nervous. What if it was a disaster?

In some ways, maybe it was a disaster. Wine spilled on one of my new rugs and left a small stain. Someone dropped one of my new plates and it chipped. Dirt was tracked in, the pillows on my couch were smooshed, and my new embroidered tablecloth was littered with crumbs. It took days for me to find the TV remote, which someone had unaccountably placed on the very top bookshelf. When the party wound down and the last guests traipsed out the door into the night, my apartment was a total mess.

And I could not have been happier.

I used to believe that filling an empty apartment meant buying furniture and decorating the walls. But I learned that what really makes a place into a home is welcoming others inside it with you.

That night, my new apartment was filled with people and food and joy. The walls soaked up their stories and laughter so that even when they left and I was by myself again, I didn't feel alone. I drifted to sleep with a smile on my face.

For the first time since I had moved in, I felt like I was home.

~Dallas Woodburn

57 Steps to Paradise

To be a queen of a household is a powerful thing.
~Jill Scott

My husband and I live in two separate condos, fifty-seven steps apart on the second floor of a two-story condo building. We're happy, practically still newlyweds, having said our "I do's" in June of 2012. I was sixty-six and Jack was seventy-five at the time of what we lovingly refer to as our "geezer wedding."

We had no attendants, no ushers, no rehearsal, no rehearsal dinner. Just the two of us walking down the aisle of our church hand in hand, married by my cousin Jerry—a monsignor in the Catholic church—with more than one hundred of our relatives and friends there for moral support.

After the church ceremony they all joined us at our condo clubhouse for the most fun wedding reception I've ever attended in my life. We had live music, an open bar and a spread of mid-afternoon finger food that could've fed an army. My kids, their spouses, grandkids, brother, sister, their spouses, and one niece surprised us with an elaborate flash mob dance to the song "Get Down Tonight." It was a magical day.

And so our marriage began and continues… in two separate condos. We sleep at his condo, where most of my clothes and jewelry live. Then we go to water aerobics across the street six days a week from 9 to 10 a.m., and go back to his condo where we have coffee (he), tea (me) and breakfast. He still eats Frosted Flakes. I make my own granola.

Right after breakfast, it's like I have a job. "Bye, honey, see you later," and I'm off to the outside walkway, past five other units to my condo just fifty-seven steps away. The place I call home. It's where I work as a writer and where I prepare my speeches for my other career as a professional speaker. It's where I fix a little snack in the mid-afternoon for myself. Jack, after all, has his own refrigerator and cupboards full of snack food, the kinds of things I don't eat like hot dogs, white bread and potato chips.

My condo is where I prepare our evening meal. And that's because I like my kitchen and my pots, pans, utensils and dishes better than his. I also like being in control of having at least one meal a day that's nutritious for both of us. My kitchen is a place filled with lovely spices, bottles of sweet red chili sauce and a great collection of various flavored olive oils and balsamic vinegars—condiments that my meat-and-potatoes man wouldn't think of putting on a salad or on fresh veggies.

My condo is where I play on my computer after my workday is done. It's where I read books, pay my bills, paint my toenails, organize my stuff, make photo albums, read my mail, paint jars and watch the TV shows that I enjoy. If there isn't a ballgame on TV after dinner, my husband will come into my lanai, where my only TV lives, and watch a show or two with me. But the minute a baseball, football, hockey or basketball game comes on, and he gets that look in his eye, I smile sincerely at my beloved husband and say, "Bye, honey… see you around 11. Or maybe I'll be over earlier and we can play cards while you watch the game."

I can almost see the relief in his eyes as he gets up from one of the two recliners in my lanai and practically trots out the front door, down those fifty-seven steps to one of his three TV sets where he can settle in and do what God put him on this earth to do… watch sports from a recliner. In fact, at Jack's retirement party years ago, before his beloved wife of forty-three years passed away, she regaled the audience by telling them that Jack was "a recliner that farts."

Jack and his first wife had a wonderful, happy marriage, and to be perfectly honest that is one reason I married the man. He's a good person who knows how to make a marriage happy and calm. When he agreed that we would live in both condos I knew he was a keeper.

At our ages, another thing I didn't feel like combining was our names. I just couldn't face the work of changing my name, again. Like many couples our age who had been married before, I wasn't about to change all my medical, financial, social security, business, social, church and passport records. Besides, as the author of thirteen books, my byline is pretty important to me and I'm keeping it forever, thank you.

When I moved to Florida in 2004, I left a six-bedroom home in Oak Creek, Wisconsin, the home where I lived for twenty-four years and where I raised my four children. After the kids were all out of the house, through college and on their own, I decided to sell the place and buy a two-bedroom condo in Florida. So I sold or gave away two-thirds of everything I owned. Thank goodness my children wanted some of my things, because now I can visit those treasures in California, Ohio and Wisconsin.

Because of all that purging, when I moved into my condo in Florida, I only brought the things I loved and wanted around me for the rest of my life, including some antiques and heirloom furniture that my parents had given me during my early married years. I wanted to display the hundreds of brightly colored painted jars I'd made over the years. I wanted my crock collection. Over a dozen crocks in sizes from one gallon up to twenty-five gallons. Three of those crocks, the twenty-five-, twenty- and twelve-gallon crocks, are used as end tables in my living room. My dad made round solid oak tops for them, and they are not only utilitarian because they store my out-of-season decorations, but they are also great conversation starters.

Jack, on the other hand, is a more modern-furniture kind of guy. He actually has good taste when it comes to decorating… it's just not my taste exactly. So why shouldn't he be in charge of decorating his condo and I be in charge of mine? It sure works for us.

Another reason we live in two condos is that after raising four children, mostly as a single parent, and spending most of my life running, running, running to various activities those four kids were involved in, I have come to discover that I love being alone. Alone in a quiet condo. No music, no TV, just me and whatever I want to do.

As a woman who can organize a dozen people to meet for lunch or dinner at various restaurants, yuck it up every day at water aerobics class and speak from the podium to 300 women and then chit-chat with them later, I find it an enigma that I am basically a loner. But I honestly find my own company more comforting than mixing with others, even one man, 24/7. I love being alone in my own condo much of the day.

And I'm sure Jack would say the same thing about his alone time during the day. As president of our condo association, president of the small pool and clubhouse association and head usher at our church, he has plenty to keep him busy during the day in his own condo.

Don't get me wrong. I love my husband with all my heart and enjoy the time we spend together… always from 11 p.m. until 11 a.m., and often more than that. We're back and forth between the two condos three or four times a day. Jack often brings my mail over and stops for a chat in my writing room office. Or I stop by his place to put on my swimsuit so we can go for an afternoon swim together. Or we go the movies mid-afternoon.

But the fact remains that I love being head of my household. I like knowing that I can buy new bookshelves for my office or new expensive windows in the dining room and kitchen without even discussing the price with Jack. I pay for everything that involves my condo and he pays for everything in his.

It's just that when one or both of us has the need to be alone, we can do it without hurting the other's feelings. If I had to watch him watch sports on TV so many hours a day I'd scream and think he needed to get a life. But this way, we each have our own space that we're in charge of. And we can do exactly what we want in our own homes. And by late afternoon I always look forward to seeing my man come in the door to have dinner with me.

I think he's happy, too, to hear me come in his door at night, ready to relax, stretch out on our comfy king-size bed and do what we do every night of our married life... kiss goodnight and reach for each other's hand before falling asleep.

~Patricia Lorenz

Cupboard Space

The only difference between men and boys is the cost of their toys.
~Author Unknown

I believe my kitchen has the standard amount of cupboards. Not banks and banks of them like those dream kitchens featured on HGTV, but definitely a normal amount. As a matter of fact, I'm positive that I'd have ample storage space if it weren't for a certain husband I live with, a certain husband named Mark who can't seem to breathe quite right if there isn't a pair of pliers or a flashlight within his reach at all times.

It doesn't matter that there's a workroom in the basement, mere steps away from the kitchen, loaded with saws and hammers, levels and files. Nor does it seem to matter that said workroom is all his. I haven't tried to use his workbench or decorate the basement windows with cute curtains or do anything to impinge on his man space. His workroom is as macho as he is, with a concrete floor and cinder block walls, and that's just how Mark likes it. I've given up any claim on his workroom. I wish I could say the same about my kitchen.

"I just need one drawer in the kitchen to store a few of my tools," he told me shortly after we'd moved in.

"Why do you need to store tools in the kitchen?" I asked.

Looking at me as if I'd asked him why it was necessary to drink water, Mark replied, "It makes sense to keep duplicates of tools I use all the time upstairs so I don't have to run down to the basement whenever I need a hammer or a nail."

"One drawer," I conceded. "This is the first kitchen we've ever had where I won't have to keep the Bundt pan on top of the refrigerator. I need all the cupboards for storage."

"One drawer," he promised.

Knowing I should know better, I reluctantly agreed. Quickly, Mark filled his allotted drawer to the very brim with vital things like sandpaper, screwdrivers, and roll after roll of duct tape. I stepped in as he tried to jam a cordless drill on top.

"One drawer," I reminded him.

"I know." Mark flashed me his familiar smile, the same smile that got me to agree to paint the bedroom my least favorite color and go on vacation to Arkansas in August. "One drawer is all I need." Pause. "Well, maybe two drawers would be a better idea. Then I could definitely store my new flashlight charger in here. The kitchen is a good place to keep a flashlight charger."

And so it went. Before I could say "Hot Springs National Park," my mixer was sharing a shelf with boxes of bolts. My dishcloths nestled next to tubes of caulk. And my poor Bundt pan was relegated to an empty spot in the laundry room. I got used to looking for the blender and finding a staple gun. It seemed normal to stow the cereal boxes beside paintbrushes. And, in a warped way, it did make sense for Mark to store everything upstairs, saving himself from that long trek down the basement.

Then came the day when I opened a skinny cupboard wedged between the dishwasher and the refrigerator and discovered that it was empty. That particular cupboard had somehow escaped our notice. Staring in delight, I tried to decide just what might fit in the small, awkward space. Aluminum foil? Waxed paper? Perhaps the Bundt pan if I stood it on its side?

Mark strolled into the kitchen, interrupting my reverie. "Hey," he commented, "I didn't realize that cupboard was empty. It's the perfect spot for my new airless—"

I slammed the door shut. I had had enough. "This cupboard is taken," I informed him. "The only fingerprints I want to see on it are mine and Betty Crocker's."

Seeing that I meant business, Mark backed down. "You keep it," he told me generously. "After all, this is your kitchen."

I'm thinking of having husband-proof locks installed. And I know just who to hire to install them.

~Nell Musolf

Wired for Sound

Everybody needs beauty as well as bread, places to play in and pray in,
where nature may heal and give strength to body and soul.
~John Muir

Porches have always been my favorite part of any house. Lofty front porches shaded by massive ferns. Back porches where chest freezers hum and dance, and string mops are hung to dry. Wraparound porches crowded with rocking chairs and potted geraniums.

But the best porch of all is a screened porch. Whether on the front, back, or side of a house, all it takes is a roof, some fine-gauge mesh and a slamming door to create the most popular room in any home.

My family just added a screened porch to our 1840s farmhouse, and we are already wondering how we ever got along without it. It's on the east side of the house, positioned just right to catch the morning sun while enjoying a wake-up cup of coffee. Shaded by a giant maple tree that's reputed to be even older than the house, the porch is impenetrable even to high-noon summer heat.

A six-foot-long, don't-make-me-ever-get-up-swing hangs at one end. In the middle is a big round table, which—when it's not being used for a meal—usually has a game of *Monopoly* or Chinese checkers going on. The porch is filled with the intoxicating aroma of honeysuckle and wild roses and, at dusk, with the smell of supper sizzling on the grill.

Conceding to the twenty-first century, the porch has electricity that powers two big white ceiling fans and the reading lamps that flank the swing. Not long after the porch was built, a friend stopped by to visit. He was thrilled to learn that the porch was electrified. "You should buy a little flat screen TV and set it up there in the corner," he said. "And get some stereo speakers and wire the porch for sound."

Wire it for sound?

I just looked at him and laughed.

Would there be any point explaining to him that the finest stereo system in the world couldn't compare to what I hear every evening on that porch as I sway in the big swing, iced tea in hand and a magazine lying unopened on my lap?

The swing's heavy metal chains creak steadily against giant eye-bolts and the ceiling fan paddles whir softly as they stir the night air. Hard-backed beetles, wanting to share my lamplight, slam against the screen. Across the road, a neighbor's cow lows deep and plaintive, the unmistakable sound of imminent calving. The herd answers and the pasture is suddenly alive with noise. Canada geese honk and circle, trying to decide which of the many ponds in our valley would make the best overnight motel.

The screen door bangs as my son rushes in to find a jar for lightning bugs. The dog, who doesn't understand screens at all, scratches and whines to be let in. As the last smidgen of daylight disappears, birds bid each other goodnight. All around us, frogs and crickets and katydids join in a symphony that must surely be so harmonious because it's been rehearsed just this way for countless centuries.

So I smile and tell my friend no, we really don't need a flat screen TV or a fine stereo system for our screened porch. It's already wired for sound.

~Jennie Ivey

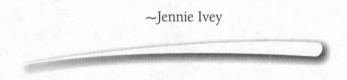

Do-It-Myself

A happy marriage is the union of two good forgivers.
~Ruth Bell Graham

I knew I wasn't marrying a do-it-yourself kind of guy, but that was okay. When we got married I couldn't do some things too. I couldn't iron a man's shirt or cook a great steak. I assumed that when I married my husband both he and I would learn how to do things that we had never done before, and the best part was that we would learn together. We would grow as a couple. We would grow with each other, for each other.

Part of the deal was that he was in charge of the tools—tools like a screwdriver, not a Cuisinart. And because I was so thoughtful, I went to The Home Depot and bought him an electric screwdriver so his wrist wouldn't get tired when he worked around our new house. Like, for example, when he needed to hang the new curtains and curtain rod I had just bought for the dining room.

When I brought the screwdriver home and tried it out I realized how lucky he was. Learning how to cook had nothing on plugging in the electric screwdriver, squeezing the trigger, and feeling the power.

I mentioned to him that evening that everything was ready. His part of the deal was on deck. How about next weekend, I suggested?

"Uh, okay," he said.

That weekend came and went. And the next one. And the one after that. There were no curtains hung. There was no initiative. There was no appreciation for the new screwdriver. So although I began with gentle reminders, I realized that gentleness was over-rated.

The next Saturday I found my husband halfway up the stepladder, staring at the wall, armed with the screwdriver in his right hand and a screw in his left.

"How's it going," I asked cheerfully.

"Well, honey," he replied, taking a deep breath. "I'm not so sure."

I peered around his body to find a three-inch hole where the screw was supposed to go. I could see the pink insulation peeking out from inside the wall. He saw me looking at the insulation.

"I'm not really sure what happened," he explained.

He wasn't really sure what had happened? He had put a hole the size of a tennis ball into our dining room wall.

To my credit I remained silent. I turned around and walked into another room to think. Otherwise I might have ended up in prison for killing my spouse.

It was all wrong! How could it have gone so wrong? How could he not be able to hang a curtain rod? What did this mean for us? For our marriage? For our future? Could we not work together? After a few minutes alone I had talked myself out of divorce court. I realized that hiring a handyman really wouldn't be so bad. It wouldn't be that expensive… And that, yes, our marriage quite possibly might make it.

I came back into the dining room and told my hangdog husband that it was all right. I knew that he had done his best, and that I could find someone to fix the hole. He appeared quite relieved.

Two days later, while I watched a handyman fix up the hole and hang the curtain in a jiffy, I realized that some people are just better at some things than others. How could I expect my husband to do something he wasn't very skilled, nor practiced, at doing?

And then, I actually felt a little bad. In the time we were married I still hadn't managed to cook him a steak the way he likes it, nor had I ever agreed to iron his shirts.

~Jennifer Quasha

A House Without a Chimney

Even as an adult I find it difficult to sleep on Christmas Eve.
Yuletide excitement is a potent caffeine, no matter your age.
~Terri Guillemets

I couldn't sleep. Wide-eyed, I stared up at the ceiling. "It's not fair," I whispered. "Uncle Ed's house has a chimney. Uncle Marty's house has a chimney. Grandpa's house has a chimney. Why doesn't ours?"

I clutched my blue blankie to my chest.

"Well, I'm not going to lie here and let Santa Claus skip my house just because we don't have a chimney."

I kicked off my covers and sat up. With my blue blankie draped around my neck, I leapt from my bed. In the pale glow of a cheap, drugstore nightlight, I tiptoed around the pieces to Mr. Potato Head. Then I slowly pushed the door open.

I stuck my head into the hallway and peeked left.

I could hear faint noises coming from the kitchen. Who was up this late on Christmas Eve?

I stepped into the hallway, and crept toward the noises. Meanwhile, the footies in my jammies made a funny sound "skish" on the hallway's wooden floor.

At the end of the hallway, I halted and peeked around the corner.

"John?"

I froze.

Mom asked, "What are you doing up?"

I stepped into the kitchen, replying, "Mom, I can't sleep."

"Well, you better get your little butt to bed," Mom countered, "or Santa won't come."

"I know, I know."

Mom folded her arms across her chest and began tapping her right foot.

So I asked, "Um, Mom… can I… uh… take one more look at the tree?"

Mom sighed.

"Okay, I guess so," she said. "But then you go straight to bed."

"Yes, ma'am," I replied. I scampered across the kitchen's linoleum floor.

Then I hit the living room's carpet and continued my trek to see the tree—just like I had told Mom I would. But I stopped in the middle of the living room and looked over my left shoulder.

Mom was puttering around in the kitchen.

The coast was clear!

I bolted to the front door, reached up, and grabbed the knob. I silently rotated it, barely cracking open the front door.

"There," I whispered. "Our house not having a chimney won't stop Santa now."

Then I retreated from the scene of the crime and began my trek back into the kitchen. When I reached the linoleum, I actually did turn around and look at our Christmas tree. It was beautiful, but it would look even better tomorrow morning with all the presents under it.

I turned around to go back into the kitchen—only to run headlong into Mom.

"John, please watch where you're going," she commanded, balancing a glass of milk and a plate of cookies.

"I'm sorry."

Mom traipsed to the living room's coffee table, where she set those items down. Then she stood erect, and started back to the kitchen — but lurched to a halt.

Uh oh.

Mom furrowed her brow.

I bit my lip.

"I feel a draft," Mom mumbled.

"Oh no," I groaned.

Mom looked around and then asked, "Well, who left the front door cracked open?"

I hung my head. Then I watched Mom troop over to the front door, slam it shut, and lock it.

Dang it. Santa was never going to get in.

After Mom returned across the carpet, she placed her right hand upon my shoulder and steered me into the kitchen. There, she pointed down the hallway and said, "Go!"

With my blue blankie dragging on the floor, I returned to my bedroom.

Christmas morning, I awoke to find a million presents under our tree! But I wasn't surprised. To this very day, Mom doesn't know that — on the way to my bedroom — I unlocked the back door.

~John M. Scanlan

Bad Feng Shui

My view on feng shui:
don't put your bed in front of the door because you won't get in.
~Jonas Eriksson

I have bad feng shui. I know. I shouldn't be telling everyone this—but I feel I must. I'm probably not alone.
There must be others out there suffering from the same
embarrassing condition.

It started with my sister. One day, I told her I was feeling a bit
off. Truthfully, I meant I had a cold and she should let me get off the
darn phone, but Tiffany took it to be something else. She told me the
truth. She told me I had bad feng shui.

I was shocked. Who wouldn't be? One minute your life is perfectly fine and the next you have bad feng shui. I was horrified. How
long had I been walking around like this? Were the neighbors gossip-
ing about it? Did people see me in the grocery store and shield their
loved ones from the sight of a woman with bad feng shui?

It turns out, I wasn't walking around with bad feng shui—I was
living in it. And according to my sister, I'd been living in it for a while.
How awful is that? There I was, stuck in a bad feng shui situation and
I didn't even know it.

So Tiffany happily let me know exactly what it was. And I have
to tell you, I didn't understand half of what she said. But what I did
get was that my bad feng shui had something to do with the flow

of chi—which is something you can't see, smell or vacuum up if someone tracks it in from outside.

And apparently, my chi wasn't flowing. Or maybe it was, but it was flowing right back outside. Truthfully, I'm still not clear. But I figured what the heck—if I'm going to get some chi flowing, it might as well be good chi and I probably should encourage it to flow nicely through the house.

The first thing I did was rearrange the furniture. Unfortunately that meant putting the living room couch in front of the bathroom. After all, I didn't want my good chi to go down the drain.

As you can imagine, blocking the toilet wasn't really a good thing. And I can't tell you how difficult it was to ask friends to sit on the couch sitting in the hallway directly in front of the bathroom door. So I figured that maybe I could block the drains by closing the door to the bathroom.

After I came to my senses on the drain issue, I moved to the bedrooms, only to find that every bed in every bedroom was in the something called the "death position." As bad as this sounds, it turns out that the death position means the bed is visible from the doorway.

I don't know about you, but I find it difficult to hide the view of my bed from the doorway. Beds are big. Doorways are small. No matter how much I huffed and puffed and moved the beds around, they were always in a death position. Well, I actually maneuvered Junior's bed into something I'd call a "near death" position—but that was a close as I got.

Just when I was about to give up, I found feng shui candles. So I spent a small fortune on candles that represented earth, air, water, wood and a bunch of other stuff, and scattered them throughout the house.

It turned out I was allergic to the candles. I spent a week with my nose running faster than my chi. It wasn't pleasant. I finally had to decide between good chi or watery eyes.

So I went back to the way things were, with my bad feng shui and my unblocked bathroom drains and my death position beds. And I've moved on to the garden—where my feng shui is apparently really, really bad. I learned our in-ground pool is on the wrong side of the yard. All I have to do is move it about ten feet to the right....

~Laurie Sontag

Mommy, I'm Cold

Being a mother is learning about strengths you didn't know you had,
and dealing with fears you didn't know existed.
~Linda Wooten

M y three-year-old daughter woke me up before dawn: "Mommy, I'm cold." It was January, and while we often experience warm-wind Chinooks in Alberta that warm up our winters, I could tell right away the Chinook was definitely over and winter was back full force. It was cold in the house.

Hopping out of bed to tuck her back in, the cold air took my breath away. Wow! I must have forgotten to turn the heat up before going to bed.

After getting extra blankets for my daughter and her twin brother, I turned up the thermostat—which didn't seem to be too low. I jumped back into bed to warm up and get a bit more sleep.

Waking up a few hours later with the alarm, I noticed the house was still very cold. And there was no heat coming from the registers.

After getting the kids situated with breakfast, bundled up in heavy sweaters and hats, I ventured into the basement to see if I could figure out the problem. Perhaps the furnace needed to be relit.

I had never taken the time to examine the furnace at our new home. I had limited experience with furnaces all together, but I did have basic knowledge of pilot lights and how to light them however, I was surprised to find that I did not have a furnace with a pilot light. Instead I had an electric furnace with no pilot light in sight.

I saw some lights flashing, so I grabbed the manual and deciphered the coded flashing.

Proud of myself, I declared, "Aha! It's the igniter!"

I ran upstairs to check on the kids.

"Mommy, it's cold." My son shivered in his sweater.

"I know sweetie, the furnace is broken."

"Fix it?" my daughter asked.

I could fix broken Barbie legs, broken truck wheels, and ripped books so it seemed simple to my children. If I could fix everything that was broken in their world, I should be able to fix the heat as well.

I laughed and said, "No, sweetie. Mommy is going to call someone."

I put the kids in the living room where the gas fireplace could keep them somewhat warm while I flipped through the yellow pages.

It only took me a few minutes to discover that the earliest anyone could come to fix the furnace would be in three days. Since my handy husband was out of town on business for a few days and I was alone with two very cold children in -30 C temperatures, three days was not an option!

Frustrated, I angrily asked the furnace repair man, "I have two small children and no heat! What would you suggest I do?"

"Well, I can get someone out there for $500 if it's an emergency, or I can sell you the part for $30 and you can do it yourself."

"I don't have $500," I cried.

"Well, I have the part in stock," he calmly replied.

I glanced at my children, huddled near the fireplace. I could fix the furnace if I had to, couldn't I? After all I could fix Barbie legs, broken truck wheels and ripped books. Why couldn't I fix a furnace?

"Okay, I'll be right there."

The kids were happy to get into the warm car, where the heat did work. And we made the forty-five-minute trip to the other side of the city where I received detailed instructions about handling the part carefully. It was very fragile, and any contact with my skin would render it useless.

The salesman looked at me doubtfully and almost chuckled when I told him I would be installing the part myself.

Annoyed, I paid for the part and left without receiving any instruction on how to actually install it.

Once home, I was ready to go. I was careful not to touch the igniter with my bare hands, but had forgotten how fragile the part was until it snapped in my hands when I tightened it with the screwdriver.

Back to the drawing board!

I was too embarrassed to go back to the first guy, so I searched through the yellow pages again. I lucked upon a store much closer to my home that had the part in stock. This time, I was a little humbler and asked the salesman for instructions on how to install it.

I'm sure he sensed my desperation, standing there with two small children bundled up from head to toe. He smiled and took me into the back of the shop where there was a furnace the same model as mine. He walked me through every step and showed me exactly what to do.

I dropped the kids at a neighbor's house to play while I attempted my repair for the second time. This time, I knew exactly what to do. I slowly went through every step, and when I finished I put the exterior panel back on and held my breath. Holding down the igniter button, I counted to three and let go. When I opened my eyes, I saw the glow of the igniter. I couldn't believe it. Moments later I heard the furnace pumping hot air throughout the frigid house.

I went upstairs with tears in my eyes. I was so excited! I cranked up the thermostat and left to retrieve the kids. When I told them I had fixed the heat in the house, they were both so happy. But I realized later that night, as they proudly told their daddy on the phone that I had fixed the furnace, my children had never doubted me for a minute. After all, in their eyes Mommy could fix anything.

~Elena Aitken

Meet Our Contributors

Elena Aitken lives in the shadow of the Rocky Mountains where she spends her days playing chauffeur to her twins and writing. Elena has published over eleven romance and women's fiction novels. Learn more at www.elenaaitken.com.

Karen Baker lives in Northern California with her husband and their dogs, cats, cattle and horses. She is the proud mother of a writer and artists. One story about her beloved cat is published in *Chicken Soup for the Soul: I Can't Believe My Cat Did That!* Other stories appear in anthologies about animals.

Kerrie R. Barney lives in Pullman, WA, where she enjoys knitting, gardening, and training her supernaturally smart Border Collie, MacKenna. Her book, *Life, the Universe, and Houseplants*, a collection of essays about Kerrie's adventures growing indoor plants, is now available on Amazon.

Garrett Bauman, a retired Professor of English from Monroe Community College in Rochester, NY, has published work in *The New York Times*, *Sierra*, *Yankee* and many Chicken Soup for the Soul books. E-mail him at garrettbauman@frontiernet.net.

Pam Bender is enjoying retirement with Charlie, her husband of forty-eight years. Their kids made it into adulthood unscathed by their mother's ambitious do-it-yourself ideas! Undaunted (and while Charlie golfs) the projects continue!

Paula Bicknell began her writing career as a civilian contracted to write for the U.S. Air Force's newspaper and magazines. Later, she wrote for a daily California newspaper. Paula has seven children and enjoys farming with her family in Northern California. Visit her weekly blog at http://psbicknell.com.

Jeanne Blandford is a writer/editor who, along with her husband Jack, is currently producing documentaries and creating children's books. When not in their Airstream looking for new material, they can be found running SafePet, a partnership between Outreach for Pets in Need (OPIN) and Domestic Violence Crisis Center (DVCC).

Cynthia Lynn Blatchford is the author of several stories published in numerous Chicken Soup for the Soul books. As a former foster child success story, she aspires to help others to both heal and succeed using the written word based on her own life experiences. E-mail her at cindy_700@hotmail.com.

Jan Bono's specialty is humorous personal experience. She has published five collections, two poetry chapbooks, nine one-act plays, a dinner theater play, and written for magazines ranging from *Guideposts* to *Woman's World*. Jan is currently writing a mystery series set on the southwest Washington coast. Learn more at www.JanBonoBooks.com.

Karla Brown attended St. Joseph's University, but honed her writing skills through determination and for the joy of writing. E-mail her at karlab612@yahoo.com.

John P. Buentello has published essays, memoirs, short stories, and poetry. He is the co-author of the novel *Reproduction Rights* and the short story collection *Binary Tales*. He is currently at work on a mystery novel and can be reached at jakkhakk@yahoo.com.

Miki Butterworth and husband Bob retired to Sedona in 2003 after traveling extensively buying for Miki's clothing and world artifact boutique. Before that Miki spent twenty-six years as a professional singer/guitarist. She is a mother of three grown children and currently enjoys painting, writing and volunteering.

Carol A. Cassara is a writer and sometime college professor who lives in the San Francisco Bay area with her husband and dogs when she's not traveling the world. She blogs daily on living our best lives at www.carolcassara.com and is working on a memoir.

J.D. Chaney is a retired teacher, having received his B.A. degree from San Jose State University and M.A. degree from Cal State, Dominguez Hills. He currently lives in the Bay Area with his therapist wife. J.D.'s daughter attends Oregon State University. His hobbies include traveling and running.

Emily Parke Chase has fond memories of her grandmother's home. Now she is a grandmother herself! A popular speaker at retreats and conferences, she is the author of seven books, including *Standing Tall After Falling Short* (Wingspread, 2013). Learn more at emilychase.com.

Harriet Cooper writes personal essays, humor and creative nonfiction for newspapers, newsletters, anthologies and magazines, and is a frequent contributor to the Chicken Soup for the Soul series. She writes about family, relationships, health, food, cats, writing and daily life. E-mail her at shewrites@live.ca.

Barbara Crick, a graduate of the Institute of Children's Literature, has been writing since third grade, when a teacher told her parents she showed promise. She has won several awards for her poetry through the Poetry Society of Colorado. Barbara lives with her disabled husband, who is her greatest fan. E-mail her at bjcrick@gmail.com.

Audra Easley is a graphic designer in Atlanta, GA. She loves volunteering in her community, drawing, and writing. She is at work on her second novel.

Logan Eliasen is a senior Bible and theology major at Wheaton College. He enjoys spending his free time with friends and his four younger brothers. A few of his favorite things are chai tea, classic books, and vinyl records. Logan has previously been published in *Chicken Soup for the Soul: Miracles Happen*.

Betsy Franz is an award-winning writer and photographer specializing in nature, wildlife, the environment and both humorous and inspirational human-interest stories. Her articles and photos reflecting the wonders of life have been published in numerous books and magazines. Learn more at www.naturesdetails.net.

Sally Friedman, a graduate of the University of Pennsylvania, has contributed essays to *The New York Times*, *The Huffington Post*, *The Philadelphia Inquirer*, *Family Circle* and many other publications. Many of her essays have appeared in the Chicken Soup for the Soul series. Her favorite subject is her own family. E-mail her at pinegander@aol.com.

Ron Geelan received his bachelor's degree from Providence College. He lives in New York with his wonderful wife and children, who are the inspiration behind his writing. Ron is a previous contributor to the Chicken Soup for the Soul series, and his articles and essays have appeared in numerous regional and national publications.

Kerry Germain lives on the North Shore of Oahu, HI. She is the author of the award-winning children's picture book series *Surf's Up For Kimo*. She considers herself a "tropoholic," enjoys scuba diving and dancing hula. This is her third life story written for Chicken Soup for the Soul. Learn more at www.islandparadisepublishing.com.

Golriz Golkar has been writing poetry and prose since the age of six. She studied American literature at UCLA and received her master's degree in education from the Harvard Graduate School of Education in 2007. Golriz is a primary school teacher in San Francisco, CA.

Shirley P. Gumert and husband John built a retirement home in the Texas Hill Country. They still travel, explore historical sites, and share memories with three grandchildren. Shirley has written personal essays for newspapers, magazines, and anthologies. She says yellow legal pads and stubby pencils are better tools than computers.

Hana Haatainen-Caye, speaker and writing instructor, has a copywriting, editing, and voice-over business in Pittsburgh. With over thirty children's books published, she has won awards for her poetry, short stories, and blog (www.greengrandma.org), and is the author of the nonfiction book, *Vinegar Fridays*. Learn more at www.wordsinyourmouth.com.

Judy Harch is a freelance writer and journalist. She is the author of the novel *Falling Off the Family Tree*. Her stories have previously appeared in the Chicken Soup for the Soul series. Judy lives in southern New Jersey with her husband and rescue Labrador Retriever, Charlotte. E-mail Judy at jharch1@verizon.net.

Michelle Hauser is a Canadian humorist and newspaper columnist. Having made a mid-career shift to writing, she is currently working on a collection of nonfiction essays for publication. Outside of writing, one of Michelle's favorite roles in life is to be "Joe's mom," however tough picking up after him proves to be.

Jan Henrikson is an intuitive counselor who writes and hikes in Tucson, the home of her heart, with her love, Louis.

Miriam Hill is a frequent contributor to the Chicken Soup for the Soul series and has been published in *Writer's Digest, The Christian Science Monitor, Grit, The St. Petersburg Times, The Sacramento Bee*, and Poynter Online. Miriam's manuscript received Honorable Mention for Inspirational Writing in a Writer's Digest Writing Competition.

Writer **Rebecca Hill** lives in Los Angeles with musician Tom Caufield;

both appreciate the creative haven that is Apartment #104. Rebecca has worked with *American Idol*, National Geographic, Warner Bros., and IMAX. Her stories have appeared in Chicken Soup for the Soul anthologies, a Hallmark book and *Redbook* magazine.

Judi Hockabout-Martin's story was written when she was an activity director at an assisted living facility in Omaha, NE. She and her husband are both retired and enjoy golfing, traveling and spending time with their kids and grandchildren. Judi owns her own videography business called Reflections.

Ken Hoculock, known to western Pennsylvania radio listeners as "Ken Hawk," recently retired after twenty-five years as a broadcast journalist. He resides in western Pennsylvania with his wife Margie and their daughter Savannah. E-mail him at radiohawk@hotmail.com or his Sunday blog "Ken's Korner" at BlogSpot.com.

Mariane Dailey Holbrook graduated from both Nyack (NY) College and High Point (NC) University, with degrees in education. A retired teacher, she lives with her husband, John, in coastal North Carolina. She has two sons and three grandchildren. Mariane is the author of two books, *Humor Me* and *Prisms of the Heart*.

Stan Holden has been a professional art director and cartoonist for many years. With the downturn of the economy he chose to look at other avenues of income, which included sales and marketing. A terrible event that occurred during his childhood became the catalyst for his passion to help others through his writing.

Jennie Ivey lives in Tennessee. She is the author of numerous works of fiction and nonfiction, including several stories in the Chicken Soup for the Soul anthology. Learn more at www.jennieivey.com.

Joelle Jarvis's passion has always been personal development. She has worked with many of the world's most inspirational names, including Tony Robbins, and now has her dream job as Vice President of Marketing for Chicken Soup for the Soul. Her greatest love is her son Jackson. E-mail her at joellejarvis@mac.com.

Karen Kilby is a certified personality trainer with CLASServices and a speaker for Stonecroft Ministries. She is a popular contributor to Chicken Soup for the Soul and other publications. Karen's devotional book, *Becoming a Woman of Purpose*, is available through Amazon and major bookstores. Learn more at www.karenkilby.tateauthor.com.

Mitchell Kyd is a freelance writer living in central Pennsylvania. She writes and blogs about the joys and poignant moments of small town living and is a frequent contributor to Chicken Soup for the Soul. More of her stories can be found at www.mitchellkyd.com.

Cathi LaMarche has contributed to over twenty anthologies. As a composition teacher, novelist, and writing coach, she spends most days immersed in the written word. In her spare time, she enjoys gardening, cooking, and hiking. She resides in Missouri with her husband, two children, and three dogs.

Carrie M. Leach is a missionary wife and mom-of-many in Eastern Europe. When she's not homeschooling, folding laundry, cooking, gardening, or working among the Gypsy children of her area, she is writing. Her goal is to write a book about her experiences. E-mail her at cmleach5@gmail.com.

Barbara LoMonaco has worked for Chicken Soup for the Soul as an editor since 1998. She has co-authored two Chicken Soup for the Soul book titles and has had stories published in numerous other titles. Barbara is a graduate of the University of Southern California and has a teaching credential.

Crescent LoMonaco used her knowledge from years of working behind the chair and owning a hair salon to write the "Ask a Stylist" column for the *Santa Barbara Independent*. She is a frequent contributor to the Chicken Soup for the Soul series. She lives on the South Coast with her husband and son.

Patricia Lorenz is an art-of-living writer and speaker, the author of thirteen books and contributing writer to nearly sixty Chicken Soup for the Soul books. She and her husband "hunka-burnin-love" Jack live in Largo, FL, but she enjoys traveling to other parts of the country speaking to various groups. Contact her at www.PatriciaLorenz.com.

A retired naval officer, **Ken Lynch** worked as a teacher's assistant in Pennsylvania's Pennridge School District after his career. He has had several stories published in the Chicken Soup for the Soul series and is currently writing a book about his time in the service. Ken lives with his wife and two children in Hilltown, PA.

Gloria Hander Lyons has channeled thirty-five years of training in the areas of art, interior decorating, and event planning into writing cookbooks and fun how-to books. She also writes humorous short stories and cozy murder mysteries. Learn more at www.gloriahanderlyons.com.

Judith Marks-White is a *Westport News* (CT) award-winning columnist of "In Other Words." She is the author of two novels published by Random House/Ballantine Books: *Seducing Harry* and *Bachelor Degree*. Her work appears in numerous anthologies. She teaches humor writing, lectures widely, and is working on her third novel.

David Martin's humor and political satire have appeared in many publications including *The New York Times*, *Chicago Tribune* and *Smithsonian* magazine. His latest humor collection *Screams & Whispers* is available on Amazon.com. David lives in Ottawa, Canada with his wife Cheryl and their daughter Sarah.

Lynn Maddalena Menna's young adult novel, *Piece of My Heart*, was listed on *Seventeen* magazine's list of must-read books for the summer of 2013. A song from that book, "(You Have) No Soul," is available on YouTube. Lynn and Prospero live in Hawthorne, NJ. Contact her at prolynn@aol.com or on Facebook.

Jackie Minniti is a former teacher and the award-winning author of *Project June Bug*, a novel about a student with ADHD. She is currently a columnist for *The Island Reporter*, a publication serving the South Gulf beaches in St. Petersburg, FL. She lives on nearby Treasure Island with her husband and two noisy macaws.

Courtney Mroch writes fiction in addition to blogging about travel, health and fitness. When she's not writing, it's a safe bet you'll find her on a tennis court somewhere. She lives in Nashville, TN with her husband and their two cats, Mr. Meow and Lady Tabitha Tabernathy Tabberkins Pryor (or Tabby for short).

Nell Musolf lives in the Midwest with her husband and two sons. She enjoys reading, writing and puttering around her kitchen.

Irena Nieslony was born in England, but now lives on the island of Crete, Greece with her husband and her many cats and dogs. She received her B.A. honors degree in Drama and English from the University of London. As well as writing short stories, Irena has had three novels published, all murder mysteries.

Risa Nye's articles and essays have appeared in both local and national publications and in several anthologies. She writes about the craft of nonfiction for *Hippocampus Magazine*. Her "Ms. Barstool" cocktail columns appear online at www.berkeleyside.com. She lives in Oakland, CA. Learn more at www.risanye.com.

Linda O'Connell is a multi-published writer and teacher from St. Louis, MO. She enjoys a hearty laugh, dark chocolate and walks on

the beach with her husband Bill. Linda blogs at http://lindaoconnell.
blogspot.com.

Barbara A. Page holds a Bachelor of Arts degree in computer science
from Wilkes College and spends her days as a technical writer. She lives
in Raleigh, NC with her husband and two cats. Barbara enjoys writing
personal essays, playing acoustic guitar, reading nonfiction, and walking.

Kathy Passage is a writer living in Edmonds, WA. Living with her
handyman husband, her two Elkhound pups and her adult son provide
her with hilarious life happenings to share with her readers. She writes
to get life out of her head and onto the page for a better perspective.

Chicken Soup for the Soul editor **Kristiana Pastir** earned a journalism
degree from Syracuse University in 2004. When she's not reading,
writing, or editing for Chicken Soup for the Soul, Kristiana enjoys
reading, yoga, and adventures with her husband—especially their
scuba diving trips around the world.

Andrea Peebles lives with her husband in Rockmart, GA. She enjoys
writing, cooking, travel and photography. She is still working on her
memoir and in the meantime has enjoyed writing for the Chicken
Soup for the Soul series for the past several years. E-mail her at
aanddpeebles@aol.com.

Saralee Perel is an award-winning, nationally syndicated columnist
who is honored to be a contributor to many Chicken Soup for the
Soul books. E-mail her at sperel@saraleeperel.com or visit www.
saraleeperel.com.

Connie Pombo is a freelance writer, author and speaker. Her stories
have appeared in several Chicken Soup for the Soul books and
numerous publications. Learn more at http://conniepombo.com.

Winter D. Prosapio is an award-winning humor and travel writer with a weekly family humor column, "Crib Notes." Her writing has appeared in everything from airline magazines to grocery lists. She lives in the Texas Hill Country with her husband and two daughters, and works for a water park. This is her third Chicken Soup for the Soul essay.

Jennifer Quasha is the author of over forty nonfiction books for children and adults. She has also been published in more than a dozen Chicken Soup for the Soul books! Check out her favorite books on pointynosebooks.wordpress.com.

Carol McAdoo Rehme spends her children's inheritance maintaining a demanding, historic 1887 Victorian Italianate she shares with her hard-working husband. When not repairing plaster, unearthing hidden ponds and chasing off pigeons, she authors award-winning books, mentors writers for thrills, ghostwrites for money, teaches at conferences, and edits books for variety and challenge. She is also the coauthor of *Chicken Soup for the Soul: Empty Nesters*.

Maureen Rogers is a Canadian transplant living in her new home by the sea in Seattle, WA. Her writing projects include fiction, essays and poetry. She has been published online in newspapers, and anthologies including four other stories in the Chicken Soup for the Soul series. E-mail her at tworogers@msn.com.

John Scanlan is a 1983 graduate of the United States Naval Academy, and retired from the Marine Corps as a Lieutenant Colonel aviator. He currently resides on Hilton Head Island, SC, and is pursuing a second career as a writer. E-mail him at ping1@hargray.com.

Laura Smetak and her husband Mark enjoyed five blissful years of living in their loft space before moving to the suburbs to start a family. Now they have two children, a minivan, a lawn to mow, and a constant parade of deer in the back yard… and they wouldn't have it any other way. E-mail her at lrsmetak@gmail.com.

Jeanne Jacoby Smith is a retired professor of English and Teacher Education at McPherson College in Kansas. She and her husband have two children, Adam and MiRan, plus three grandchildren. She is an avid writer and active in outreach projects in her church.

Michael T. Smith lives in Caldwell, ID with his lovely wife Ginny. He works as a project manager and writes stories for his heart in his free time. E-mail him at heartsandhumor@gmail.com.

Ruth Smith was born in Missouri and raised in Colorado. She is now living in California. Her father taught her the love of reading. Her sister told her to write. Ruth has three children, six grandchildren and seven great-grandchildren—#8 is on the way. Her goal is to continue to write for the family.

Laurie Sontag is a California newspaper columnist who also has a blog. She spends most of her time being confused by Twitter and avoiding work by posting cat videos to Facebook. Her writing has been in nine Chicken Soup for the Soul anthologies and featured on Yahoo Shine. Learn more at www.lauriesontag.com.

Joyce Stark retired from local government and started to write stories about her life and the people in it. She travels widely in the U.S. and Europe, looking and listening.

Jean Haynie Stewart still lives with her husband in their Mission Viejo, CA, home of forty-two years, and longs for that single-story house while she writes about family, travel, and history for Chicken Soup for the Soul, magazines, and newspapers; serves as a Christy Award judge; and tackles her first book.

Writer, performer, speaker **Kim Stokely's** humor blog can be seen at thechristianpulse.com. Her novel, *Woman of Flames*, a fictional account of the Hebrew prophet Deborah, is available through Amazon and Barnes & Noble. Visit www.kimstokely.com or Facebook.com/kimstokelyauthor for information on her performances and work.

Sharon Struth believes you're never too old to pursue a dream. Her first novel, *The Hourglass*, is a winner of the Chatelaine Award for Romantic Fiction. Sharon's second novel, *Share the Moon* (to be released Fall 2014 by Lyrical Press), was inspired by the closeness in her own community and scenic northwestern Connecticut.

Hope Sunderland is a retired registered nurse who hung up her enema bucket and bedpan to start writing. She writes what she hopes is humor from the South Texas Gulf Coast.

Pam Tallman holds a master's degree in theater arts, but is constantly fumbling and dropping her degree in life skills. This gives her plenty of fodder for her humorous essays. The mother of four felines, Pam enjoys baking, quilting and cat herding. She hopes to soon sell her novel. Please… anyone.

Writer, speech therapist, memoir teacher, life coach, wife and mother, **Tsgoyna Tanzman** credits writing as the supreme "therapy" for raising an adolescent daughter. Published in numerous Chicken Soup for the Soul books, her humorous essays appear on More.com and Mothering.com. Follow her blog at tsgoyna.tumblr.com.

B.J. Taylor admits she's bullheaded, though that can be a good thing. She is an award-winning author whose work has appeared in *Guideposts*, numerous Chicken Soup for the Soul books, and various magazines. Learn more at www.bjtayloronline.com and check out her dog blog at www.bjtaylorblog.wordpress.com.

Ann Thurber has a Master of Arts degree in Film Studies with an emphasis in Comparative Literature. She's a movie aficionado, devourer of books, yogi, positive thinker, and pink glitter enthusiast.

Ann has a background in screenwriting and is currently working on a Young Adult novel.

Joanne Webster made her home in Orillia, Ontario, happy with her husband, two sons, a dog, a cat and many friends. She celebrated life by teaching, writing, playing piano, singing and making pottery. The family loved their Newfoundland cottage and community. Joanne died in February 2014.

Ernie Witham writes the syndicated humor column "Ernie's World" for the *Montecito Journal* in Santa Barbara, CA. His work has also appeared in many anthologies including twenty Chicken Soup for the Soul books. He leads humor workshops around the country and is on the faculty of the Santa Barbara Writers Conference.

Raymond M. Wong earned the MFA degree in Creative Writing from Antioch University Los Angeles. His memoir, *I'm Not Chinese: The Journey from Resentment to Reverence*, is slated for publication by Apprentice House in October 2014. He lives in San Diego with his wife and two children. E-mail him at rwong@antioch.edu.

Dallas Woodburn is a Steinbeck Fellow in Creative Writing at San Jose State University. This year she is doing fifty-two random acts of kindness and chronicling her experiences on her blog daybydaymasterpiece.com. Contact her and learn more about her nonprofit youth literacy organization Write On! at writeonbooks.org.

Linda C. Wright lives on the Space Coast of Florida with her husband Richard and their dog Ginger. Several of her personal essays have been anthologized in the Chicken Soup for the Soul series. In her spare time, Linda teaches creative writing, enjoys reading, and traveling. E-mail her at lindacwright@ymail.com.

Chicken Soup for the Soul

Meet Our Authors

Jack Canfield and **Mark Victor Hansen** are the co-founders of Chicken Soup for the Soul. Jack is the author of many bestselling books and is CEO of the Canfield Training Group. Mark is a prolific writer and has had a profound influence in the field of human potential through his library of audios, videos, and articles. Jack and Mark have received many awards and honors, including a Guinness World Records Certificate for having seven books from the Chicken Soup for the Soul series on the New York Times bestseller list on May 24, 1998. You can reach them at www.jackcanfield.com and www.markvictorhansen.com.

Amy Newmark has been Chicken Soup for the Soul's publisher, coauthor, and editor-in-chief for the last six years, after a 30-year career as a writer, speaker, financial analyst, and business executive in the worlds of finance and telecommunications. Amy is a Chartered Financial Analyst and a *magna cum laude* graduate of Harvard College, where she majored in Portuguese, minored in French, and traveled extensively. She and her husband have four grown children.

After a long career writing books on telecommunications, voluminous financial reports, business plans, and corporate press releases, Chicken Soup for the Soul is a breath of fresh air for Amy. She loves creating these life-changing books for Chicken Soup for the Soul's wonderful readers. She has coauthored and/or edited more than 100 Chicken Soup for the Soul books.

You can reach Amy with any questions or comments through webmaster@chickensoupforthesoul.com and you can follow her on Twitter @amynewmark or @chickensoupsoul.

Thank You

We owe huge thanks to all of our contributors. We know that you poured your hearts and souls into the thousands of stories that you shared with us, and ultimately with other people who are making a home. As we read and edited these stories, we were truly moved by your experiences and inspired by your great advice. We appreciate your willingness to share these personal, heartfelt stories with our readers, even the ones in which you confess a do-it-yourself disaster!

We could only publish a small percentage of the stories that were submitted, but we read every single one and even the ones that do not appear in the book had an influence on us and on the final manuscript. We owe special thanks to our senior editor Barbara LoMonaco, who read all the submissions to this volume, and narrowed down the list to a manageable size. Our assistant publisher D'ette Corona did her normal masterful job of working with the contributors to approve our edits and answer any questions we had, as well as helping select many of the stories in the final manuscript. And managing editor and production coordinator Kristiana Pastir proofread and managed the metamorphosis from Word document to printed book, a process that never fails to amaze me.

We also owe a special thanks to our creative director and book producer, Brian Taylor at Pneuma Books, for his brilliant vision for our covers and interiors.

~Amy Newmark

Chicken Soup for the Soul

Sharing Happiness, Inspiration, and Wellness

eal people sharing real stories, every day, all over the world. In 2007, *USA Today* named *Chicken Soup for the Soul* one of the five most memorable books in the last quarter-century. With over 100 million books sold to date in the U.S. and Canada alone, more than 200 titles in print, and translations into more than 40 languages, "chicken soup for the soul" is one of the world's best-known phrases.

Today, 21 years after we first began sharing happiness, inspiration and wellness through our books, we continue to delight our readers with new titles, but have also evolved beyond the bookstore, with wholesome and balanced pet food, delicious nutritious comfort food, and a major motion picture in development. Whatever you're doing, wherever you are, Chicken Soup for the Soul is "always there for you™." Thanks for reading!

Share with Us

We all have had Chicken Soup for the Soul moments in our lives. If you would like to share your story or poem with millions of people around the world, go to chickensoup.com and click on "Submit Your Story." You may be able to help another reader, and become a published author at the same time. Some of our past contributors have launched writing and speaking careers from the publication of their stories in our books!

We only accept story submissions via our website. They are no longer accepted via mail or fax.

To contact us regarding other matters, please send us an e-mail through webmaster@chickensoupforthesoul.com, or fax or write us at:

Chicken Soup for the Soul
P.O. Box 700
Cos Cob, CT 06807-0700
Fax: 203-861-7194

One more note from your friends at Chicken Soup for the Soul: Occasionally, we receive an unsolicited book manuscript from one of our readers, and we would like to respectfully inform you that we do not accept unsolicited manuscripts and we must discard the ones that appear.

Chicken Soup

www.chickensoup.com

for the Soul®